My Beloved Toto

SUNY series, Women Writers in Translation

Marilyn Gaddis Rose, editor

My Beloved Toto

Letters from Juliette Drouet to Victor Hugo
1833–1882

Juliette Drouet

Translated and with an introduction, additional notes, and glossary by
VICTORIA TIETZE LARSON

French Edition
edited and annotated by
Evelyn Blewer

with a preface by
Jean Gaudon

State University of New York Press

Originally published in French as *Lettres à Victor Hugo, 1833–1882* (Paris: Jean-Jacques Pauvert et Silène-Har/Po, 1985). Revised, with correspondence from Victor Hugo, as *Lettres à Victor Hugo: Correspondance, 1833–1882, Lettres à Juliette Drouet: Correspondance, 1833–1883; Correspondence, 1833–1883 suivi de* Le Livre de l'anniversaire, 2 vols. (Paris: Fayard, 2001). ©2001 Librairie Arthème Fayard.

Cover image: Lithograph of Mlle Juliette (1832) by Alphonse-Léon Nöel. ©Photothèque des Musées de la Ville de Paris/Andréani.

Published by
State University of New York Press, Albany

© 2005 State University of New York

All rights reserved

Printed in the United States of America

No part of this book may be used or reproduced in any manner whatsoever without written permission. No part of this book may be stored in a retrieval system or transmitted in any form or by any means including electronic, electrostatic, magnetic tape, mechanical, photocopying, recording, or otherwise without the prior permission in writing of the publisher.

For information, address State University of New York Press,
194 Washington Ave., Suite 305, Albany, NY 12210-2384

Production by Judith Block
Marketing by Anne M. Valentine

Library of Congress Cataloging-in-Publication Data

Drouet, Juliette, 1806–1883.
    [Lettres à Victor Hugo, 1833–1882. English]
    My beloved Toto: letters from Juliette Drouet to Victor Hugo, 1833–1882 / Juliette Drouet; translated by Victoria Tietze Larson; edited and annotated by Evelyn Blewer; with a preface by Jean Gaudon; with an introduction, additional notes, and glossary by Victoria Tietze Larson.
       p. cm. — (SUNY series, Women Writers in Translation)
    Includes bibliographical references and index.
    ISBN 0-7914-6571-3 (alk. paper)
    1. Hugo, Victor, 1802–1885—Correspondence. 2. Drouet, Juliette, 1806–1883—Correspondence. 3. Authors, French—19th century—Correspondence. 4. Actors—France—Correspondence. I. Title: *My Beloved Toto: Letters from Juliette Drouet to Victor Hugo, 1833–1882.* II. Tietze Larson, Victoria, 1954– III. Blewer, Evelyn. IV. Title. V. Series.

PQ2295.D72313
848'.709—dc22
[B]
                                                                                                     2004065683

I live to love you, and I love you to live.
—*Juliette Drouet to Victor Hugo, 4 September 1853*

You are my life, and you will be my eternity.
—*Victor Hugo to Juliette Drouet, 21 May 1875*

Roofline of Juliette Drouet's house Hauteville Féerie in Guernsey. (Photo taken by the translator with kind permission of Richard and Elizabeth Soar).

Contents

Preface to the French Edition	ix
Abbreviations	xv
Introduction	1
Letters	45
1830s	45
Letters 1–40	47
Notes	71
1840s	81
Letters 41–77	83
Notes	106
1850s	117
Letters 78–130	119
Notes	152
1860s	163
Letters 131–67	165
Notes	187
1870s	197
Letters 168–82	199
Notes	206
1880s	211
Letters 183–6	213
Notes	215

Glossary	217
Note on the French Edition	229
List of Sources	231
Works Cited	233
Index	237

Preface to the French Edition

The trite version of Juliette Drouet's relationship with Victor Hugo endlessly rehashed by pseudohistorical and simplistic biographies is, alas, only too familiar to us. She called him "my Toto." Every day, and often two or three times, she wrote four pages to him in her cook's handwriting to tell him that she loved him. It was, in any case, always the same letter—to read one is to read them all! He liked this because he was incredibly vain. He had cloistered her in a cheap little apartment that she was not allowed to leave without him. She was jealous. He deceived her shamefully.

I trust Mme Drouet's shade will forgive this allusion to sanctimonious biographers who take the liberty of treating her with condescension and compassion. She had slight regard for "this dubious light of pity" (13 July 1851) and would have detested being pitied by muckrakers of any kind, charitable or not. Not being one to mince her words, she would certainly have had some sharp things to say about them.

When Victor Hugo became Julienne Gauvain's lover during the rehearsals of *Lucrèce Borgia*, she was not yet twenty-seven years old. In the theater she went by the name of "Mlle Juliette." In the world outside she was "Juliette Drouet," having taken the surname of a military uncle who had adopted her at a very young age. She spelled her name "Droüet" with a dieresis (testimony perhaps to a regional pronunciation), which Hugo usually observed but which has been dropped by later generations. She would be called *"Madame"* Drouet when she was an old woman, very beautiful and dignified, and continued to be so called for a long time after her death. Jean Hugo, a hundred years later, still occasionally referred to her in this way.

As a little Breton girl of very humble origins, who was born in Fougères on 10 April 1806 and orphaned before she was two years old, Juliette received a good education. However, her writing is not that of a *femme du monde* like the incredibly insipid writing of Léonie Biard. It is rather the writing of an actress—extroverted, with a grain of exhibitionism typical of those who need admiration to survive but who are misinterpreted as megalomaniacs. It seems improbable that she had already adopted this mode of writing at the convent of the Sisters of Perpetual Adoration where she received her education. Like the big, rather coarse handwriting, it must be one of the signs of her independence, dating from the time when she began to kick over the traces.

It is not known what she did after leaving the convent. However, when she made her debut in the Belgian theater under the direction of Harel, she had a little girl of three years old, "given" to her, as they say, by a fashionable sculptor, Pradier—who didn't give her much else. As far as her acting is concerned, the consensus has generally been that her modest talent would probably have gone unnoticed if she had not been so pretty. In the same view she is portrayed with an abundance of lovers—impecunious young men who cadge off her, and Russian princes who keep her in luxury. She is depicted as living in penniless splendor with a courtesan's wardrobe and pyramidal debt. Similarly, the impression given by the lithograph of Léon Noël, or by Théophile Gautier's portrait of her, is of an unintelligent vamp—more of a nincompoop than Zola's Nana in fact!

Victor Hugo's arrival on the scene would change everything. What began officially on the night of 16 to 17 February 1833, was not—although they could not know it—just a passing romance, but the affair of a whole lifetime, lasting until her death on 11 May 1883. She would very soon say that she was in love for the first time. *He* would say the same, which is more surprising. So did Hugo's letters to his fiancée, Adèle Foucher—Mme Victor Hugo since 1822—count for nothing? Certainly not, but obviously the relationship with Juliette Drouet involved something more, including, not insignificantly, sexual desire on her part as well as his.

There was a great deal of naïveté in the way in which Juliette abandoned herself very quickly to idyllic fantasies and to the spirit of self-purification. She suffered greatly and so did Hugo from the fact that the starry dream they tried to live out was completely at odds with harsh reality. There is a startling contrast between the poems that Hugo dedicates regularly to Juliette from *Les Chants du crépuscule* onward and the letters that she sends to him. On the one hand, we find in Hugo's poetry the bucolic spirit transplanted into the Ile-de-France—shady bowers and amorous euphoria that finds expression in long, disciplined phrases; on the other hand, in Juliette's letters we find overflowing passion voiced in stammering outbursts. There is also in these letters of hers a sense of revolt, weariness, discord, and a desire to flee from a love that offers no freedom. She declares Hugo's jealousy to be more unbearable than debt. The two hurt each other, tear each other apart, and rehearse separations as though planning suicide, leaving behind them what is necessary to stop the tragedy short at the last moment and transform it into a confirmation of love.

In this redemptive battle of the emotions, writing certainly plays a mediating role. The letter seems often to refine and soften what might sound brutal or overly simplified if said aloud. In the minutes that follow a quarrel between them, Juliette will write a letter to explain and defuse what she has said, without, on the other hand, recanting it. Of course Juliette knows how to say she was wrong, but she also knows how to say, even in the midst of declarations of love, what is very soon true: that Hugo does not have enough time for her. She understands and respects his work, but suffers from the fact that the writer's calling brings with it distractions and worldly obligations. Sometimes her suffering takes on an accusatory form: "What use will have been my trust in your love, my faith in the future, and my courage? You always abandon me at the moment of danger! Oh Victor, Victor, you are truly at fault, and I am truly unhappy!" Juliette's ideal is very simple: love in a thatched cottage with reams of paper, pens, and an inkpot. He would write. She would copy. What use are the Bertin family, Dorval, the royal family, politics? Just let the great man do his job as a writer and give his Juju what her body and soul desire! In fact the trips they made together, despite their discomfort, almost succeeded in doing this.

There was also the complicated matter of the family. Not surprisingly, Juliette was rejected outright, but from the beginning she pretended desperately otherwise, referring to Hugo's children by their nicknames, Didine, Dédé, Toto, and Charlot, and taking an interest in their illnesses and scholarly achievements. She even gave them presents. One wonders whether they ever reached their intended destination. After the death of Léopoldine she is to be found alluding to "your dear children, whom I love as though they were my own flesh and blood." This osmosis, if there can be osmosis without a receptive counterpart, arose perhaps from the desire to get closer to Hugo, perhaps from the security that she received in November 1839 from a strange event that she described quite simply as a "marriage" (termed by some a "mystic" marriage, although this is a concept that hardly suited Juliette's temperament). By the same token Hugo "adopted" Juliette's daughter, the thirteen-year-old Claire, who called him "Monsieur Toto." Perhaps, after all, that was the receptive counterpart.

The letter mediates but also compensates. It expresses regrets and fills voids, while occupying the mind. Juliette hardly ever went out except accompanied by her gallant escort. If he did not come, or if he did not have time, she stayed at home—hence the innumerable "scribblings," which give such an extraordinary background to her biography.

If it is indeed true that Hugo was caught in flagrante delicto with Léonie Biard on the night of 4 to 5 July 1845 (although the date is not absolutely beyond doubt), then we must recoil at the irony of the letter written by Juliette on the morning of 5 July—Juliette is making him some tea! There is the same feeling of tragic irony about the letters written on the morning of 28 June 1851—essentially letters about strawberries in syrup—when we know that a few hours later Juliette will receive from Léonie the letter informing her that Hugo has been her lover for seven years, proof enclosed.

After exile there would be other crises that would shake the long-standing relationship, and one can understand how Juliette considered the period in the Channel Islands a blessed time. Oh, but even then she was not completely at peace! There were still too many female visitors from England and France, whom she always imagined to be charming, but in general there were fewer obvious threats. Furthermore, in relation to the legitimate family she had acquired a (literally) marginal relationship, and her existence was acknowledged. Being modest and discreet, however, her initial reaction to any gesture of acknowledgment was to turn it down. But the sons got into the habit of going to her house, and Mme Hugo, shortly before her death, took steps toward a rapprochement with her that must have been carefully negotiated.

Conflicts remained, however. While Hugo and Juliette in their old age went gaga together over the two grandchildren, their relationship with the children's mother, Alice, widow of Charles Hugo, was far from perfect. Furthermore, Hugo's love for Blanche Lanvin caused a tremendous crisis in 1873. Once more Mme Drouet carried the day. By now deprived of illusions, she became openly tyrannical. In some ways she was more beautiful than ever.

It is almost a pity that the addressee of Juliette Drouet's letters is called Victor Hugo and that one is led, despite oneself, to be more interested in his biography than in the talent of his correspondent. He himself made no mistake about it, and if he encouraged Juliette to write to him, it was not because he was unable to live without the smell of incense, but quite simply because, as a master craftsman, he knew the value of her prose: it even happened on occasion that the roles were reversed and that he in turn copied extracts from her letters.

These letters, of which there must be at least twenty thousand, are neither more nor less monotonous than those of Mme de Sévigné. Both of them have to resolve the same problem: how to keep on saying "I love you." Both have the same skill in surmounting this obstacle, but Juliette has an additional difficulty: it is easier to ring the changes when the letter writer is at a distance and the letter can become a sort of journal, than when it is merely a connective tissue that helps to give consistency to daily life. It is impossible in this case to resort to novelistic tricks, and that is a serious drawback. It is a pity that this epistolary flow, this Mississippi of ink—of which the small number of letters published gives a very poor account—cannot be reproduced in its entirety. Contrary to the judgments of those with pretensions to taste—who, having no time for Hugo, keep a little of their dissatisfaction for Juliette—these letters are marvelously varied. I mentioned Mme de Sévigné. Juliette refers to de Sévigné on several occa-

Introduction

Victoria Tietze Larson

On 22 November 1835 Juliette Drouet, aged twenty-nine, wrote to Victor Hugo, renowned poet, novelist, and dramatist, and her lover of two years: "It's my love that will make me immortal. When I am dead, I will love you still. My body and my life will be used up before one single particle of my love disappears" (*MUL*, 77).[1] By 1883 when Drouet died at seventy-seven after a lifetime of passionate love for Hugo, it had long been clear that this early description of the intensity and durability of her love was no exaggeration. Just as she had predicted, it would be this love, expressed in some twenty thousand love letters written over a period of fifty years, that would make her and her relationship with Hugo "immortal."

Juliette Drouet was born Julienne Gauvain on 10 April 1806 in Fougères, Brittany.[2] Her parents, Marie and Julien Gauvain, were artisans of peasant stock who made a humble living in the town's weaving industry. They died in 1806 and 1807 respectively, both at the age of about thirty, leaving behind four orphaned children: three girls, Renée (born 1800), Thérèse (born 1801), and Juliette (or Julienne as she was christened), and one boy, Armand (born 1803). Renée, aged six when her parents died, was sent to a local hospice run by a religious order, while her younger siblings were farmed out to foster mothers. Thérèse would also end up in the hospice and die there in 1813 at the age of eleven. Armand became completely separated from his two surviving sisters and grew up apart from them.[3] It is unclear what happened to baby Juliette immediately after she left the wet nurse who looked after her following her parents' death. In the long term, however, she seems to have had a slightly luckier fate than her two sisters in that she was taken into the care of her mother's sister, her Aunt Françoise, and her Uncle René-Henry Drouet.

René-Henry was in the Army, but also worked for part of his married life as a printer. Drouet always remembered him with affection as "uncle by name, but father in heart," and she adopted his surname (*MUL*, 617). For her aunt, however, she never had much good to say. The couple probably first sent her to a local convent in Brittany and then took her with them when they moved to Paris in 1815. In Paris, René-Henry (now retired from the Army on a very small pension) hoped, perhaps, for help from his brother, who had been living there for some time. Juliette was placed, once again, in a convent, and her aunt and uncle separated. Her aunt, who appears to have gained some kind of marginal footing in Parisian artistic circles after her separation, gave birth to an illegitimate daughter, Eugénie, in 1816.[4] To judge by subsequent events, Juliette emerged from the convent with considerably more education and polish than had been afforded to her elder sister. After leaving the hospice in 1812 at the age of twelve, Renée remained in Brittany and was probably sent into service by her Aunt Françoise. She ended up with a level of education considerably inferior to Drouet's, and her letters written as an adult are semi-illiterate.[5]

The story is that Drouet was allowed to leave the Parisian convent in 1821 on the eve of taking orders, having discovered that she had no vocation for the nunhood.[6] Virtually nothing is known about Drouet's life in the next five years, but it must have been, as Gaudon puts it, a life that "bordered on prostitution" (*LJD*, 11). Later in a letter to Hugo, Drouet would thank him for having saved her from "poverty and prostitution,"[7] and as Drouet herself would admit, before she met Hugo she had been "a woman whom necessity can throw into the arms of the first rich man that wants to buy her" (*MUL*, 40). Some idea of the joys and of the much more obvious sorrows of living such a life are given by Hugo's description in his novel *Les Misérables* of the four *grisettes*, Dahlia, Zéphine, Favourite, and Fantine, as well as of Eponine and Azelma. Perhaps the sympathy with which Hugo portrays them owes something to what he knew of Drouet's past life.

In 1826 at the age of twenty Drouet gave birth to an illegitimate child, Claire, the daughter of Jean-Jacques Pradier, a sculptor who called himself James and was sixteen years older than Drouet. This was doubtless not Drouet's first liaison before she met Hugo, and there would be others after it, but it was the most important of the several relationships she had before she met Hugo because of the lasting consequences it would have on her life.

Born in 1790 in Geneva to French Huguenot parents, Pradier came to Paris around 1808 to join his brother, Charles-Simon, who had, like himself, been trained as an engraver.[8] He became a student at the Ecole des Beaux-Arts where he studied sculpture. He won the prestigious Prix de Rome in 1813, spent some years in Italy as a consequence (1814–1818), and subsequently kept a studio in Paris. He had soon acquired all the symbols of success within the establishment—exhibiting annually at the Salon, becoming a member of the Académie des Beaux-Arts (1827), professor at the Ecole des Beaux-Arts (1827), chevalier de la Légion d'honneur (1828), officier de la Légion d'honneur (1834), and obtaining numerous important commissions from the State for public buildings and monuments.[9] While now an unknown name, Pradier considered himself, and was considered by others, to be among the foremost sculptors of his time.[10] He specialized in erotic female nudes in marble, which he turned out in mythological guises in the hundreds. In the opinion of some, Drouet may have modeled for one of these, the *Satyre et Bacchante*,[11] a sculpture that many contemporary critics found indecent.

The reminiscences of his acquaintances allude to Pradier's flamboyant sartorial style and taste for frequent and extravagant entertainment.[12] A self-portrait[13] shows Pradier every inch the poseur, self-consciously enveloped in his trademark cape,[14] accompanied by a large greyhound. Since he assiduously tended his social and political connections, Pradier frequently threw parties, on which he spent exorbitant sums of money. One of his guests was Gustave Flaubert, who became acquainted through Pradier with the poetess Louise Colet, who was to become his mistress and "Muse."[15] Furthermore, Pradier's eventual wife, the reckless Louise d'Arcet, would provide the model for Emma in Flaubert's novel *Madame Bovary*.[16] Pradier had musical aspirations as well as artistic ones, dabbling on the piano, guitar, organ, and harp, and composing ballads, and was friends with a number of prominent composers of the time.[17] The cover of the score of one of his ballads, entitled *Le Chagrin de l'absence*, features a prominent dedication to Drouet "by her very humble servant" and a Pradier drawing of a romantically-cloaked man looking for all the world just like the self-portrait described above.[18]

Pouchain (*JDD*, 35) speculates that there are two possible ways in which Drouet could have been introduced to Pradier: either during the course of her artistic studies with Pierre-Joseph Redouté, a teacher of drawing, who must have known Pradier and may possibly have introduced her as a potential model, or, alternatively, through Drouet's friendship with Laure Krafft, a musician, who may have taken her to one of Pradier's musical soirées.[19] Another possibility is that, like her cousin, Eugénie, Drouet was first introduced into the artistic world—if only for the exploitation of her beauty as a model—by her manipulative aunt-cum-stepmother.[20] Like Drouet, Eugénie ended up with an illegitimate child fathered by an artist, Jules Ziegler. In any event, however Drouet may have met Pradier, she eventually became his model and therefore, as so often with Pradier, also his mistress.[21] Indeed, the narrow dividing line between sex and art in Pradier's studio is underlined by Arsène Houssaye, friend of Victor Hugo and onetime director of the Comédie-Française. In his memoirs he describes meeting in 1832 (almost at exactly our period) two *grisettes* who had been modeling, "naturally as goddesses or demigoddesses on Olympus," in Pradier's studio, and who were "not ashamed to undress before a bunch of prying men who wouldn't pretend to be artists except for the nude models."[22] Drouet claimed to have been the model for the city of Strasbourg, one of the two statues that Pradier executed for the place de la Concorde in Paris representing France's important cities.[23] She doubtlessly modeled for other well-known Pradier sculptures too.

Within Pradier's flamboyant and boastful bohemian facade there lurked a circumspect, bourgeois soul. Pradier had no intention of marrying Drouet, albeit the mother of his daughter. Any marriage he might make would be calculated to support his lavish lifestyle and social status. His marriage in 1833 to the wealthy nineteen-year-old, Louise d'Arcet (although it proved to be a grave mistake that Pradier would greatly regret, especially financially),[24] must have been based on just such a calculation. A marriage with Drouet could only be a marriage of love, although if Drouet ever felt any love for him it was probably quickly extinguished. Pradier's letters to her convey a picture of a man who was vain, self-centered, and self-righteous. Drouet would later feel nothing but contempt for him, describing him in one letter to Hugo as "a miserable imbecile, a stupid rogue, the vilest and most foolish of men."[25] In any case, the arrival of the baby Claire must have introduced a note of harsh reality into the relationship that brought it to an end. The most Pradier was willing to do was to put in a word for her later with contacts that might help launch Drouet's theatrical career[26] and to provide grudging and sporadic support for his daughter. This very rich man could never find the ready cash to pay for her upkeep on time, yet, as Houssaye tells us, he could spend ten thousand francs on one party.[27] Pradier's response to Drouet's cries for help was only to prevaricate concerning the money and to send pompous letters filled with gratuitous advice: "Come, come, now, courage and mint pastilles!"[28]

Before Drouet's theatrical career was to begin, however, Claire would be boarded out with a wet nurse (*JDD*, 41), and by 1827 Drouet was involved in a liaison with a married man with consequences far more important than the affair itself. This man was Scipion Pinel, a wealthy doctor in his early thirties with a specialization in psychiatric disorders and an interest in the arts.[29] Pinel presented Drouet with jewelry and Indian cashmere amounting to the value of twenty thousand francs, an enormous sum of money that was too much even for the affluent Pinel to afford: to finance the purchase of the gifts he borrowed money from a dealer in cashmere (*JDD*, 148) called Mme Ribot or Ribou. Subsequently Pinel found himself unable to repay the money as contracted, and by the beginning of the following year newspapers carried accounts of the legal case brought against Pinel by Ribot. The next months were spent by the two lovers in Frankfurt-am-Main in Germany, perhaps to avoid the possibility of further legal action. While they were there, Pradier wrote Drouet letters of paternalistic advice.[30] By October 1828, however, Drouet's affair with Pinel had finished. She was now on her own financially and physically and must take drastic measures to earn enough money to live and make at least some gestures toward paying off her large debts. She went to Brussels where she initiated, without any dramatic training whatsoever, a career in the theater. Why Brussels? It was a cosmopolitan cultural center with many links to Paris. Drouet may also have been helped to break into theatrical circles there by Simone Luigi Peruzzi, the ambassador for Tuscany in Brussels and Paris, with whom she had a liaison, which was in full swing by January 1829 (*JDD*, 83). The debt to Mme Ribot, which Drouet had honorably assumed after the end of her relationship with Pinel, and the debts to her many other creditors, would continue to haunt her, however, for many years to come.[31]

Drouet's theatrical debut—under the stage name "Mlle Juliette"—occurred on December 6 1828, in a play by Scribe and Courcy called *Simple Histoire* at the Théâtre du Parc in Brussels.[32] It was a theater that specialized in vaudeville—short, comic, lighthearted plays, often with some topical relevance and interspersed with songs. Drouet played the role of Miss Milner in this vacuous story of the love affair between Lord Frédéric, "so well-known for his duels and gallant adventures," and his seventeen-year-old pupil. This play, like nearly all the plays in which Drouet would hold a role of any importance, was of second-rate literary merit by now forgotten dramatists.[33] The reviews in the press of her first ever appearance on stage, however, were encouraging and all of them remarked on her beauty.

Without a doubt, Juliette Drouet was a beautiful woman. In a description that originally appeared in *Les Belles Femmes de Paris* (*The Beautiful Women of Paris*), Théophile Gautier, friend of Victor Hugo, Parnassian poet, novelist, and journalist, said of her:

> Mlle Juliette's face is beautiful in a regular and delicate way . . . Her nose is purely cut and finely chiseled. Her eyes are sparkling and limpid . . . Her mouth, which is of a dewy rose and lively in expression, is always small, even in bursts of the greatest gaiety. All these features, which are so charming in themselves, are contained within an oval face of the smoothest and most harmonious outline. A smooth and serene forehead like the white marble pediment of a Greek temple luminously crowns this delightful face. Abundant black hair with a wonderful shine sets off marvelously, by contrast, its diaphanous glow.
>
> Mlle Juliette's neck, shoulders, and arms are of quite classical perfection. She could be a worthy inspiration to sculptors and compete with the beauty of the young Athenian women who cast off their veils before Praxiteles as he contemplated his Venus.[34]

Drouet's stay in Brussels turned out to be a short one. By April 1829 she was back in Paris and, possibly with the help of Pradier, managed to secure a role at the Théâtre du Vaudeville which, true to its name, specialized in staging vaudevilles. Her debut on the Parisian stage on 29 July 1829 was in *Kettly ou le retour en Suisse* by Duvert and Paulin. In this play Drouet played the part of Kettly, the young, female love interest and a role in which she was required to sing some duets. Her connection with this theater, too, did not last long. The Théâtre du Vaudeville was in financial difficulty, and Juliette Drouet left it after just a few months to make her debut on 27 February 1830 at another Parisian theater, the Théâtre de la Porte-Saint-Martin.

Like the Théâtre du Vaudeville this theater catered to popular (although more middle-class) audiences, with a specialty in melodrama: sensational plays with some incidental music and often a strong moral component.[35] Drouet began in the box office success *L'Homme du monde* by Ancelot and Saintine and then appeared, beginning in April, in *Shylock* by Dulac and Alboise. This sensational melodrama was described by one drama critic as "horror from beginning to end. Not a smile, but constantly cries of rage, vengeance, cruelty, despair, tears, sighs, pain, misery. First of all tempests, shipwrecks, abductions, then a deathbed, a funeral procession, secret meetings in underground caverns, a trial, finally the frightful triumph of hatred and vengeance in the heart of the Jew."[36] Drouet played the part of Jessica, the young daughter of Shylock, who falls in love with a young gentile Venetian, Lorenzo. The couple attempts to elope by sea, but a storm wrecks their ship. The play ends climactically with Jessica's confession to her father of her love for Lorenzo and her conversion to Christianity. Shylock is about to run her through with his sword when she is saved, fainting, by Lorenzo and Bassiano. The spirit of Shakespeare was a long way from this melodrama, but the public loved it.

Drouet stayed just over a year at the Porte-Saint-Martin and, excluding one benefit performance, played seven different roles in as many different plays. The last new role that she took was the young love interest, Clémence, in *Napoléon ou Schönbrunn et Sainte-Hélène* by Dupeuty, Régnier, and Detourbey—one of the several dramatizations of the life of Napoleon popular in theaters at this time. She would perform the part of Clémence more than a hundred times.

In April 1831 Drouet left the Porte-Saint-Martin for the Odéon, a first-class, state-subsidized theater. Pouchain speculates (*JDD*, 75) that one reason Drovet moved there may have been the prospect of being able to play the female lead alongside Frédérick Lemaître, one of the most celebrated actors of the time, and of putting a distance between herself and Marie Dorval. Dorval was the principal actress at the Porte-Saint-Martin and one of the leading actresses of her day. Drouet would show some jealousy of her seductiveness and powers as an actress in her letters to Victor Hugo (L. 17). Drouet imitated Dorval's acting style in her role as Antonia in the melodrama in which she appeared at the Odéon on 28 May 1831. This was *Le Moine* by Louis-Marie Fontan, one of several stage versions of the sensational 1796 Gothic novel *The Monk* by the English novelist Matthew Gregory Lewis (1775–1818).[37] The plot of *Le Moine* has some similarities to the story of Hugo's perverted archdeacon, Claude Frollo, and his love for Esmeralda in his novel *Notre-Dame de Paris*, which appeared this same year, 1831. In *Le Moine* a Franciscan monk, Ambrosio, has been tricked by the Devil and made to fall in love with Antonia. Seeking to possess her, Ambrosio creeps in on Antonia while she is sleeping (as does Claude Frollo on Esmeralda). Antonia is defended by her brother, whom Ambrosio kills before abducting her. The play concludes with a duel between Ambrosio and the Devil, which the Devil wins. Drouet would receive good reviews for her performance of this part and she would play it again when she returned to the Porte-Saint-Martin the following year, performing the role all in all some fifty times.

Drouet's time at the Odéon turned out to be even shorter than her previous stint at the Porte-Saint-Martin. In October of 1831 the newspapers reported that she had decided to break with this theater. She left it perhaps for the Florentine palazzo of Simone Peruzzi, the above-mentioned ambassador for Tuscany, whose unedited diaries reveal a whirl of daily cultural and social activity, including ambassadorial parties that he attended in the company of Juliette Drouet. There appears to be no evidence, however, for the tenacious story that while in Florence Drouet belonged to the theatrical company of a Russian prince, Demidoff. The story—which has been repeated by most of Drouet's biographers since Paul Chenay, the son-in-law of Victor Hugo, alleged that Drouet was protected by "a fabulously rich Russian prince, owner of mines in Siberia"[38]—seems to date back to a gossipy article about Drouet that appeared in 1832 in the theatrical magazine *La Rampe et les coulisses*. In this article it was claimed that "authors, directors, stockbrokers, Russian aristocrats, and even a certain *Préfet de police* were hot on her heels" (*JDD*, 86). In any case, Drouet returned to Paris in January 1832 after a three-month stay in Florence, and Peruzzi would return three months later.

On her return Drouet signed up not with the Odéon, the theater she had left for Italy, but once again with the Porte-Saint-Martin. She began with a part in the sensational melodrama *Shylock*, a part she had played more than forty times in her previous stint at this theater. Drouet's next role at the Porte-Saint-Martin was in a production by Scribe and Terrier called *Dix ans de la vie d'une femme*. The play began in March 1832 with Mme Zélie-Paul playing the part of Sophie Marini. Drouet at this point had no part in the play—luckily for her, as the audience judged the play with its female "nudity" too indecent, and the actresses, including Marie Dorval, were booed off the stage. Responding to the criticism, the dramatists made some changes to the play that must have satisfied the public, as more than fifty performances followed with Drouet now playing Sophie Marini. However, an epidemic of cholera struck Paris at this time and severely diminished the size of audiences, while a more personal form of misfortune struck Drouet in particular. The enormous debt to Mme Ribot, incurred by her former lover Pinel, but assumed by Drouet in 1830, now caught up with her. Ribot sued Drouet for failing to make payments on the eight thousand francs for which she had taken responsibility, and which represented almost three years' salary (*VS*, 4:48). Drouet lost the case and was ordered to repay the debt with interest.

Drouet had no means to repay the money except by incurring further debt since she was already living beyond her means and was already in debt to many other people, including the furniture dealer,[39] the jeweler, the glover, the dressmaker, the cosmetician, the laundress, and two other dealers in cashmere besides Ribot (*VS*, 4:49). Actresses were required to furnish their own lavish costumes, which were extremely costly. Furthermore, Drouet had an expensive apartment and a social life to maintain where she had to keep up appearances. So it is not surprising to find at this time signs of stress in reviews that allude to slipshod, lackluster performances in which she did not know her words and read them from the back of a fan or written on letters used as props! Moreover, just at a time when she most needed the money, Drouet began to find that she could not keep up with the grueling schedule of performances night after night. The stress was beginning to tell mentally and physically, and reviewers were not kind. Yet the test was just beginning. As she was in financially desperate straits, Drouet needed to perform as much as possible. Accordingly Drouet engaged upon what Pouchain calls "a stupefying theatrical marathon" (*JPD*, 100), acting between August 1832 and the end of 1833 in a dozen or so different plays and in nearly five hundred performances. On more than a hundred occasions she performed in two or even three plays on a single night.

However, by the end of 1832 Drouet was beginning to get a taste of what her career might have become if she had not met Victor Hugo. In November she appeared in the part of Marie in the drama *Perrinet Leclerc* by Lockroy and Anicet Bourgeois, which, catering to the taste for historical drama with lavish costumes and staging that Hugo would exploit so well, was set in fifteenth-century France in the context of the feud between the Armagnacs and the Burgundians. The play was a tremendous success, and the theater was full to overflowing night after night. Even though Drouet did not have the leading part, even though she had received some negative reviews for her lack of theatrical technique, and even though her fatigue, in the eyes of some, had begun to take a toll on her acting and her looks, she had achieved star status. She was a celebrity whose doings were the fodder of gossip columns in newspapers and magazines and the subject of satirical plays and novels. Like the image of a modern pop or screen idol, Drouet's portrait (a lithograph in these predaguerreotype days) appeared that autumn in the magazine *L'Artiste,* accompanied by a lengthy eulogy.

Separated by a few pages in the same magazine there appeared a lithograph by the same artist, Léon Noël, of another celebrity, the thirty-year-old Victor Hugo. Drouet and Hugo were not yet acquainted with one another, but they would be very soon! In the meantime, however, Drouet had become involved in a new liaison, this time with Alphonse Karr, drama critic for *Le Figaro,* who had been following her career with interest for some time. In his reviews Karr had highly praised not only Drouet's beauty but also her acting. It was Karr who had written the article that accompanied the portrait of Drouet in *L'Artiste* in which he says, in part:

> Some of our actresses may perhaps compete with Mlle Juliette for the prize for beauty; but not one has this purity, this youthfulness, these artless contours which recall Greek sculpture, and, at the same time, this poetic and expressive face that brings to mind

Shakespearean heroines. Thus M. Léon Noël, whose talent the readers of *L'Artiste* have already come to appreciate, must regret the impossibility of capturing on stone this face that is in turns passionate and deadly, witty and biting. There are limits to art and the finest heads of Van Dyck do not speak to us. Only Lawrence could have rendered these features, pure and smooth. (*JPD*, 105)

Unsurprisingly, Alphonse Karr was another disappointment. While alluring Drouet with promises of marriage, he demanded from her—as she staggered under her own burden of debt—loans of money that he would never pay back. The relationship was very short-lived. By the beginning of the next year, 1833, Drouet was ready for an affair that would last for the rest of her life.

Drouet and Victor Hugo met on 2 January 1833 at the Théâtre de la Porte-Saint-Martin. Hugo was there to read to the actors his sensational and bloodcurdling prose drama *Lucrèce Borgia*, in preparation for their performance of it. Twenty-two years later in a New Year's letter dated 31 December 1854, he reminisced to Drouet: "The day after tomorrow, 2 January, it will be twenty-two years since I saw you for the first time. Do you remember? Since that moment it has been 2 January (and not the first) that has started the year, or rather life itself, for me" (*LJD*, 212).

Notwithstanding the importance in retrospect of this initial meeting, or of the fact that this was Drouet's first part in a play that could lay claim to literary merit, Drouet resigned from the theater. The papers said that she found her role as the Princesse Negroni insultingly small.[40] Then, perhaps because the director, Harel, called her bluff by accepting her resignation, Drouet quickly returned and accepted the role, declaring, so the legend has it, that "there is no small role in a play by Victor Hugo."[41] Before the play even opened, however, Drouet found herself summoned to court on 23 January to answer charges brought by Mme Ribot who, hearing the press reports of Drouet's imminent appearance in this play with its eminent author and celebrated actors, Frédérick Lemaître and Mlle George, had decided that the time was opportune to make another attempt to recoup the money Drouet owed her. The case was referred to another court before which she would be called to appear on 8 February. The press was titillated by the spectacle of the young star in trouble with the law, and Hugo, along with the rest of the world, could not have failed to be aware of the situation. If her outstanding beauty had not already brought her to his attention during rehearsals, then surely "the prestige of this great misfortune" must have. As Drouet would remark ruefully in years to come, Hugo, who had already written a play about a redeemed courtesan, *Marion de Lorme*, never could resist the sight of a young woman in trouble, or as Drouet later acidly put it, "a tart in a bind" (L. 175).[42]

The play had its premiere on 2 February 1833 and was a tremendous success with the theater packed to capacity. Several eulogistic accounts of Drouet's performance appeared in the papers, but the most evocative account of Drouet's presence in the play is that of Théophile Gautier:

It was in the small role of the Princesse Negroni in *Lucrèce Borgia* that Mlle Juliette cast the most dazzling light. She had only a couple of words to say and really only crossed the stage: but with such little time and with so few words she found a way to create a ravishing figure, a real Italian princess with a gracious and deadly smile, her eyes full of treacherous inebriation . . .

Her costume was ravishing in its character and taste: a dress of pink damask with a silver floral pattern, feathers and pearls in her hair; all that in a capricious and Romanesque style like a drawing by Tempeste or della Bella. She was like a snake standing upright on its tail, so undulating, supple, and serpentine were her movements. Through all her grace how well she conveyed something venomous! With what disturbing and mocking agility did she slip away from the prostrate adoration of the handsome Venetian noblemen![43]

In her appearance in court on 8 February Drouet had been ordered, once again, to pay the eight thousand francs with interest for which she had assumed responsibility three years previously. Her situation was such that she had already had to sell and pawn her belongings. Prison was a possibility if she did not come up with the money. So as the eighty performances of *Lucrèce Borgia* got underway, Drouet maintained a punishing schedule, appearing also on other nights in other plays that were already running at the Porte-Saint-Martin: *Le Moine*, *L'Homme au masque de fer*, *Jeanne Vaubernier*, *Térésa*, and *Perrinet Leclerc*. She appeared, as Pouchain calculates, in more than one hundred performances in three months[44] and, from 1 May 1833 onward, acted in two plays every night. After her evening performance at the Porte-Saint-Martin she would rush to the Théâtre Molière and perform late at night in *Le Fils de Zambular*. It is no surprise to find her letters from this time referring to a breakdown in her health, and in the context of such overwhelming stress the theory (*JDD*, 115–7) that Drouet audaciously appealed to Hugo for help is not at all difficult to believe.

In any case, the sophisticated boldness of one of Drouet's earliest letters to him, possibly dated 16 February 1833, and miraculously preserved, bears the legend out (L. 1):

Come for me this evening at Mme K's.

I will love you until then just to stay patient. See you this evening! Oh, this evening will be everything!

I will give myself to you completely.

It was the night of 16–17 February 1833 (or so they always said) that

Drouet and Hugo first slept together, and it was also Mardi Gras. They would memorialize this night for the rest of their fifty years together (L. 80, 135, 142). Drouet kept under her pillow a red book they called the *Livre de l'anniversaire*, in which, beginning in 1835 and ending in 1882, the year before she died, Hugo wrote a few lines each year to commemorate the moment.[45] Hugo evocatively described their first night together in his entry in the *Livre de l'anniversaire* for 1841:

> Our first night was a carnival night, the night of Mardi Gras 1833. They were giving in some theater or other some ball to which we were both supposed to go, and which we both missed . . . Your little bedroom was full of an adorable silence. Outside we could hear Paris laughing and singing and the masqueraders passing by with loud shouts. In the midst of the general festivities we secluded and concealed in the shadows our own sweet festival. (*LJD*, 336–7).

When he came to write his monumental novel *Les Misérables*, which was published in 1862, Hugo made Mardi Gras, 16 February 1833, the day on which the young hero and heroine, Marius and Cosette, were married and consummated their love. The carriages taking the wedding party to church thread their way through Parisian streets thronged with masqueraders celebrating Mardi Gras. Like Marius and Cosette, it seems, Drouet and Hugo sensed on that first fateful night the presence of "the forms of the night, the unknown winged ones, the blue passersby of the invisible, bending in a crowd of somber heads around the luminous dwelling—satisfied, offering benediction."[46] Similarly, in a letter written sixteen years after their first night (20 February 1849, *LJD*, 181), Hugo poetically evokes the morning after:

> I'll never forget that morning as I left your place, my heart bedazzled. The day was just beginning, it was pouring rain, the masqueraders, in tatters and covered with mud, were yelling as they came down from La Courtille and flooded into the Boulevard du Temple. They were drunk, and I was too—they with wine, I with love. Through their shrieks I heard a song that I had in my heart. I didn't see all these specters around me, specters of a joy that had died away, ghosts of an orgy that was over—I saw you—you, sweet shadow shining in the darkness, your eyes, your forehead, your beauty, and your smile as inebriating as your kisses. O morning, icy and rainy in the sky, radiant and ardent in my soul! Memory!

Aside from Drouet, could any reader of *Les Misérables* on its publication in 1862 have recognized the symbolism of the hero and heroine's marriage date? Undoubtedly Mme Hugo will have done so, for as she will have remembered, her marriage of eleven years' standing was in serious trouble by this point. By February 1833, Adèle Hugo and her husband's best friend, Charles-Augustin Sainte-Beuve—poet, literary critic, and admirer of Hugo's work—had been carrying on an affair for at least the previous two years, which would continue until 1836.[47] Mme Hugo had terminated sexual relations with Hugo after the birth of their last child, Adèle.[48] There would be gossip later that Sainte-Beuve was not only this girl's godfather, but her biological father too.[49] In any case, Hugo's marriage had deteriorated since 1822 when he had married Adèle Foucher, a childhood sweetheart, and by 1833 it seemed to be maintained only for the sake of appearances. Yet it was a complex relationship. Hugo's letters to her, written touring France or farther afield with Drouet, while admittedly rather like travelogues, are wonderful examples of his skills as poet, novelist, and artist. Their correspondence, while difficult to analyze completely, seems to give evidence of mutual affection. Hugo assures Adèle in 1835 while on vacation with Drouet: "I still love you more than anything in the world, you can believe me. You are my life itself" (*CF*, 2:235).[50] Adèle, simultaneously away from home to attend a wedding in the company of Sainte-Beuve, goes out of her way to assure Hugo that she is sharing a bedroom with her daughter, not Sainte-Beuve (*CF*, 2:223, 229). Both spouses emphasize how much they miss each other. But Adèle's tone with Hugo is often self-righteous and sometimes accusatory.[51] The prosaic banality of her letters makes one feel that, in contrast to Drouet, she must have poorly appreciated his artistic genius. In any case, a childhood torn between two warring parents, each with an extramarital relationship, combined with his present marital situation, had made Hugo insecure. He needed a solid relationship with a motherly woman to reaffirm his self-esteem. Concomitantly, Drouet needed a father figure to protect her in her current financial crisis and to provide her in general with the parenting that, as an orphan, she had never received. Drouet and Hugo would, in a sense, give each other exactly what each needed. No doubt that is why the relationship would last a whole lifetime.

What Hugo needed, in fact, was that Drouet should need him entirely. He therefore wanted her to give up her theatrical career. While she may, in the short term, have been glad to be released from the exhausting grind of too many performances, Drouet would eventually bitterly regret her break with the theater. She continued to perform at the Porte-Saint-Martin for about a year after meeting Hugo until the end of her contract, which occurred on 30 March 1834. She could hardly have suspected it at the time—after all she had a new contract starting 1 April with the prestigious Comédie-Française—but she would never again appear onstage after her last performance that night as (once again) Antonia in *Le Moine*. She had appeared during her six-year theatrical career in at least thirty-four different roles and had performed onstage more than a thousand times.

In some respects, however, the end of Drouet's dramatic career had already occurred on 7 November 1833. On this date Drouet appeared at the Porte-Saint-Martin in the premiere of Hugo's play *Marie Tudor*. It was an experience so excruciatingly embarrassing that the memory of it would last a lifetime.

On the night of the performance the audience arrived in the mood for a fight—perhaps with latent hostility toward Hugo and sensing another "Battle of *Hernani*."[52] The atmosphere had been primed by the knowledge that the playwright had given the young female lead, Jane, to his mistress, Mlle Juliette, piquing the jealousy of fellow actresses Mlle George and Mlle Ida. There had also been disagreements between Hugo and the theater director, Harel. The audience tangled with police outside the theater and, once inside it, behaved like animals. A journalist's account describes "shrieks, barking." He continues: "There was a gentleman in the second tier who could take off a dog to perfection and who gave us the proof of his talent for mimicry five or six times. We were also subjected to the *Marseillaise* sung out of tune by two hundred rather discordant voices . . . Added to this prologue there was a little entertainment, a shower of pieces of paper, inoffensive enough, but not so were the crusts of bread, apples, hats, and other projectiles thrown at the women."[53]

Any actor would have been disconcerted by such a brouhaha taking place during his or her performance. Drouet was already nervous after the weeks of backbiting and hostility to which she had been subjected during rehearsals. She was also acutely desirous of doing justice to her lover's faith in her acting. She lost her nerve. Almost all the newspaper reviews of the performance the next day lambasted her performance and commented on the way she had acted with her head lowered throughout the entire play. She looked, when her back was to the audience, as though she had been decapitated, one reviewer wrote scathingly![54] Hugo must have been similarly dismayed by her performance, for the very next day Drouet found herself out of the play and replaced by Mlle Ida. She would continue to perform until the end of her contract in the other plays in her repertoire at the theater, but her confidence was broken, as she herself said (*MUL*, 45). Hugo was anxious for her to abandon her career and willing to provide for her. The Comédie-Française, which seems to have engaged her only under pressure from Hugo, never offered her any roles (L. 20). The combination of these factors sufficed to prevent her from returning to the stage ever again.

For some years after her last appearance, however, Drouet would continue to hope for a comeback. There would be one brief moment of ecstasy in 1838 when Hugo promised Drouet the role of the Queen of Spain, Doña Maria de Neubourg, in his play *Ruy Blas* (L. 31), but it was quickly scotched by Mme Hugo. Unbeknownst to Hugo and Drouet, she wrote to the director of the Théâtre de la Renaissance to suggest that Mlle Juliette might compromise the success of the play. The role went instead, with no protest from Hugo, to Mlle Beaudoin, the mistress of the male lead, Frédérick Lemaître.[55] After this final blow Drouet felt that her morale had been destroyed forever—"I'm demoralized to the point that I wouldn't dare to perform, no matter what the role or whose play it was," she said (L. 34). With the years she would gradually come to accept her retirement from the theater. For someone who had made her name in parts contingent on youth and beauty the passage of time made it inevitable.

Once Drouet had retired from the theater, the contrast between her previous life as an actress and her life as Hugo's mistress became stark. Whereas she had previously led a busy independent life in the center of Paris's social maelstrom, glamorous and desired both onstage and off, and had lived in a relatively luxurious apartment on the rue de l'Echiquier, Drouet gained in return for being Hugo's lover a parsimonious and solitary existence that she would describe at times as the life of "a squirrel in a cage."[56] Her social circle was reduced to one. Hugo, who was intensely jealous and possessive, would not allow her to leave her apartment without him or open her own letters, even from her daughter.[57] Despite Hugo's famed dictum, "Oh! n'insultez jamais une femme qui tombe!" ("Oh, never insult a woman who falls!" *Les Chants du crépuscule*, XIV), and despite the sympathy he would show later in *Les Misérables* for the plight of the young unmarried mother, Fantine, at his worst moments he also raked up Drovel's "sinful" past and demanded that she atone for it. (L. 4). Throughout the letters that Drouet wrote to Hugo over fifty years, she often compared him to God (L. 32, 49, 55, 97, 99, 105, 115, 118, 122, 133, 144, 145, 152)[58] or to Jesus Christ (L. 145, 164, 177).[59] She, on the other hand, was cast in the role of Mary Magdalene (L. 105), as Hugo began to congratulate her on her moral "ascension" (*LJD*, 109) and on her "devotion, resignation, and virtue."[60] Accepting the role of redeemed harlot, Drouet writes in a letter dated 2 May 1837:

> I am in ecstasy as I contemplate the thought of you and your adored image. I see what you are, that is to say, God-made-Man, to redeem me and save me from this infamous life to which I was enslaved for so long. What Jesus Christ did for the world as a whole, you have done for me alone. Like Him you have redeemed my soul at the expense of your repose and your life. (*VHJD*, 2:335)

In Hugo's view, Drouet's past sin had taken two forms, sexual and financial. In fact he saw these as being two sides of the same coin.[61] She would be redeemed in his eyes by practicing total monogamy and stringent economy. When Hugo met Drouet she was not only being sued for debts she was unable to meet, but she had no financial records of her own affairs, no record of what she had paid for purchases, no clear idea of whom she owed what. This was a situation that shocked the bourgeois in Hugo. All his life he wrote down every day every penny he spent (including on prostitutes) and was always very frugal, even after he had become an extremely wealthy man. Complete financial dependence on Hugo required that his money be accounted for, as Drouet complained, down to the last carrot in her stewpot.[62] From now on, instead of being surrounded by luxurious furnishings in a luxurious apartment, wearing the finest clothes and jewelry, she would have to make do with bare necessities in much more humble quarters. Indeed, some of her letters show her referring to economizing on firewood (L. 20) and owning only the dress she has on her back

(L. 42, 47, 73). In order to set off on trips with Hugo she has to borrow a hat, shawl, even a corset, from a friend (L. 30, 42).[63]

The first couple of years of the relationship were stormy with constant rows, often arising from Hugo's unfounded suspicions of Drouet's infidelity. Matters reached a head with Drouet's flight to Brittany with her daughter, Claire, in August 1834 (L. 11), where she stayed with her sister Renée and her brother-in-law, Louis Koch. Hugo followed her. There was a passionate reconciliation and a meandering return—which became the prototype for a tradition of annual pleasure trips—and then an idyllic interlude in the forested countryside outside Paris in a village called Les Metz (L. 14). Drouet lived in a little cottage Hugo had rented for her, and he stayed with his family not far away at the country home of the cultured family of François Bertin, editor of *Le Journal des débats*. The two lovers met each day in the woods and left notes for each other in the hollow trunk of a chestnut tree. The idyll would be repeated in the autumn of 1835.

During this second idyllic interlude Hugo writes on 25 September 1835, after a meeting in the forest the day before:

> Let us never forget this terrible storm of 24 September 1835 that was so full of divine things for us. The rain fell in torrents, the leaves of the tree served only to bring it down more cold upon our heads, the sky was full of thunder, you were naked in my arms—your beautiful face hidden in my lap turning only to smile at me—and your wet blouse clung to your shoulders.

This was a love with a vision of itself, and a strikingly modern—in fact, Romantic—one at that. Indeed, what else from the leader of the French Romantic movement? Clearly, in order to properly romanticize itself such a love needed the written word and a lover who could respond in kind.[64] Hugo agreed with Drouet: "You're right. We must love each other, and then we must tell ourselves we love each other, and then we must write it to each other" (*LJD*, 32). Drouet was the perfect correspondent. As Hugo was writing his description of their lovemaking in the rain, Drouet had also committed hers to paper:

> My dear beloved, my Victor, I would not give this day and especially the moment when I trembled with cold upon your lap for the finest and most radiant of summer days. It seems to me that we were reborn in this baptism, showered on us by Heaven and presided over by Love." (*MUL*, 86)

Drouet felt from the very beginning a need to write down her feelings about Hugo and observations that she would have made to him in person, had he been there. She wrote her first letter of this kind the morning of 17 February 1833 after their first night together, and such letters served, she said, as "a kind of electric wire by which my soul felt connected with your soul when you were far from me" (*MUL*, 606). But writing letters was not only a substitute for being together. It was also a necessary adjunct to it. The "epistolary prodigality" (*VHJD*, 2:261) for which Drouet was already apologizing in 1833 would continue and grow, with Hugo's encouragement, for the next half century.

If we are to judge by Drouet's letters and the course of events, for Hugo—who could find sexual appeal only in very young women—the relationship appears to have lost its sexual excitement, although certainly not its poetic and moral interest, quite soon. Many of Drouet's letters in the first two decades of their relationship, perhaps, indeed, the majority, complain about how very little time Hugo spends with her. The state of incarceration imposed on her by Hugo now becomes unbearable as Hugo's visits become shorter and shorter (and often occur in the middle of the night—L. 44, 47). She finds herself going days, even weeks or months, without setting foot outdoors. She must wait for Hugo to find time to take her out, whether for a walk or for essential business, such as visiting her daughter in the pension or making purchases (*VS*, 1:69–72). She lives all year waiting for their annual trip and the chance to be with Hugo for a few days at a time. Despite Hugo's obvious sexual appetite for other women and numerous letters in which Drouet openly describes her sexual desire, many of Drouet's letters from early on testify to little sexual contact in the relationship, or what she calls "the scandal of two lovers living in a state of atrocious chastity" (25 November 1834 [*VS*, 1:20]).[65] In one letter she asks, "When are you going to come and sleep with me?" (7 March 1837 [*MUL*, 115]) or, "When is the orgy? When . . . ??????"[66] In another letter (19 December 1848 [*LVH*, 122]) she complains about the fact that Hugo has refused to have sex with her. In other letters she promises sexual delights if only Hugo will take advantage of them.[67] "I have a burning heart and lips on fire," she writes on 30 May 1842, "why do you condemn me the whole year through to the punishment of Tantalus?" (*VS*, 1:53). In a letter dated 11 March 1852 (L. 100), she comments ironically vis-à-vis an ailment of Hugo's, "It appears you must double your chastity, which won't be difficult as far as I'm concerned, for you only have to continue the continence you have observed with me so scrupulously for what will soon be two months, although I could even say for what will soon be *eight years*." With hindsight, and the decipherment and publication of Hugo's encrypted notations on his sex life, we know that Hugo's prodigious sexual appetite was finding other means to express itself. Drouet's had to remain unsatisfied.[68]

On 17 November 1839 when the relationship was six years old, Hugo promised Drouet, in return for her promising to abandon all intentions of returning to the stage, that he would never leave her and that he would support her and her daughter, Claire, for the rest of their lives (L. 37, 38). This was a promise that Hugo kept, and both saw it as a kind of marriage between them. But perhaps it also extinguished the last vestiges of the sexual interest of the relationship for Hugo: Drouet was now fully and safely his in every sense of the word and the excitement of the chase was truly gone.

Many of the letters Drouet wrote in the 1840s reflect her unhappiness with the situation. At the beginning of the decade she writes on 20 July 1841, "This year is one of the saddest, coldest, and most denuded of any kind of happiness that has ever weighed on my life."[69] On 16 February 1843, the anniversary of their first night of love, which was usually for her an occasion for rejoicing, she writes:

> Always to be sacrificed to everything: to business, to pleasure, to family affections—this is not living. May God forgive me what I'm going to say if it's blasphemy, but if I had known ten years ago what I know today, I would have rather killed myself than have accepted my life as it is now.
>
> I'm all ready in fact to renounce this life. The most miserable condition is preferable to the life that I lead. I'm like a poor starving person condemned to live in the midst of painted game, pâté, and fruit, and whatever the merit of the painting might be, it's difficult to restrict oneself to food for the eyes alone. I have only painted happiness and cardboard pleasures. (*MUL*, 252)

In this letter Drouet dates the beginning of her insufferable existence to three years previously and remarks, "It's very clear that you no longer have any love for me." Notwithstanding the fact that Drouet made observations of this kind many times, especially during the 1840s, and whatever the exact chronology of Hugo's feelings for her may have been, it does seem that a turning point was reached in the years 1843–1844 that would permanently change the nature of their relationship. It was heart wrenching for Hugo when his treasured nineteen-year-old daughter, Léopoldine, got married (L. 50). A few months later, she drowned with her husband, Charles Vacquerie, in a boating accident. Hugo learned of the accident by chance as he read a newspaper at an inn, while away on a trip with Drouet (L. 53, 54).

This event may have been partly the catalyst, if not the motivation or the justification, for his first serious affair since he had met Drouet eleven years previously. The affair began probably in 1844 with a woman named Léonie Biard (née d'Aunet)[70] who was married to an academic and fashionable painter of about the same age as Hugo. She had moved into the luxurious residence of the wealthy society painter when she was between sixteen and seventeen years old (1837–1838) and had already acquired some celebrity by accompanying him on a voyage to Spitsbergen in the Arctic. Léonie d'Aunet was pregnant by François Biard when she married him in 1840. At twenty-four years old she was fourteen years younger than Drouet and eighteen years younger than Hugo. Ironically, Hugo probably met her through Pradier, whose house and studio he often visited as a friend and as an advocate of Drouet, mother of Pradier's daughter.[71]

To Léonie Biard Hugo wrote passionate love letters as spontaneous as those Drouet wrote to him, and strangely reminiscent of them. Just as Drouet declares in her letters her unbearable longing for Hugo's presence, which sanctifies as religious relics even the traces of disorder left in the room behind him, so Hugo repeats the same sentiment to Biard;[72] just as Drouet compares Hugo to God and declares her willingness to die for him, so Hugo repeats the same sentiment to Biard.[73] Yet in 1847 at the height of his affair with Biard, and unknown to both her and Drouet, Hugo attempted to initiate an affair with the actress Alice Ozy, who was at the time mistress of his son Charles.[74] As Arsène Houssaye acutely commented with reference to Hugo, "There are some men whom it is impossible to contain within the laws of family and society, because they comprise several men."[75]

The Hugo-Biard relationship would continue for seven years and Drouet would not know about it, even though in 1845 Hugo and Biard would be caught together in flagrante delicto and arrested after Biard's husband had hired a private detective (L. 57). The incident was reported in the newspapers, and yet Drouet—who did not read them, or perhaps read only what Hugo allowed her to read—had no inkling of the event that reached even the ears of her sister and brother-in-law in Brittany. When that brother-in-law, Louis Koch, brought the news to her attention, albeit in a very oblique kind of way, she chose to dismiss it (L. 58). Perhaps it was imperative to believe that Hugo could not be unfaithful to her, since as she frequently said, infidelity on his part would have killed her (L. 58). "I know you are incapable of lying to me, because *I* always tell *you* the truth," she wrote (L. 59). Unfortunately, Drouet's confidence in Hugo in this respect was grossly misplaced. And yet maybe, at a subconscious level, Drouet did suspect the truth. Certainly she refers to the possibility of infidelity on Hugo's part many times, especially in the 1840s. For example, in a letter dated 20 September 1845, some two months after Hugo's arrest in flagrante delicto, Drouet writes:

> I had a bad night, complicated . . . by frightful dreams. I woke up several times sobbing. Every time I dream of you, which I do almost every night, I have terrible dreams . . .
>
> I hope that these hideous dreams are the opposite of reality, for if they aren't, I would be in despair and would kill you without pity.
>
> It's true that all these horrible dreams are lies, isn't it? It's true that you love me and are very faithful to me, isn't it?" (*VS*, 3.32)[76]

On 28 June 1851, Drouet wrote two witty letters (L. 81, 82) to Hugo about a dish of strawberries that she had sent to his house by her servant, Suzanne, for him and his family to enjoy, concluding with the line: "As long as you are completely faithful to me and love me, I permit you everything." Sometime shortly afterward that day she received in the mail a package of love letters written by Hugo to Léonie Biard over the course of the preceding seven years. Biard had sent them to her with a note saying that the relationship was still flourishing. Drouet's feelings as she opened the package and read the letters can only be imagined. But she did not die. From then on more than ever, it was Drouet's conviction and pride that her love for Hugo was a greater love than any other.[77] While she may not have been able to compete in life with the beauty of women years younger, in death the beauty of her loving soul would outshine all others (L. 83). Nevertheless, as she wrote on 28 December 1851, she felt that there was "something dead in the depths of [her] soul" that would never revive.

Why did Drouet tolerate Hugo's treatment of her? A pragmatic answer is that Drouet was entirely financially dependent on Hugo and had no hope of earning any income as an actress by this point in her life. Moreover, Hugo's dual standards were merely the norm, as the literature of the period abundantly testifies. Indeed, reading accounts of extramarital relationships of the time, such as Arsène Houssaye's self-glorifying and callous description of his treatment of Marie Garcia,[78] one is tempted to conclude that Hugo's behavior was actually rather more decent than the contemporary norm. But aside from practical considerations and social mores, Drouet had made loving Hugo her life's work. "I live to love you and I love you to live," she wrote on 4 September 1853 (*LVH*, 190) or, on 1 January 1868: "My virtue is to love you. My body, my blood, my heart, my life, my soul are employed in loving you. Beyond my love, I am nothing, I understand nothing, I want nothing. Loving you, loving you, loving you, that is my one and only perfection" (L. 141). Finally, she needed Hugo to provide her with the psychological security that her orphaned childhood had not given her. This need was to become even stronger after 1846 with the death of her daughter, Claire, from tuberculosis (L. 62, 63, 64, 65).

The story of Claire Pradier's life makes for painful reading. She spent her whole short life farmed out to strangers, incarcerated in pensions, or boarding schools, first as a pupil and then, ultimately, as a student teacher—sad, lonely, waiting for opportunities to see her mother and father, both of whose approbation she desperately desired. Indeed, it seems that it was partly shame at having failed her parents by failing her teacher's examinations for a second time that caused Claire to fall seriously ill in March 1846.[79] She died three months later. It was clear too that although she already had a tubercular infection, Claire's illness was exacerbated by "sorrow," and after her death Drouet admitted that Claire must have had a desire to die.[80]

Boarding at a pension outside Paris at Saint-Mandé, she saw her mother every two weeks, if Drouet was not away on a trip with Hugo, and she would hope—often without result—to see her father also. When her mother left on a trip of several weeks, Claire was left behind. She longed for an affectionate relationship with her father, James Pradier. While he did do some charming sketches of her,[81] he was inadequate and irresponsible in his relations with her, often refusing her mother's request for money to pay the school fees, rebuffing all Claire's attempts at affection, and even eventually forbidding her to use his surname.[82] Although Claire was deeply hurt by this, her instinct throughout her life was to adore him.[83] In tragic letters (*MUL*, 325, 326) Drouet describes how brief visits by Pradier to Claire's deathbed were the only thing that could arouse her from her apathy, bringing a glow of joy to her face. Even after Claire's death, Pradier failed her. Having promised that he would design a monument to mark her grave, he never did so.[84] He even took his time paying her doctor.[85] Shortly after her death in June 1846 it was discovered that Claire had written her will the previous November, surely an unusual act for a twenty-year-old.[86] In it she bequeathed some mementoes from her small possessions to her two half sisters, Charlotte and Thérèse Pradier, but strangely enough made no mention of her father.

Claire was fond of Hugo, calling him "Monsieur Toto," and it is to Hugo's credit that he was affectionate toward Claire. For the rest of her life Drouet would commemorate the anniversary of Claire's death, and it was a convention between her and Hugo to invoke at solemn moments in their letters the spirits of their two dead daughters, Léopoldine and Claire, the two "angels" (L. 123, 135, 141). Around Claire's memory Drouet erected a monument to virginity, which contrasts strangely with the sensuality and enjoyment of sexuality that is both implicit and explicit in her letters to Hugo.[87] The contradiction only underlines the inherent paradoxes in the nineteenth-century role of women, which Hugo would do as much as anyone to perpetuate. While his diaries reveal relations throughout his life with an astonishing number of prostitutes and various other women, he also cultivated the concept of the virgin—worshiped by him in his own daughter Léopoldine—but also memorably enshrined in *Les Misérables* in the figure of Cosette.

The year 1851 was a turning point in France and for Drouet and Hugo in their lives and relationship, a year that Hugo would describe as "a year of pain, a year of struggle, a year of trial" (*LJD*, 197). It was the year of the coup d'état that brought Napoleon III to power, and it was the year in which Drouet and Hugo went into exile. It was also quite possibly this event that saved their relationship. Who knows whether Hugo would have chosen Drouet over Biard, if it had not been for the coup d'état, which made Hugo's swift departure from France, leaving Biard behind, a necessity? Hugo's politics had made him anathema to the regime that came to power, and it was only because of Drouet, as he believed, that he was not deported or killed.[88] Hugo left on 12 December under an assumed name and with a false passport. Drouet joined him on 14 December, carrying a trunk containing Hugo's manuscripts (L. 97). They would not return for nineteen years. They went first to Brussels, and when they were no longer welcome there, they went to Jersey in the British Channel Islands. From there too they were obliged to leave in 1855, and they spent the remaining fifteen years in Jersey's neighboring island, Guernsey. It was in Guernsey that Hugo would write some of his greatest works. Drouet had Hugo to herself without serious threat from competing relationships, and during the extended absences of Adèle Hugo, almost became his surrogate wife, or what she called "temporary *Grande Dame* of Hauteville House" (*MUL*, 622). There she would be most happy and write some of her most delightful letters. It was a period in their life that would seem like "paradise" in retrospect (L. 169). In fact, Drouet openly celebrated the anniversary of the 1851 coup d'état, which had sent them into exile (L. 146, 162), and the visitor to Saint Peter Port and to the spot where Drouet and Hugo lived, so little changed today, can see how the beauty of the island must have contributed to the charmed life they led there. As Hugo wrote in one of the Latin tags with which he decorated his home, Hauteville House, "Exile is life."[89]

In Guernsey Hugo and Drouet lived a small life on a small island in close proximity—for most of the time close enough to wave or to signal to one another from their respective houses (L. 141, 147, 154, 157, 160, 163, 174). Hugo deployed his vast energy writing some of his greatest work—*La Légende des siècles* (1859), *Les Misérables* (1862), *William Shakespeare* (1864), *Les Chansons des rues et des bois* (1865), *Les Travailleurs de la mer* (1866), *L'Homme qui rit* (1869)—fraternizing with other exiles, decorating his house (L. 116), and seducing the servants who worked for him. He lived in a large house at 38 Hauteville Street, which he called Hauteville House, purchased with the proceeds of the sales from his collection of poetry *Les Contemplations*. For the fourteen years (1856–1870) he lived there, he spent a great deal of time, energy, and money covering every inch of the interior with decor of his own design. Every detail of every room, it seems, bears the mark of Hugo: in the form of ornate carvings, screens, tapestries, or tiles that he bought in his travels across the island or abroad under the protection of "the good fairy Bric-a-Brac,"[90] or in the form of carvings he commissioned his carpenter to make, all of them then arranged by Hugo and in some cases "signed" by his initial *H*, or "annotated" by his Latin and French inscriptions. As Charles Hugo so aptly put it in *Chez Victor Hugo par un passant*, Hugo's house would be "for his biographers a veritable autograph on three floors, something like . . . a poem in several rooms."[91]

From 1856 until 1864 Drouet lived in La Fallue, a small house down a small alley that runs at right angles to Hauteville Street and Hauteville House. From the dormer window of La Fallue, her "lookout," she could see Hugo in his lookout only yards away and look down into the Hugos' garden. In 1864 Hugo purchased for Drouet a much larger and more elegant house (in which he himself had lived for the first few months after his arrival in Guernsey), about a hundred yards down the hill from Hugo's house. They called it "Hauteville-Féerie." From here her vision of Hugo was more limited, but Drouet was still able to look through her window in the morning and see Hugo's towel tied to the balcony that ran around his lookout, signaling to her that he had got up. Here too at Hauteville-Féerie, Hugo let his imagination run riot as he decorated this house, like his own Hauteville House, with an abundance of chinoiseries and signed it with the ubiquitous *H*.

When Hugo moved to Guernsey he insisted that his adult children, Charles, François-Victor, and Adèle, twenty-nine, twenty-seven, and twenty-five years old respectively, move with him. Playing the part of paterfamilias and *Maître* ("Master") was vital to Hugo's sense of security, and it was a role that he played out, or attempted to play out, in many ways all his life. However, his wife and children submitted to their roles in the drama with less enthusiasm than Drouet (L. 122). All of them suffered in one way or another from Hugo's overwhelming omnipotence, and concomitantly, all of them were dependent on him. His sons, who were quite accomplished writers and journalists in their own right, were completely overshadowed by Hugo, and he supported them financially for the length of both of their short lives. Furthermore, being used to the sophistication and excitement of metropolitan Paris, they were not impressed by this English-speaking, sleepy backwater. All members of Hugo's family eventually began to spend long periods of time abroad, especially in Brussels, where the sons acted as unofficial agents in Hugo's business relations with his publishers, who were based there.[92] Charles moved there in 1861, where he married and had two children. François-Victor and Mme Hugo left for Brussels permanently in 1865 after François-Victor's fiancée, Emily de Putron, died. Emily, a native of Guernsey and daughter of a shipowner, had worked with him on his translations of Shakespeare.

Part of Mme Hugo's desire to leave Guernsey related to her anxiety about finding suitable marriage prospects for her daughter Adèle, who had refused several marriage proposals in Guernsey and was showing signs of depression. Adèle's life was to turn out almost as dramatically as a Hugolian novel.[93] In 1863 she ran away in pursuit of a British officer, Lt. Alfred Pinson, whom she had first met in Guernsey. She followed him to Canada and then to Barbados (L. 148). Her obsessive pursuit of Pinson, a kind of sad parody of Drouet's devotion to Hugo, did not end until 1872. Adèle was brought back to France from Barbados after nine years' absence by her black servant, Mme Baa. In the interim her mother (1868) and her brother Charles (1871) had died. She was interned for the rest of her life in a psychiatric institution on the outskirts of Paris. Ironically, she outlived all the Hugo family, surviving until 1915, lost in a world of insanity.

Toward the end of her life Mme Hugo officially met Drouet, and formal courtesies were exchanged. Adèle Hugo had known about her husband's affair with Drouet from very early on in the relationship.[94] She had even acquiesced in her husband's relationship with Léonie Biard, entertaining her in her own house (L. 101), no doubt with the thought that Biard might be the means to break the link with Drouet. We have little evidence that Adèle directly tackled her husband on the subject except for a letter written by Hugo, dated 24 January 1851, in reply to one from his wife. Clearly Adèle was dismayed to see that Drouet had followed them even to Brussels and was going to be with them in exile, but Hugo's response,[95] in which he credited Drouet with saving his life, was of a kind to put an end to discussion. Adèle's increasing absence from Guernsey, leaving Drouet and Hugo together sometimes for years at a time, was a kind of tacit acceptance of, maybe even an ultimate indifference toward, the situation.⁹⁶ Both her sons, Charles and François-Victor, had known Drouet since 1859 (L. 124, 125, 126) and were in the habit of dining with her. It is inconceivable that, living at such close proximity and in a town as small as Saint Peter Port, Adèle Hugo and Juliette Drouet were not well acquainted with each other, at least by sight. However, the first step in Mme Hugo's official recognition of Drouet seems to have been the act of sending her in 1863 a signed copy of her biography of Hugo, *Victor Hugo raconté par un témoin de sa vie* (L. 162). As a second step, Mme Hugo invited Drouet on 20 December 1864 to attend the Christmas dinner for the poor children of Saint Peter Port, whom Hugo was in the habit of entertaining once a month.⁹⁷ Drouet wrote back graciously declining this invitation. However, during a visit with Drouet to Brussels to visit his wife and sons from June to October 1866, Hugo's diaries make it clear that Drouet dined *en famille* with the Hugos several times.⁹⁸ The visit that made the relationship official was the one made on 23 January 1867 by Mme Hugo to "Mme Drouet" at her house at 20 Hauteville Street, not in the anonymity of Brussels, but under the judgmental gaze of the bourgeoisie of Guernsey (L. 163). During the visits to Brussels that Drouet and Hugo made to visit his wife and sons in the summer of this year and the summer of the next, Drouet read to Adèle Hugo. Adèle's eyesight had diminished to the point where she could not see well enough to read (*JDD*, 322, 324).

It was during the second of these visits, on 27 August 1868, that Mme Hugo died. Drouet's grief is expressed in her letter of 28 August (L. 166). Hugo wrote on the back of his wife's deathbed photograph, "Dear departed one, pardoned and blessed!"⁹⁹ Nineteenth-century gender roles were such that Adèle's fling with Sainte-Beuve, forty years before, weighed more heavily in the scales of sin than Hugo's entire married life committing adultery.

Juju would now have another fifteen years to live with her Toto. Although they did not marry after the death of Mme Hugo, Juliette as "Mme Drouet" assumed more and more the mantle of Hugo's official consort and hostess. Eventually, after they returned to France, they lived under one roof, although on separate floors. Ironically, however, Drouet would be less happy than she had ever been.

When the Franco-Prussian War broke out in 1870, Hugo, having scorned Napoleon III's earlier "amnesty" (L. 128), decided that the symbolically right moment to return to France had come. He returned to France on 5 September 1870, the day after the proclamation of the beginning of the Third Republic, to overwhelming acclaim and popularity. His life became a perpetual round of entertaining and socializing. In addition, he now also had a political career. He was elected a Deputy in 1871 and Senator in 1876. Drouet was called on to be his unofficial housekeeper and secretary, opening and answering an avalanche of Hugo's mail each day, arranging and hosting large dinner parties, and overseeing the accounts of the household, while fearfully trying not to exceed the parameters of his stringent parsimony (L. 183, 184) or infringe on his superstitions by inviting thirteen guests to dinner (*MUL*, 758). Her health was not as robust as Hugo's, who was boasting about running upstairs at the age of seventy-two (*CL*, 82) and was still keeping records of sexual encounters at the age of eighty-five in the month before he died (*HS*, 134). She was exhausted by the pace of Hugo's life, which was now more hectic than it had ever been, and she was demoralized by Hugo's physical and spiritual remoteness (L. 181). While in Guernsey they had shared, tête-à-tête as it were, a little universe, a "little pocket-sized fatherland" (*JDD*, 320) "so luminous and so radiant" (*MUL*, 652). Back in Paris Hugo's attention was distracted by the flattery and the popularity, by his political career, and by a seemingly inexhaustible supply of women anxious to attract his sexual attention. He was also in the midst of his long-lasting relationship with Blanche Lanvin, who was twenty-three to Hugo's seventy-one.

The affair had begun in Guernsey, where Blanche, the illegitimate granddaughter of the Lanvins (whom Drouet had known since the 1820s as servants to Pradier), was acting as lady's maid to Drouet. When he had written the play *Hernani* in 1829, the twenty-seven-year-old Hugo had presented with comic revulsion the idea that the young Doña Sol could be affianced to the "old" man of sixty, Don Ruy Gomez de Silva, "decrepit, venerable, and jealous" (I.1). Now that Hugo himself was in his seventies, the idea seemed far less repellent.

A depressingly large number of the letters that Drouet read for Hugo in her role as secretary made her only too aware of the extent of Hugo's past and present "grave wrongs" to their relationship (*CL*, 182). Hugo's infidelities were nothing new—Guillemin speculates that they existed already in the first year of their relationship (*HS*, 21). The difference was that Drouet now had the humiliation of being brought face to face with them. She writes Hugo letters of lashing contempt (L. 171, 175), but her pain is tangible (L. 176, 178). Whereas Hugo's passion for Drouet had evolved into something sexless many, many years before, Drouet, on the other hand, still loved him, as she herself puts it in a letter of 1872 (L. 171), "with the same ardent and jealous passion" as she had in 1833. In 1873 she makes one last dramatic stand against such treatment, echoing her flight of four decades before. After reading a letter to Hugo from an admirer, she leaves for Belgium without telling him.[100] Hugo is devastated and feverishly beseeches her to return with magnificent and sincere love letters—"To lose you is to die." He promises fidelity on the head of his son François-Victor, who is ill with renal tuberculosis and will die three months later.[101] After her return he keeps his promise for exactly two days, and then continues as before (*HS*, 114). Drouet is too old, tired, and often ill to take any further stands. On 9 March 1880 she writes:

> My heart has received so many bruises over such a long period of time that there is no more room for wounds. I forgive you the old ones and no longer fear those to come, whatever they may be. All the water of the sea could not add a single drop of bitterness to a sponge that is already saturated. (*CL*, 159)

There is comparatively little joy in the letters Drouet wrote after the return from exile. Hugo and Drouet had been anticipating for many years the union in Heaven of their souls with those of their daughters, Léopoldine and Claire. In the letters of the 1870s, however, and after the death of Mme Hugo as well as of Hugo's two sons, Charles (1871) and François-Victor (1873), death begins to take on a new reality for them—especially for Drouet, who in some letters openly wishes for the repose of death. One of the most terrible letters of this kind is that of 8 February 1881, in which she writes in part:

> You do well to continue your good night and to keep your eyes and ears shut to the wind and the storm. As far as I am concerned, who have slept very little and very badly, I much prefer to see and hear these meteorological nightmares than to remember those that haunted me last night. I'm in a hurry to be done with all dreams, those of the day as well as those of the night. I'm in a hurry to rest in the honest repose of death, even if I am never to wake up elsewhere. I feel tired of life and uninterested in everything, in good as in bad. I desire nothing more; I hardly dare hope for anything. I smile without joy and cry without sorrow. I do my duty without virtue and love without happiness. That is the real truth. (*CL,* 168)

Yet, even fifty years earlier, Drouet had written Hugo letters alternating between ecstatic happiness and suicidal despair, and even now she could do the same. Moreover, it was Hugo as ever who, just as he could cause her the greatest sorrow, could bring her the greatest joy, making her young and healthy again. A letter from Hugo could still draw from Drouet declarations of her undying love, and her admiration for his "divine" genius was undimmed. For her he was still a god, and she was Psyche, clinging to his wings as he ascended to his celestial sphere. In a letter dated 30 May 1882, written one year before she died, she writes at seven o' clock in the morning, after having stayed up until three reading Hugo's newly published play *Torquemada*:

> How beautiful, how great, how sublime and divine it is!!! I emerge from this reading radiant and transfigured as though I had drunk all the elixir of your ardent poetry at once. My staggering soul clings to your great wings in order not to roll down from your high starry peaks into the deep chasm of my ignorance.
>
> I was afraid to disturb your sleep by the rustling of the pages I was cutting and devouring with a frenetic appetite without noticing the time passing and dragging the day behind it.
>
> Finally, fearing that you would catch me by surprise, I decided at three o'clock to go to bed, and here I am already up, triumphant,

in complete health, in complete love, rejuvenated by this Fountain of Youth of the mind and the heart that your inexhaustible genius pours out at every moment for a human race that is amazed, touched, and gratified! (*MUL*, 826)

Drouet died on 11 May 1883, and Hugo two years later. Drouet's last letter in this collection, written on 11 July 1882 forty-nine years after their relationship began, reaffirms her love, unchanged after half a century, ending with the line: "I love you, I admire you, I venerate you, and I adore you." Her last ever letter to Hugo, written on 1 January 1883, reads: "Dear beloved, I don't know where I will be next year at this time, but I am happy and proud to sign for you my affidavit of existence for this year with just these words: 'I love you.'" Hugo wrote back to her on the same day: "When I say to you, 'Bless you'—it is Heaven. When I say to you, 'Sleep well'—it is Earth. When I say to you, 'I love you'—it is I" (*LJD*, 329).

Hugo felt obsessively compelled to express himself in writing—not only in the form of some of the world's greatest ever poems, plays, and novels—but also in the form of notes on his day-to-day expenditures, sexual encounters, sayings, doings, and feelings. So also Drouet felt compelled to express her life's great "work," her love for Hugo, in written form. She wrote letters to Hugo when he was away from her (although never far away), but she also wrote to him on occasion even when he was with her (L. 167). Letter writing was not simply a means to communicate with an absent Hugo. Indeed, most of the letters Drouet wrote were not actually mailed to him and therefore, in that sense, lacked any utilitarian function. After writing a letter on a piece of paper folded often into four pages, she would write Hugo's name, or some appellation such as "For my beloved," on a blank outside page and place it (without an envelope) in a container on her mantelpiece for Hugo to retrieve—which sometimes he was slow to do.[102] He would then read the letter in situ (*MUL*, 438) or take it away with him to read later.[103] Drouet's letter writing was most importantly a means to make a work of art out of her love for him. Indeed, Drouet cultivated her love as Hugo cultivated his art, and in her humble way, Drouet saw her role as lover as a kind of counterpart to Hugo's role as artist.[104] Her letters were thus the artistic expression of her love.

Despite Drouet's many self-deprecating comments about her "poor pieces of twaddle without head or tail" (*MUL*, 476), which she felt could give Hugo about as much pleasure as she received from "the continual barking of the big dog opposite,"[105] her letters often reach the level of poetry. Images run like leitmotifs through a whole lifetime of correspondence and recur every time in a slightly new and beautiful form. Take, for example, the image of her love as a form of vegetation—an image that Hugo also uses in his letters, but more rhetorically and less vividly.[106] An early example occurs in a letter of 31 October 1837 where Drouet writes: "The sad season of affairs has arrived, that is to say, the cold, the rain, the wind, and the snow. Love must remain torpid under all of that, like the sap of the tree until next spring."[107] On 19 September 1847 she writes:

> The more I go on, my sweet Toto, the more I love you. My love, having invaded me completely, has outgrown my life and attaches itself to everything you like, everything you touch, everything that surrounds you. I love the floor on which you walk, the things your eyes have seen, the objects your hands have touched. All this luxuriant vegetation of love that issues from my heart could cover the earth and rise up to the sky without being in the least exhausted. I love you with the sap of youth and with the deep roots of an oak several centuries old . . . My soul turns toward you, my radiant sun, with a tender impatience. (*MUL*, 346)

Similarly, in her letter of 4 March 1851 she says: "Happiness grows tired and dies, love survives and increases and takes root to the point of absorbing the heart in its entirety. I do not complain, because it is the natural law of this species of vegetation" (L. 80). Again, on the first day of 1854 she writes: "By dint of loving you, my enchanting beloved, I no longer know what to say to you. Like branches that bend under the weight of too much fruit, my poor mind is close to breaking under the weight of too much love" (*MUL*, 459). In another New Year's letter, this time in 1856, she writes: "I smile at you through the twenty-three years that protect you and shelter us under their branches of love against the storms and tests to come" (*MUL*, 479). In this same year she writes on 6 April: "My love is like the natural fruit of my soul. I love you as apple trees have apples" (*MUL*, 482), and on the thirtieth of this same month, describing her pleasure at receiving *Les Contemplations* three days before, she writes: "I love you still more, if it's possible, these last three days because all the flowers of my love have blossomed at once, just as a rose bush is more a rose bush when it covers itself with roses" (*MUL*, 483). Nearly twenty years later in letters in which Drouet bewails the infirmity of her old age vis-à-vis Hugo's vitality, we find her returning to the image. On 22 February, 1874 she writes:

> My soul drags itself after you, repentant and blessing you.
>
> I say "repentant" . . . Of what? Of loving you too much. I don't blame myself for it, however, any more than the tree that blooms again in winter blames itself for the flowers it bears, which must kill it. (*MUL*, 711)

And the image of her love as a flower recurs again in a similar context a year later in a letter of 27 July 1875:

As for myself I go along more and more haltingly every day. But I don't care, for I have never had my heart more full of the sap of love, and it senses a flora of everlasting flowers bursting into bloom inside me one by one with which I will make the bouquet of our eternal Hymen in Heaven. (*MUL*, 733)

Most striking of all is the wonderful immediacy of the letters that conveys the sights and sounds of the "here and now" of a century and a half ago. We hear the barking of Hugo's dog, Chougna, grow fainter as he follows his master into town (L. 120), and we see Hugo's wife, dressed in her finery, walk past the window with Vacquerie (L. 109); we see the sun strike the rocks outside Drouet's window (*MUL*, 446), the bright whiteness of a cloth tied to Hugo's balcony as the early morning sun strikes it (L. 157), her cat sleeping on the rug (L. 107), or her cherry tree blooming outside, the hens clucking, and patches of sunlight streaking her neighbors' gardens (*MUL*, 508). Quite a number of the letters finish abruptly with the exclamation "Here you are!" as Hugo arrives at her house or comes into the room, surprising her in the middle of writing a letter (L. 55, 61, 94, 96, 110, 117, 120, 167). In the middle of writing one letter (L. 141), Drouet hears Hugo opening his window and puts down her pen to run to her window to wave to him.

The letters are full of variety, running the gamut of emotions and corresponding diction from religious and elevated (L. 88, 105, 121) to comic to raucous and crude (L. 22, 23, 25, 26, 35, 39, 44, 47, 48, 73, 74). Drouet had a wonderful sense of humor and some of her most pithy letters are those in which she unleashes her most colloquial vocabulary: when, for example, she piles up assonant adjectives to convey her contempt for the "bearded, crooked, mossy, hairy, hunchbacked, obtuse" ("barbus, crochus, moussus, poilus, bossus et obtus") political exiles in Jersey (*MUL*, 446). Drouet contrasted self-deprecatingly the clumsy Breton clogs of her letters with the gentility of the famous letter writer, Mme de Sévigné (*MUL*, 114). She compares her attempts to express her love to Hugo to the language of the "lowliest shopgirl to the head clerk" (ibid.), and says in the same letter that she can only really express herself with her clothes off.[108] Yet the fact is that it is often the spontaneous earthiness of her language that makes her letters so compelling. In a second letter evoking the storm of 24 September 1835 described above and replying to the letter Hugo had written her about it, Drouet comments:

You see, my dear Victor, I don't have the resource of a beautiful style, big words to describe the impressions of my heart and the joys of my soul. I offer you all of that crude and natural, like colonial commodities before the refiner and the merchant have crystallized and refined their merchandise. I love you purely and simply. (*MUL*, 86)

In another letter she says:

> I leave others who know how to *write well* to construct their sentences with perfect balance and choose their words with the postures dictated by the dictionary and the grammar book.
>
> *I* write for my pleasure, at random and at full rein and with all the energy of my love. If, in so doing, I jump over the hurdles of spelling, and if I gallop across fine language, splashing mud on it here and there as I go with vulgar and slangy expressions, I don't give two hoots, since I have no other pretension than to love you better than anyone. (*MUL*, 339)

Drouet well knew, in fact, that "talking dirty" appealed to Hugo's refinement. She was not only Mary Magdalene to his Christ. Their relationship also played out parallel fantasies of nature versus civilization, Breton peasant versus aristocratic Viscount,[109] *grisette* versus upper-class lover, Muse versus *Maître*, Marion de Lorme versus Didier,[110] Cosette versus Marius. The romances of many of Hugo's plays and novels revolve around sexual relationships across barriers of class, power, or moral stature.

Above all the letters are honest and give the lie to the conventional wisdom that Drouet's relationship with Hugo was a simple one of worshiper at the shrine. Though Drouet did, as already mentioned, many times compare Hugo to God and Jesus Christ, she was also quite capable of showering him with withering contempt, sometimes ironic, sometimes bitter, most often in relation to Hugo's weakness for women. Take, for example, her letter of 11 March 1852 (L. 100), which begins with a statement of dissatisfaction at their sex life and finishes:

> So have the courage, once and for all, of your physical and moral infidelity! What is a love that has a need for a third to satisfy it? What, you need several bodies for a single love, when mine would like two souls to love you better? What a profanation of love! How disgraceful all these miserable treacheries are that deceive no one and satisfy no one! It's time for us to be completely sincere toward each other, it's the only end worthy of us, worthy of this love that circulates in my veins along with my blood, that regulates the beating of my heart, that is the soul of my soul, that is more me than I myself, that is everything, that wants everything because it gives everything, that prefers nothing to something! Keep your generosity, your devotion, your pity, your gratitude, if you think you owe me them, which I deny, and let me die in peace far away from you—this is the only favor that I ask!

Or take the witty and crude sarcasm of her letter of 28 May 1855, written at the beginning of Jersey's bathing season:

> If this is the way you reward women who have head colds, better not to have them, that at least is my humble opinion. In any case, I'm not surprised at your absence since the appearance of the women's cabins at the *Hot Sea Bath [sic]*. You are too polite not to have attended *in person* the inauguration of the first naked asses of the season. You could not have done less, and you have, perhaps, done much more. *Let's hope so.*" (*LVH*, 235)

Then there is the reaction in a letter of 24 July 1880, written early in the morning after a night of insomnia while Hugo was still asleep, to a poem Hugo had written for the young Judith Mendès (daughter of Théophile Gautier), one of his senile flirtations:

> The sublime wretch who wrote that and the one to whom it is addressed are both in marvelous health, for nothing fattens and conditions the body and soul like treachery. Misfortune is reserved for those imbeciles of love and good faith. Which explains why I am so sick this morning, in body, mind, and heart." (*MUL*, 808)

At the age of seventy-four, Drouet's writing style had lost none of its pungency or force.

Hugo encouraged Drouet to write letters to him. Indeed he even insisted on them, jokingly describing them as a kind of debt for which they would coin the name "restitus," a neologism apparently based on "restituer," "to pay back" (L. 115, 120, 129, 183, 184, 185, 186). He described them as "his treasure, his jewel box, his richness." "Our life is there," he says, "laid away day by day, thought by thought. All that you have dreamed is there, all that you have suffered is there. They are as many charming little mirrors, each one of which reflects a side of your beautiful soul" (*LJD*, 101).

Drouet generally wrote twice a day, once in the morning and once in the evening, just as Hugo generally visited her twice a day at these times and would then read the letter she had written, anticipating his arrival. Drouet many times asked Hugo's permission to stop writing.[111] Toward the end of her life there were occasional periods when she laid aside the habit for some time,[112] but she never abandoned it, except in the last four or five months of her life, when she was too ill to write. In one letter she admitted that writing the letters represented for her "sweetness and pleasure in doing what pleases me the most after the happiness of being with you." "All that I say to you about them," she continues, "is a way of excusing myself for something that I am burning to do and that I would do even if you opposed it. What does it matter to me to be ignorant and stupid, since I love you?" With a reprise of the vegetation image, she asks, "Does the vine need education to seep its sap? Does the heart need syntax to give its love? So I give you mine in abundance and in the form that God has made it" (*MUL*, 449).

The 280 letters by Hugo to Drouet edited by Jean Gaudon (*LJD*) represent the entirety of those preserved by her (*LJD*, 12). Since, as Gaudon points out, Drouet treasured everything that she received from Hugo, we can assume that these represent close to the totality of the letters that she received from him (apart from six months' of his letters that she burned after a quarrel in the first year of their relationship [*LJD*, 29]). Whereas most of Drouet's letters were collected by Hugo when he came to visit her, many of Hugo's letters in the preexile period were mailed to her, and the envelopes and postmarks survive to prove it. During exile when they lived in close proximity, Hugo's letters to Drouet were often delivered by a servant, and after exile Drouet and Hugo virtually lived with one another, so delivery was no longer an issue. After the beginning of the relationship when Hugo must have written more frequently, and except for unusual occasions such as when Hugo was ill and wrote letters to keep Drouet informed, Hugo's letters were sent, for the most part, as commemorations for special events in the calendar of their anniversaries—such as New Year's Eve, 16–17 February (the day of their first "kiss"), Drouet's birthday, and her feast day, Saint Julie's day, in May. While most of Juliette's letters in this collection were written in the morning when she got up, many of Hugo's (in the preexile and exile period) were written late at night after he had closeted himself up to work. As the mail was delivered with extraordinary rapidity and, it seems, on every day of the year, Hugo could mail a letter in the small hours of the morning and have it reach Drouet later in the morning of the same day. By comparison with Drouet's letters, Hugo's letters—especially after the first couple of years—are as Gaudon points out, "always astonishingly reserved . . . [Hugo] never confides or explains himself." The purpose of them appears to be, as Gaudon puts it, "to wrap the loved object in harmonious tissue . . . to respond to the daily confidence with noise, which in the ears of his lover is the most touching and grandiose of harmonies."[113] Concomitant with the reserve of Hugo's letters is an obvious rhetorical artifice that contrasts with the apparent spontaneity of Drouet's letters, as well as with the spontaneity of those Hugo wrote to Léonie Biard. Yet rhetorical artifice came naturally to Hugo, and his letters to Drouet are no less beautiful or sincere for that. Each of his letters to Drouet is a poem by Victor Hugo dedicated to their love and cherished by Drouet as such. Take, for example, just one line from a letter written on Saint Julie's Day 1875, which even in translation retains its beauty: "You are my life, and you will be my eternity" (*LJD*, 300).

The letters translated here are all derived from two public collections: the vast majority from the Biliothèque nationale and a few from the Maison Victor Hugo, with the exception of L. 7 (the whereabouts of which is not now known), which is reproduced as published by Paul Souchon in his collection *"Mon grand petit homme . . .": Mille et une lettres d'amour à Victor Hugo (MUL)*. They are a translation, with the kind permission of the Librairie Arthème Fayard and Evelyn Blewer, of a collection edited by Evelyn Blewer entitled *Lettres à Victor Hugo, 1833–1882*, first published in 1985 by Jean-Jacques Pauvert et Silène-Har/Po. This was reissued in 2001 by Fayard (*LVH*), with some additional letters, notes, and emendations by Blewer as a companion edition to Jean Gaudon's *Lettres à Juliette Drouet (LJD)*, also a reissue with additions and emendations of an edition originally published in 1964. The present collection consists of 186 letters out of a total of perhaps twenty thousand written during Drouet's fifty-year relationship with Hugo.[114] After her death the letters passed into the hands of her heirs and into other private collections. The Bibliothèque nationale acquired its collection of 16,228 letters in 1969 as a result of purchasing the collection of private collector Louis Icart. However, many (perhaps hundreds) of other letters written by Drouet to Hugo remain in private hands, while others dealing with delicate matters were doubtless destroyed by Drouet's executors, especially Paul Meurice, before they ever reached the collectors (*VS*, 4: 90–2). Besides Blewer's collection of letters translated here, other collections are to be found: in the second volume of Louis Guimbaud's *Victor Hugo et Juliette Drouet (VHJD)*, in Paul Souchon's collection of letters mentioned above (*MUL*), in Jean Massin's complete works of Hugo, *Oeuvres complètes (OC)*, and in Jacques and Simonne Charpentreau's *"Je ne veux qu' être aimée": Cinquante lettres de Juliette Drouet à Victor Hugo (CL)*. Clearly, by far the largest part of Juliette Drouet's correspondence with Hugo remains to be published. In English, other than this translation, there exists to my knowledge only Lady Theodora Davidson's 1914 translation of Guimbaud *(VHJD)*.

Translation is always an art, and translating Juliette Drouet's letters presents some problems of its own. The letters were not intended for publication. They were private musings written for the very specific recipient Victor Hugo, and therefore do not strive to make themselves intelligible to a general reader. They do not seek to provide context or elucidate allusions or jokes, the meaning of some of which must now elude us. The French language has evolved in the century and a half since the letters were written, some words, especially slang, dropping out of usage, others changing their value. Drouet invented some words and misspelled others, sometimes deliberately, to mimic an amusing accent or pronunciation, and sometimes unintentionally, as when she ventures into English, a language that she did not know. Private jokes involving spoonerisms and puns—particularly salacious ones—in the French of a century and a half ago present an especial challenge, since low diction is always less well documented than high and changes more rapidly. Even when the double meaning of a pun is obvious, it is usually impossible to preserve it in English, since the joke resides in the coincidence of two meanings with a single sound that is lost in translation. Furthermore, the variety that makes Drouet's letters lively, charming, and interesting also makes them difficult to translate. Within a single letter there are many registers of tone—often ranging from the sublime to the ridiculous, from the high to the low—with diction to match. She will address Hugo with the formal *vous* at one moment and with the informal *tu* at another,[115] a subtlety that English cannot render. In order to give the flavor of the colloquial and sometimes downright earthy or crude tone of the letters, I have occasionally used slang that is anachronistic and/or uniquely British or American in usage rather than fail completely to convey the tone of the original. "Boo-boo" (L. 124, 139, 164), for example, may not have been current in nineteenth-century American slang and never in British, but it captures better than any other word the feeling of "bobo." The British slang word "swot" (L. 47, 76, 156, 171) may not be common currency in America, but it is the only word that approximates to "piocheur."

For the reader interested in pursuing further reading in English on or by Juliette Drouet, the bibliography is unfortunately extremely limited. As mentioned above, to my knowledge only one other English translation of a collection of her letters exists—Davidson's translation of the second volume of Guimbaud (*VHJD*), the second volume of which contains a selection of the letters. Davidson's translation omits some of the letters in the Guimbaud edition and, obviously with an eye to contemporary Anglo-American prudery, omits anything suggestive from what is already a highly censored selection of letters. There is no full-length biography in English of Juliette Drouet. Anglophone readers must glean what they can from biographies in English of Victor Hugo, best of which is Graham Robb's *Victor Hugo* (*VH*). *Rage and Fire*, Francine du Plessix Gray's biography of Louise Colet, gives a good picture of the kind of life led by James Pradier and his scandalous wife, Louise d'Arcet. Concerning Hugo and Drouet's life in the Channel Islands, there is much of interest in the bilingual book by Gregory Stevens Cox, *Victor Hugo in the Channel Islands*. John McCormick's *Popular Theatres of Nineteenth-Century France*, while it does not mention Mlle Juliette, provides information on the theatrical world to which she belonged.

In French there is of course more available, although even then there is little written specifically about Juliette Drouet. There are a few full-length biographies of her, but with the exception of Pouchain and Sabourin's *Juliette Drouet ou "la dépaysée"* (*JDD*), they are not always factually reliable, and some are even "outrightly mendacious" (*LJD*, 19). Gérard Pouchain has recently published a collection of letters, *Lettres familiales* (*LF*), written by Drouet to her sister's family, the Kochs, in Brittany, along with a valuable biographical commentary that adds to our knowledge about Drouet's life. Douglas Siler's meticulously annotated edition of the correspondence of James Pradier provides much valuable incidental information on the life of Juliette Drouet and on people with whom she was closely associated. The handsome edition of fifty of her letters by Jacques and Simonne Charpentreau (*CL*) is valuable even to an Anglophone reader for its illustrations, including photographs of the original letters in Drouet's handwriting, complete, in some cases, with her own illustrations. Guimbaud (*VHJD*) also has some interesting illustrations, including some drawings of Claire Pradier by her father, as well as a useful list of poems by Hugo that were inspired by Drouet (501–3). Another source of wonderful illustrations, pertaining mainly to Hugo but of relevance also to Drouet, is the catalog of the exhibition *Victor Hugo: L'homme océan* held by the Bibliothèque nationale de France to mark the bicentenary in 2002 of Hugo's birth. Information about Juliette Drouet's (and Victor Hugo's) relations with James Pradier and many illustrations of his work are available in the catalog of the exhibition of Pradier's sculpture, *Statues de chair*, that was held in Geneva and Paris in 1985–1986.

In many places I have supplemented Evelyn Blewer's notes with my own additions (printed in bold) where I have felt that Anglophone readers would require more information. I have also incorporated, as appropriate, emendations made by Blewer to the text of the letters, or additions made by her to the notes on the text in her recent edition of the letters (*LVH*), which was published while this work was in progress. The numbering of the letters, designed to make cross-referencing easier, is my own. Where references were made by Blewer to Gaudon's 1964 edition of Hugo's letters, I have substituted references to the more readily available edition of 2001 (*LJD*). My glossary provides information about all the works by Hugo mentioned in this book, as well as information about people mentioned in the text or of importance for understanding the life of Drouet or Hugo. For a more complete list of Hugo's vast literary oeuvre the reader may consult Robb (*VH*, 550–2).

All translations from French, unless otherwise noted, are my own.

I would like to thank Evelyn Blewer for her permission to translate her edition of Juliette Drouet's letters, and for help with difficulties of translation and with understanding the context in which the letters were written. I am grateful too to have been able to consult my colleague Elizabeth Emery when particularly stumped by Drouet's wit and wordplay and to my colleague Avram Segall for clarifying aspects of French nineteenth-century law pertaining to Drouet's debts. I wish, especially, to express my gratitude for the hospitality of Richard and Elizabeth Soar, the present owners of "Hauteville-Féerie" in Saint Peter Port, Guernsey, where Hugo briefly lived in 1855–1856 and where Drouet lived from 1864 until her return to France in 1870. Mr. and Mrs. Soar kindly allowed me to see the interior of their house and to look through the window (with original shutters) from which Drouet had a view of Hugo's "lookout," and from which she peered anxiously each morning for a glimpse of the towel tied to the railing that signaled Hugo had got up. Thanks finally to Boris, Margaret, and Kristen for accompanying me twice to Guernsey and enduring three visits to Hauteville House in two days! I dedicate this book to them.

Notes

1. Paul Souchon, *"Mon grand petit homme...": Mille et une lettres d'amour à Victor Hugo* (Paris: Gallimard, 1951), abbreviated henceforth as *MUL*. Louis Guimbaud (*Victor Hugo et Juliette Drouet: D'après les lettres inédites de Juliette Drouet à Victor Hugo et avec un choix de ces lettres*, 2 vols. [Paris: Auguste Blaizot, 1914], 1:77), dates the letter to 1837. This work will be abbreviated henceforth as *VHJD*.

2. The most reliable details about the early life of Juliette Drouet are given by Gérard Pouchain and Robert Sabourin, *Juliette Drouet ou "la dépaysée"* (Paris: Librairie Arthème Fayard, 1992), abbreviated henceforth as *JDD*. Part I, sections I–III (13–248) are written by Pouchain, part II, sections I–II (265–425) are by Sabourin. The following information about Drouet's childhood and young adulthood are derived, ibid., part I, chapters I–III, unless otherwise noted.

3. Gérard Pouchain has discovered that, unknown to his sisters, Armand grew up to be a miller and lived all his life not far from Fougères, dying in 1876—Gérard Pouchain, ed., *Lettres familiales*, by Juliette Drouet (Condé-sur-Noireau: Charles Corlet, 2001), 12, n. 7. This work will be abbreviated henceforth as *LF*.

4. For Drouet's negative opinion, see Douglas Siler, ed., *Correspondance*, by James Pradier, 3 vols. (Geneva: Droz, 1984–1988), 3:215, n. 1. For Françoise Drouet's familiarity with artistic circles, see below, n. 20.

5. Examples of her letter writing are to be found in *LF*.

6. Richard Lesclide, *Propos de table de Victor Hugo* (Paris: E. Dentu, 1885), 65–7.

7. "Sunday evening, half past 8:00, 1835," cited by *JDD*, 32 and n. 14.

8. The fullest and most accurate recent accounts of Pradier's life and career are provided passim by J. de Caso, G. Garnier, C. Lapaire, I. Leroy-Jay Lemaistre, and D. Siler, *Statues de chair: Sculptures de James Pradier* (Paris: Editions de la Réunion des musées nationaux, 1985) and by Siler, *Correspondance*.

9. See Garnier in *Statues de chair*, "La carrière d'un artiste officiel à Paris," 78–96.

10. Baudelaire, for example, calls him (albeit ironically) the "king" of sculpture, going on to criticize him for his "cold and academic talent." "He has spent his life," alleges Baudelaire, "fattening up a few ancient torsos and adjusting on their necks the hairdos of kept women" ("Salon de 1846," in Baudelaire, *Oeuvres complètes*, ed. Marcel A. Ruff [Paris: Editions du Seuil, 1968] 257–8). For Pradier's eminence, see also Garnier, "La carrière d'un artiste officiel," 86–7, and also in *Statues de chair*, Leroy-Jay Lemaistre, "Pradier et les musées de France," 105. It was Flaubert's opinion too that Pradier was "the foremost sculptor of his time"—letter to Louise Colet, 9 June 1852, see *Statues de chair*, 370, #212, "Flaubert à Louise Pradier, Croisset, 12 juin 1852."

11. Cf. the comments of David d'Angers on Pradier's sculpture: "The poses, the lines of his statues, are lascivious, but the figures have no life ... Lasciviousness is not

passion"—cited by de Caso, "Comprendre Pradier," in *Statues de chair*, 39 and n. 82. Pradier's sculpture *Satyre et Bacchante* caused a sensation when it was shown at the Salon of 1834 and was considered by many to be indecent—*Statues de chair*, 124–5, #6.

12. *JDD*, 35. Cf. also Arsène Houssaye, *Les Confessions: Souvenirs d'un demi-siècle*. 6 vols. Vols. 1–4, 1830–1880; Vols. 5–6, 1830–1890 (Paris: E. Dentu, 1885–1891), 1:388–9.

13. *VHJD*, opposite p. 8.

14. Cf. de Caso, "Comprendre Pradier," 38 and n. 76.

15. See Francine du Plessix Gray, *Rage and Fire: A Life of Louise Colet: Pioneer Feminist, Literary Star, Flaubert's Muse* (New York: Simon & Schuster, 1994).

16. The anonymous *Mémoires de Madame Ludovica* (Douglas Siler, ed., *Flaubert et Louise Pradier: Le Texte intégral des* Mémoires de Madame Ludovica [Paris: Minard, 1973]), an account of Louise's marriage with Pradier found among Flaubert's personal papers, seem to have furnished his model for Emma Bovary. In any case, as Siler points out, ibid., 5, Flaubert knew Louise well and they had a brief sexual relationship in 1853.

17. *Statues de chair*, 345–6, #180, "Le chagrin de l'absence."

18. Cover of ballad: *JDD*, opposite p. 228. For other portraits of Pradier, see *Statues de chair*, 324–5 (#151–2), 326 (#153), 333 (#165), 334 (#167), 347 (#181), 349 (#184), 350 (#187), 363 (#203), 364 (#204).

19. The most complete information on Laure Krafft is to be found in Jean Savant, *La Vie sentimentale de Victor Hugo*, 6 fascicles (Paris: Chez l'auteur, 1982–1985), 4:75–80 (this work abbreviated henceforth as *VS*), as well as Jean Savant, "Madame Krafft et Madame Luthereau," *L'Intermédiaire des chercheurs et curieux*, September 1979, cols. 884–6.

20. This is the supposition of Jean Savant, *VS*, 1:10, 4:4, who sees Françoise Drouet as responsible also for her daughter, Eugénie's, liaisons with two artists, Ziegler and Victor Vilain. Drouet refers with pity to Eugénie's sad life made more difficult by her mother. See Siler, *Correspondance*, 1:162–3, nn. 1–2; 174, n. 4; 3:215, n. 1. For more on Eugénie, see Glossary. For Françoise Drouet's familiarity with artistic circles, see *VS*, 4:4, 69.

21. De Caso, "Comprendre Pradier," 39, n. 81, cites David d'Angers who says "Pradier always had for mistresses servants, models, actresses . . . He has no soul."

22. Arsène Houssaye, *Man About Paris: The Confessions of Arsène Houssaye*, trans. and ed. Henry Knepler (New York: William Morrow, 1970), 15.

23. Drouet makes this claim in a letter dated 5 September 1870 to Victor Hugo (cited by Paul Souchon, *La Servitude amoureuse de Juliette Drouet à Victor Hugo* [Paris: Albin Michel, 1943], 24, n. 1, as belonging to Gérard de Berny). However, in a letter to Drouet dated 15 July 1838 (cited *VHJD*, 11, n. 1), Pradier discusses this statue but makes no mention of her having been the model for it. Lapaire (*Statues de chair*, 326, #154, "Portrait de sa femme Louise") and de Caso (ibid., 186, #25, "La ville de Strasbourg") also contest the identification of Juliette Drouet as the model for the

Strasbourg and believe that Louise Pradier was probably the model instead. Cf. also Siler, *Correspondance*, 2:108, n. 9.

24. Louise Pradier had multiple affairs with other men while married to Pradier, and only one of the three children born during their marriage was Pradier's. She ran up enormous debts, which she attempted to cover by various financial deceptions of both Pradier and others. Pradier eventually hired a private detective to stalk her, and the dramatic escape of Louise and her lover by rooftop from their love nest was reported in the press. Louise and James Pradier legally separated in 1845. See de Caso et al., *Statues de chair*, especially 340–70 (#175–212).

25. Dated 27 April 1845 by Siler (*Correspondance*, 3:184). In a letter written to Hugo on the following day Drouet also calls Pradier "a stupid cretin" (ibid., n. 2).

26. Some of the letters Pradier wrote to Drouet show him attempting to help her career through his contacts—for example, Siler, *Correspondance*, 1:165, 168, 179 (dated 10 November, 11 November, 21 December, all in 1828).

27. For Pradier's wealth, see his marriage settlement with Louise (Siler, *Correspondance*, 1:315–6, n. 1), his will (de Caso et al., *Statues de chair*, 368, #210), and the legal deposition Pradier made showing that his income in 1844 was Fr 94,800 (Siler, *Correspondance*, 3:125). Pradier refers also to the fact that he inherited fifty thousand francs from his father (ibid., 3:300). For Houssaye, see *Confessions*, 1:389.

28. Siler, *Correspondance*, 1:171. Cf. also, ibid., 165, 168.

29. The following details on the affair with Pinel are drawn from *JDD*, part I, section I, chapter IV (39–43) unless otherwise noted.

30. See Siler, *Correspondance*, 1:158–61.

31. For example, in a letter dated 10 June 1841 (*MUL*, 214) Drouet refers to the fact that her debts are still far from paid off. Extensive details of Drouet's debts are to be found in *VS*, fasc. 4.

32. The dates, roles, and theaters of all of Drouet's debuts are provided by *JDD*, 435–9. Details of her acting career before she met Hugo are to be found there also in part I, section II, chapters I–VIII (47–109), and my information is based on this source, unless otherwise noted.

33. She did hold some very small parts in a few performances of plays by the classical dramatists Racine (1639–1699), Molière (1622–1673), and Voltaire (1694–1778). She performed in plays by Racine (*Britannicus*) and Voltaire (*Alzire*) in March 1829 at the Salle des Beaux-Arts in Brussels—*JDD*, 53—and played, on one occasion only, the part of Mariane in Molière's *Tartuffe* on 15 October 1830 in a benefit performance (*JDD*, 72). She also played the small part of *porte-seringue* in a few performances in November and December 1833 of an extract from Molière's *Le Malade imaginaire* (*JDD*, 148). Even her part in Hugo's *Lucrèce Borgia* (see below) was a very small one.

34. Théophile Gautier, *Victor Hugo par Théophile Gautier* (Paris: Charpentier, 1902), 268–9.

35. On the nature of the Théâtre du Vaudeville and the Théâtre de la Porte-Saint-Martin, see John McCormick, *Popular Theatres of Nineteenth-Century France* (London: Routledge, 1993), 20, 25–7. On the "social melodrama," see ibid., 180ff.

36. *Journal des comédiens,* 4 April 1830, cited by *JDD,* 63.

37. Several dramatic adaptations were made of this novel, see McCormick, *Popular Theatres,* 172, 202, 204.

38. Paul Chenay, *Victor Hugo à Guernsey: Souvenirs inédits de son beau-frère Paul Chenay* (Paris: Félix Juven, n.d), 158. For a fairly recent biography incorporating the Demidov story see, for example, Jeanine Huas, *Juliette Drouet: Le Bel Amour de Victor Hugo* (Paris: Gaston Lachurié, 1985), 54–60.

39. See below, L. 3 and n. 2

40. The details on Drouet's role in *Lucrèce Borgia* and of her other roles at the Porte-Saint-Martin thereafter until 1834 are derived from *JDD,* part I, section II, chapters IX–XIII (110–64), unless otherwise noted.

41. *VHJD,* 1:26–7. Guimbaud gives no source.

42. Cf. also her letter of 20 August 1842 (*MUL,* 244) where, discussing the duchesse d'Orléans, she describes her as being "in the prestige of a great misfortune, which is to say, after physical beauty, what you [*scil.* Hugo] find the most seductive." On *Marion de Lorme,* see Glossary.

43. Gautier, *Victor Hugo,* 267–8.

44. *JDD,* 452, n. 1.

45. The entries in this book are to be found in *LJD,* 332–56. The problem with the date is, as Bernard Fertel has pointed out ("Hugo, Juliette, lettres détruites," *L'Intermédiaire des chercheurs et curieux,* September 1979, cols. 894–5), that 16 February 1833 was a Saturday, not a Tuesday, and therefore not Mardi Gras. He is of the opinion that the first night of their love affair was actually the nineteenth, that is, Mardi Gras. This view is substantiated by the fact that Hugo and Drouet had been invited on 19 February 1833, in celebration of Mardi Gras, to a masked ball at the Gymnase theater to which they did not go, spending their "first night" instead in Drouet's bed—as described by Hugo in a letter dated 17 February 1841 (*LJD,* 336). Originally the invitation to the ball, which Drouet had saved, was stuck to the first page of the *Livre de l'anniversaire*—see *LJD,* 332—whence it later became detached. Of course it is possible that the date Hugo and Drouet commemorated was correct and that it was not in fact Mardi Gras, but as Fertel points out, this seems a much more unlikely lapse of memory. If Fertel's suppositions are correct, Drouet and Hugo carefully celebrated in their *Livre de l'anniversaire* the wrong date for fifty years! Hugo also made the same "mistake" in *Les Misérables* where he makes the marriage of Marius and Cosette occur on Mardi Gras, 16 February 1833. Jean Savant, *VS,* 5:55–8, is of the opinion that 16 February was indeed the couple's first night of love, but that they also spent together the night of the nineteenth, Mardi Gras, when, having at first quarreled over the issue of the masked ball to which Drouet did not want Hugo or herself to go, they then made up and retired to bed together instead of attending it.

46. Victor Hugo, *Les Misérables*, ed. René Journet, 3 vols. (Paris: Garnier-Flammarion, 1979), 3:409.

47. Paul Souchon, *Les deux femmes de Victor Hugo* (Paris: Jules Tallandier, 1948), 21.

48. Substantiation for Adèle's cessation of sexual relations is found in a letter by Hugo to his wife dated 17 July 1831 in which he refers to "this bed where you could be (although you don't want to be anymore, bad girl!)"—*Correspondance familiale et écrits intimes*, ed. Jean Gaudon, Sheila Gaudon, and Bernard Leuilliot, 2 vols. (Paris: Robert Laffont), 2:52 (henceforth abbreviated as *CF*).

49. Prosper Mérimée, *Correspondance générale*, ed. Maurice Parturier, 17 vols. (Paris: Le Divan, 1941–1964), 4:202, 16 October 1844.

50. *CF*, 2:235. Cf. also the letter of 15 June 1836 in which, on the eve of another trip with Drouet, Hugo says, "You were the first and you will be the last love of my life," ibid., 2:276.

51. See, for example, the letter written 10 September 1836 (*CF*, 2:238) in which Adèle says with reference to expenses she has incurred: "Instead of apparently bearing me resentment for the expense, you should see that I am doing what I can, and that I sacrifice the tranquillity that is now the only happiness in my life for my home and my children. I would like, my friend, to see *you* working. I assure you that I do my duty on my side for my children, and that I sacrifice myself greatly. Do a little on your side, I beg you! I don't often talk to you about this, but I'm sad because it seems to me that you are doing little at the moment for your family. I love you nonetheless. Good-bye. Come back when you want."

52. The "Battle of *Hernani*" is the term used to refer to the two riotous first performances at the Comédie-Française of Hugo's play *Hernani* (see Glossary), on 25 and 27 February 1830. The new, daringly "Romantic" play attracted an audience of traditionalists determined to boo it and a crowd of Hugo's admirers, led by Théophile Gautier, who succeeded in applauding them into submission.

53. *L'Impartial*, 9 November 1833, cited by *JDD*, 140.

54. *Le Courrier des théâtres*, 9 November 1833, cited by *JDD*, 141.

55. See below, L. 31 and n. 1, L. 34.

56. For example, below, L. 107; *LVH*, 128; *MUL*, 337. Also, bird in a cage, *MUL*, 300.

57. See Souchon, *Servitude amoureuse*, 77–9. Cf. also, below, L. 45.

58. Cf. also *MUL*, 115, 122 ("I think that if God ever shows himself to me it will be in your form, for you are my faith, my religion, and my hope"). Cf. letter dated 7 January 1844, cited *MUL*, 278 ("I cannot compare you to any man, you are a piece of God, if not God Himself") and, ibid., a letter dated 23 January 1844: "Just think that you are my life, my hope, my religion, and my God!" Cf. also *MUL* 467 ("My love is the telescope through which I see God as I see you"), 754 ("Dear beloved . . . I cry to you from a distance that I love you, that I admire you, that I venerate you, and that you

have never been greater, more sublime, and more God than now, and that I feel beat in me the great heart of humanity that blesses you and adores you").

59. Cf. also *MUL*, 109 ("You are my savior, my *Christ*"), 426 ("My beloved Victor, the crown of glory is made with thorns for all sublime martyrs since Christ, and the rays of yours have sunk deep into your great forehead and made it bleed since long ago"), 411 ("You are my living Christ, you are my faith, you are my God, Whom I adore on my knees and for Whom I want to live, suffer, and die"), 509 ("I kiss your divine forehead under the crown of thorns that tear it, and I adore you on my knees"), 696 ("Your birth [is] more luminous and useful for mankind than that of Christ. In another era dates will be traced from Victor Hugo as they are dated now from Jesus"). Cf. *VHJD*, 1:113 ("If you only knew how happy I am when I have won a soul, a mind, an emotion, or an admiration for you! I feel as though I'm accomplishing my mission like the apostles with Christ"), and *JDD*, 269 ("Sometimes you feel the supreme lassitude of Christ mounting his true cross on Calvary; I am the humble woman who stanches the sacred sweat of your brow and kisses with devotion your venerated footsteps").

60. See below, L. 55, n. 1. Cf. also *LJD*, 81, 109, 112 ("I took you as a woman from men and I will return you as an angel to God"), 151. Alphonse Karr satirized their relationship in these terms—see *JDD*, 158.

61. See, for example, *MUL*, 43, where Drouet refers to the fact that Hugo has alleged that she is "a woman without a soul, without honor, dry and vain," and that the debts that overwhelm her arise from her "misconduct" and from her "coquetry."

62. *MUL*, 193. Cf. L. 33.

63. Cf. L. 73, 104. Hugo was equally stingy with himself, however. Cf. *MUL*, 288 (Hugo's shoes with holes), and a letter dated 2 June 1881 when Hugo, at the height of his fame and fortune, is urged by Drouet to buy new clothes since "it is impossible to keep any longer your worn-out, faded, and stained clothes" *("Je ne veux qu'une chose, être aimée": Cinquante lettres de Juliette Drouet à Victor Hugo,* ed. Simonne Charpentreau and Jacques Charpentreau [Paris: La Maison de Poésie, 1997], 178, henceforth abbreviated as *CL*).

64. The astute Arsène Houssaye noticed that the Drouet-Hugo relationship resembled a novelist's creation. He comments in *Confessions,* 5:299–300: "What Mme. Drouet could tell so well, but what she never tells, is her novel with Victor Hugo. How many pages of passion! How many troubles! How much despair! But they came back together again through all the obstacles, because the fateful hand of destiny had bound these two existences in turn by the heart and mind, by the aspirations of the soul, and by the violence of terrestrial joys. Who will write this novel? I have seen it page by page, but why open a book that death has closed? Let us therefore write it in a single line: They loved each other!"

65. Cf. L. 18. Savant in *VS,* fasc. 1 provides passim numerous examples of Drouet's complaints on this score. Cf. below, n. 68.

66. Dated 19 February 1837 (cited *JDD,* 182 and n. 11).

67. For example, the letters in which she promises oral sex, such as, *VS,* 1:60: "I've discovered a way to drink colchicum wine. It's to drink it from the *barrel* itself by

the little *tap. Mm, mm, rascal.* In this way I'm sure it won't go flat. Bring me your *nectar. You'll see how I'll* savor it" (27 July 1842).

68. See Henri Guillemin, *Hugo et la sexualité* (Paris: Gallimard, 1954), cited henceforth as *HS*. For an admittedly later period Guillemin found only two references to sex with Juliette Drouet in Hugo's records of his sexual activity for 1860–1870 (p. 98) and only three after 1870 (all in 1873, *HS*, 139, and n. 1). Hugo's casual sexual contacts with other women (servants, prostitutes, actresses, etc.) were numerous and frequent, however, especially beginning with the period of exile (see Raymond Escholier, *Un Amant de génie: Lettres d'amour et carnets inédits* [Paris: Librairie Arthème Fayard, 1953]). For other references in Drouet's letters to her sexual dissatisfaction, see *VS*, 1:30, 37–8, 39–40, 43–4, 53, 56–60, 62–4.

69. Cited by Souchon, *Servitude amoureuse*, 97.

70. The fullest treatment of this affair and of the life of Léonie Biard is to be found in *VS*, fasc. 2 and 3.

71. In a deposition dated December 1844 (Siler, *Correspondance*, 3:113) Pradier lists François-Auguste Biard as one of the people, along with Victor Hugo, who most often visited his house. Evidence for Hugo meeting her at Pradier's and carrying on a flirtation with her there is provided also by a letter from Gustave Flaubert to Louise Colet, cited by Siler, ibid., 3:44, n. 3. Numerous letters (ibid., passim) are evidence that Hugo, at Drouet's request, attempted to advance Pradier's career with favorable reviews of his work and other interceptions on his behalf (cf. also, below, L. 29). Drouet's motive was to ensure Pradier continued to support Claire financially and, for Claire's sake, recognize the obligations of his paternity.

72. Victor Hugo, *Lettres de Victor Hugo à Léonie Biard*, ed. Jean Gaudon (Paris: Claude Blaizot, 1990), 76.

73. Hugo, *Lettres à Léonie Biard*, 31, 62.

74. *HS*, 25–6; *VS*, 5:74–7; Graham Robb, *Victor Hugo* (New York: W. W. Norton, 1997), 260–1. Henceforth abbreviated as *VH*.

75. *Confessions*, 5:300.

76. Cf. also, below, L. 56, 66.

77. *MUL*, 266: "I love you as no man has ever been and ever will again be loved by a woman." Cf. below, L. 53. Jean Savant is of the opinion that the Biard-Hugo affair had been over since 1849, Léonie had returned Hugo the letters he had written her, and that it was actually Charles (with the complicity of his mother, who wanted to be rid of Drouet) who sent Drouet the package in revenge for his father's involvement with Alice Ozy, *VS*, 3:60–1.

78. *Man About Paris*, 270–83.

79. The first time she failed, Claire wrote to her mother: "I would have given anything to have had a little success granted to me for you, my beloved mother, for you who have sacrificed everything for me . . . I dread seeing my father, for one must love me as you love me to say only gentle and encouraging things to me," cited by Siler,

Correspondance, 3:198, n. 3. Drouet comments in a letter to Hugo dated 16 April 1846: "I think that you have guessed better than anyone the origin of this child's illness. Everything obviously comes from the disappointment of her exam"—cited by Siler, ibid., 3:271, n. 1.

80. "The more I think about this death, the more I find it bitter and unjust that my poor beloved should have desired death, for it is only too sure that she did desire it, and that God granted her her wish"—cited by Siler, *Correspondance*, 3:271, n. 1. Both Drouet and Pradier refer to the part played by sorrow ("chagrin") in precipitating her illness—Siler, ibid., 3:276, n. 1.

81. See *VHJD*, plates opposite pp. 128, 131, 133, 152.

82. In a letter dated 25 April 1845—Siler, *Correspondance*, 3:182. In defense of Pradier, Siler (*Statues de chair*, 345, #179, "Victor Hugo à Pradier") points out that Pradier forbade the use of his surname only at the time when he was initiating proceedings to separate legally from his wife, on the grounds that "that could give substance for chicanery on the part of a lot of people," and that he expressed genuine sorrow in a letter to Claire when he realized that he had hurt her. Siler also asks the question (ibid.): "Claire spent her whole life in the pension. Could not Juliette have kept her with her if she had wanted to?" A legitimate question.

83. As Drouet said to Hugo of Claire's love for her father: "It is impossible to love any more [than she does] a less lovable father" (10 August 1844—Siler, *Correspondance*, 3:76). For other evidence of Claire's great love for Pradier see, for example, ibid., 3:45 and n. 1; 3:50; 3:57–8, n. 2; 3:76; 3:79, n. 1; 3:101; 3:145; 3:160; 3:166, n. 1; 3:275, n. 1; 3:277, n. 3.

84. *VHJD*, 1:155–7; Siler, *Correspondance*, 3:313.

85. Siler, *Correspondance*, 3:341 and n. 3.

86. Given by *VHJD*, 1:153–4.

87. For example, Juliette ordered her nephew, Louis Koch, who had been kind enough to plant a red rose on the site of Claire Pradier's grave, to remove it immediately and replace it with a white one to symbolize Claire's virginity—*LF*, 237.

88. See below, L. 95, n. 2.

89. But the tag has an ambiguity that must have pleased Hugo. It can also mean "life is exile." See also the catalog of the exhibition in Guernsey (7 May–31 August 2002) commemorating the bicentennial of Hugo's birth—Sheila Gaudon and Danielle Molinari, eds., *Exilium vita est: Victor Hugo à Guernsey* (Paris: Paris-Musées, 2002). Hauteville House is open to the public as a museum. None of Drouet's residences is open to the public. Some of the furnishings of her house Hauteville Féerie are now exhibited at the Maison de Victor Hugo in Paris.

90. Letter from Hugo to François-Victor, 22 April 1861, quoted in Sophie Grossiord, *Hauteville House: Guide général* (Paris: Paris-Musées, 1994), 11.

91. Cited by Grossiord, *Hauteville House*, 12.

92. Nearly all of Hugo's letters to his adult sons (as also to his wife) contain references to the money he provided. The letters written to his sons in Brussels also make frequent requests for help in negotiations with his publishers—see, especially, Victor Hugo, *Correspondance*, ed. C. Daubray, 4 vols. (Paris: Albin Michel; Imprimerie nationale; Ollendorf, 1947–1952), vols. 2 and 3, passim.

93. For a biography, see (in English) Leslie Smith Dow, *Adèle Hugo: La Misérable* (Fredericton, Canada: Goose Lane Editions, 1993).

94. Evidence of just how early she knew about it is provided by a letter written 27 June 1833 by her father, Pierre Foucher, to his sister-in-law in which he refers to Hugo's affair with "the beautiful lady at the Porte-Saint-Martin . . . the princesse Negroni" (*CF,* 2:127).

95. See below, L. 95, n. 2

96. Her presence in, and absence from, Guernsey is tabulated by Gregory Stevens Cox, *Victor Hugo in the Channel Islands* (Guernsey: The Guernsey Press, 1996), 58. She was absent, for example, from January 1865 until January 1867 and from March of that year until she died in Brussels in August 1868.

97. See below, L. 153 and n. 1.

98. See below, L. 163, n. 1.

99. Arnaud Laster, *Victor Hugo* (Paris: Pierre Belfond, 1984), 142.

100. See below, L. 175, n. 2.

101. See below, L. 175, n. 2; 176 and n. a; 177 and n. 1.

102. A physical description of Drouet's letters is to be found in Souchon, *Servitude amoureuse,* 135–67. Photographs of representative letters written by Drouet to Hugo are to be found in *CL.* For Drouet's complaints that Hugo does not retrieve the letters she has written, see Souchon, ibid., 146–9. On 18 May 1840, for example (ibid., 149), she complains that he has not retrieved the letters she has written him for eight days.

103. See, for example, *LJD,* 144 where Hugo castigates himself for having forgotten to take home her letters to him.

104. For example *MUL,* 189: "I hurry to take refuge in my love because there I have no equal and I am just as great as you."

105. Undated letter cited by Souchon, *Servitude amoureuse,* 150.

106. For example, *LJD,* 88, 113, 115, 122, 125.

107. Escholier, *Amant de génie,* 194.

108. "It's only in bed that I feel equal to competing with you in variety and richness of expression, which fails me completely when I've got my shoes and corsets on."

109. Baron Hugo became Viscount Hugo on the death of his brother Eugène (1800–1837). These titles were obtained by virtue of those conferred on the service of his father, who was of humble origin, in Napoleon's army.

110. Drouet openly identified her relationship with Hugo with Marion's relationship with Didier (on Hugo's play *Marion de Lorme*, see Glossary), as when she says in a letter dated 9 November 1836 (cited by Souchon, *Servitude amoureuse*, 202): "Marion is not a *role* for me, it's *I* myself, it's us, it's all that's most fervent, loving, and virtuous in me."

111. Many examples provided by Souchon, *Servitude amoureuse*, 149–52.

112. See, for example, *MUL*, 775, 823.

113. Jean Gaudon, ed., *Lettres à Juliette Drouet, 1833–1883. Le Livre de l'anniversaire*, by Victor Hugo (Paris: Jean-Jacques Pauvert, 1964), xiv.

114. Jean Gaudon's estimate (see above, Preface, p. xii). Savant estimates twenty-five thousand (*VS*, 4:90).

115. See below, L. 66 and n. a, 136 and n. a.

1830s

Letter 1

[16 February 1833][a]

Come for me this evening at Mme K's.[1]

I will be loving you until then just to stay patient. See you this evening! Oh, this evening will be everything!

I will give myself to you completely.

J.

[Addressed] M. Victor.

Letter 2

Sunday evening, 4 o'clock *[1833]*

I have come back home very sad and discouraged with everything. I'm suffering, I'm weeping, I'm lamenting loudly and softly—to God, to you—and I would like to die once and for all, to be finished with all the misery, all the disappointments, all the pains. It's as though my happiness has vanished with the fine days, and to expect them to come back—both it and them—would be almost madness, for as I look around myself and inside myself I find the season late for fine days and happy days. Poor silly to be surprised to see me hanker so bitterly for a day of happiness! It's easy to see *you* didn't wait until the age of twenty-six for the happiness of loving and being loved. Poor poet who composed *Les Feuilles d'automne*[a] in the midst of love, children's laughter, black eyes and blue, brown hair and blonde, and happiness in plenty! You haven't noticed how much a sad and rainy day like today yellows the greenest and most firmly attached of leaves and makes them fall. So you don't know how much a day without happiness like this one can detract from one's trust in, and strength for, the future. You don't know it, because you're surprised when I cry, you're almost annoyed with my grief. So you see you don't know what my love is, you see I'm right to regret loving you so much, since this love is useless and tiresome to you. Oh, I love you, that's certainly true! I love you despite you, despite myself, despite the entire world, despite God, despite the Devil, who also has a hand in this. I love you, I love you, I love you! Whether I'm happy or unhappy, gay or sad, I love you. I love you, do with me what you will.

Letter 3

Saturday morning, 2 o'clock *[1833]*

You crazy, naughty child—haven't I suffered a hundred times more than you and more than I have the strength for? You are breaking my heart.

I have troubles from a thousand other quarters, and a thousand times more than my poor soul can bear. I hide them from you so as not to trouble you. Every feeling I have is crushed and bruised, and you abandon me today when you're my only happiness and the sole nourishment of my life. You abandon me shamefully when I'm so discouraged! Victor!

I thought your soul was greater and more worthy of mine, for I have loved you with all the love there is in my heart. You're killing what life I still have, you blow everything away with one puff as though it were a mere spider's web. I have nothing left in the world, nothing left in life. You love me, and yet you are killing me. You destroy my happiness and your own. I was beginning to amass in my heart so much love and happiness. You are crazy and I am crazier still. But don't you know that I belong to you body and soul? Like a woman who has made a pact. If my happiness alone depended on your love, I would run away from you, for one can do without happiness—and, besides, in this area I haven't developed any bad habits—but your love is necessary to me for life itself. I love you with all my strength, away from you I die.

I have a terrible fever. I'm going to take a bath at eight o'clock, perhaps it will calm me.

Why don't you want to understand that I love you? You love me, and yet you kill me. See you tomorrow, my Victor, I love you, I forgive you.

Juliette

[Addressed] Monsieur Victor Hugo.
In town

Letter 4

Monday morning, 10 minutes to 1:00 *[September 1833]*

I have been at my window all this time, my soul stretched toward you, my ear attentive to the slightest sound, fearing all the while that your courage might abandon you before the end of your painful journey. Soon it will be half an hour since you left. I have listened closely. I don't think I've heard anything to make me fear you didn't have enough strength to get home. I hope that at the moment I write these lines, you're already experiencing the relief that bed and rest will bring to your suffering. I can find no words to express to you my regret, my remorse, my despair for everything that happened this evening. I do not exclude your offences. I ask you pardon for those as for mine. After what has happened between us, I ask you to forgive me for having agreed to belong to you. I should have foreseen what would happen, what *has* happened. God knows I courageously resisted and only yielded because of the sacred and solemn promise you made me never to speak of the stains on my past life, as long as my behavior was honest and pure. My life for the last seven months *has* been honest and pure! Have you kept *your* promise?

Besides, if I were just suffering alone I would resign myself to it, but you are as unhappy as I am, you are as ashamed of the insults that you heap upon me as I am myself to receive them.

Now that I know how gangrenous our relationship is, I must arrest the progression of the disease by cutting off my life and my soul to save what can still be saved of you and me. Listen, Victor, I ask you not to withhold your support in carrying out what I think is necessary, indispensable, for our mutual honor. If anything can give you courage, it should be to know I have never been unfaithful to you during the last seven months. It's really true, I have never been unfaithful to you, it's really true, oh, it really is true! And yet during these seven months how many terrible scenes there have been like this one tonight! You see there are no two ways about it. I'll leave by the first stagecoach to Saumur, my daughter's health will be the pretext.[1] Once I'm with her, I'll be able to ponder on my situation and on what should be done to make it tolerable. If, as I think necessary, I were to break with the theater, the furniture would cover my debt to Jourdain,[2] and if you didn't want to have the trouble of dealing with the matter, I could have some agent sell it to repay the debt to Jourdain, which is the only one for which you are guarantor. As for myself, I would go abroad. Such as I am at this time in my life, I can still earn my living there— which is all that matters, isn't it? But none of this is important. The important point is this: to leave as soon as possible and on this very day, in order to protect us both from our awful lunacy.

I hope to see you before I go, unless you are feeling even more ill, which is a terrible thought when I consider that I'm the cause of it. But whether I see you or not, whether or not you are the victim of my madness, I hand over to you as I go away all love and all happiness. I don't even hold on to hope. I leave you my soul, my thoughts, my life; I shall carry away only my body. Don't regret it.

Juliette

Letter 5

[1833]

My Victor, my love, my angel, I love you still more since our love has been threatened. The impairment of my health, proof proof *[sic]* of my anxiety and sorrows, can't be the result of an ordinary love. I love you, my Victor, more than I can say. My life belongs to you, do with it what you want.

I'll wait a year if I have to for one of those moments, so brief and full of agitation but also full of tenderness and happiness.

I love you. I swear that I shall never belong to anyone but you. And you do too, don't you? You wouldn't deceive me, you would tell me if you couldn't be entirely faithful to me. Isn't that so, you would tell me, you wouldn't want to deceive me? I love you so much, with the idea that I am your woman—your only woman—in the matter of love.

Good-bye my darling! May the future be less gloomy than our present! I kiss your eyes, your feet, and the rest. I kneel before you. I adore you.

Juliette

I'm too sad not to see you, so if I go to Mme K's, you can come and find me there.

[Addressed] For my beloved.

Letter 6

Quarter past 4:00 *[just before 16 December 1833]*

I am back. You are still not here. My God, I really needed to see you! The most sinister thoughts tug and tear at my heart. Tomorrow, tomorrow perhaps, opprobrium will have succeeded misery and shame. My God, Victor, what are you doing at this hour when I am dying of pain and fear?

8 o'clock

Still not here, and it's today that you fail me when you are all my strength, all my courage, all my faith. Victor, Victor, Fate is indeed cruel toward me! My God, my God, what am I going to do, what is to become of me?

Tomorrow I have to attend the criminal court *in person,* perhaps to be convicted of the unlawful removal of effects from my home and sentenced to two years' imprisonment.[1] My God, since the conference I've just had from two till four with my bailiff and lawyer, I've been *crazy, crazy.* I really feel my mind can't take any more, and to cap the day, you haven't come and won't come. What use will have been my trust in your love, my faith in the future, and my courage? You always abandon me at the moment of danger! Oh Victor, Victor, you are truly at fault, and I am truly unhappy!

Oh, I am suffering! Forgive me this letter, its disorder, its expressions, and know that whatever happens, I'll always love you passionately.

Juliette

Half past 8:00

[Addressed] For M. Hugo.
2nd letter

Letter 7

4 July 1834

To my beloved.
Here are a thousand kisses.

My beloved Victor, I'm still so moved by our evening together yesterday. For lack of a female friend and a heart that understands me into which to pour the overflow of my happiness, I write this to you—"that yesterday, the third day of July, one thousand eight hundred and thirty-four, at half past ten in the evening, in the inn called Ecu de France at Jouy,[1] I, Juliette, was the happiest and proudest of women in this world, and I declare that until then I had not felt in all its fullness the happiness of loving you and being loved by you."

This letter, which is just like a deposition, is indeed a testament to the state of my heart. This deed drawn up today must serve for the rest of my life in this world. On no matter what day, at no matter what hour or minute it is presented to me, I engage to remit the said heart in the same state that it is today, which is to say, filled by one sole love, which is for you and by one sole thought, which is for you.

Composed in Paris, this fourth day of July, one thousand eight hundred and thirty-four, at three o'clock in the afternoon.

Juliette

Hereunto subscribed as witnesses: the thousand kisses with which I have covered this letter.

Letter 8

Saturday evening, 10 o'clock *[After 16 July 1834]*

"For he had been brought up with certain bad habits that spoiled his natural dignity more often than they should."

Claude Gueux, V.H.[1]

I also have been brought up with certain bad habits that spoil my natural dignity more often than they should. It's because I also have fate and society to blame: fate, because it cast me into a situation beneath my intelligence; society, because it takes away every day from the portion of love and happiness that you share so generously with me, my beloved Albin. Oh, I love you yet more since I have been ungrateful toward you, and esteem and respect you yet more since I have been unjust and at fault toward you! Forgive me!

"Doesn't love make us spiteful?"

Marie Tudor, V.H.[2]

My beloved, my Victor, don't abandon me! Love me! If I die before my time, I want my heart to be brought to you, as poor Claude carries his last piece of bread to Albin on the last day of his life. I want my heart to be brought to you, which you must keep even beyond my life itself.

Love me, forgive me, do with me what you want!

I love you.

Here is my life   here are my kisses

                        everywhere my love.

Juliette

[Addressed] To you my beloved.

Letter 9

Friday morning, 2 o'clock *[18 July 1834]*

My poor beloved, I don't know from what *camp* the painter of your portrait hails,[1] whether he pays his *dues*, or whether he has used *superfine* colors to *execute* it. But what I do know is that it doesn't look the least bit like, which makes me very sad, since after *you*, it's *that* that I would have most loved. But then I was silly to think that your likeness could be made. It's not in this world that the paintbrush and colors will be found to reproduce the original that is already a masterpiece. In any case, such as it is, I'm keeping it, and foolhardy will be the person who comes to takes it back. Besides, the background to this portrait is not without interest for me. It reminds me of our day yesterday: Victor Hugo and Juliette at Notre-Dame, 17 July 1834.

Thank-you anyway, my dear beloved. Good-night, I'll see you tomorrow! Sleep well, don't suffer!

Juliette

The little house[2] is charming, *everything included*.

[Addressed] 16th *[letter]*

For my dear *original*.

Letter 10

Sunday morning, half past 1:00, 18 July 1834

My beloved Victor, today is your feast day.[1] I would like to have celebrated it for you worthily by giving you a wonderful surprise. But as you know, my Victor, we're rich only in love and poetry. This richness, the wealth of lovers, is not for sale at any shopkeeper's. That's why, my poor beloved, I give you nothing. In any case I can't give you my heart, which has belonged to you since I've known you, nor my gaze, which has belonged to you since I first saw you, nor my breath, which has belonged to you since the day I first breathed upon your mouth, nor my soul, which has belonged to you since the day you deigned to take it.

I give you nothing, because everything belongs to you.

But I love you! I love you so much that this love alone would suffice even for God Himself on His feast day.

I love you. I send you a million kisses, which I beg you not to consign to *an unhappy fate.*

See you soon! *Here* or *yonder, close* or *afar,* I love you.

Juliette

[Addressed] 20th *[letter]*

To the most beloved of men.
To my Victor.

Letter 11

Saturday, noon, 2 August 1834

Farewell forever, farewell for always!

It was you who said it! Farewell then, and may you be as happy and admired as much as I'm unhappy and cast down.

"Farewell." This word contains all my life, all my joy, all my happiness. Farewell!

Juliette

I'm leaving with my daughter. I'm going right now to get her and book our seats.[1] As far as the Comédie-Française is concerned, it cannot make me perform without having first assigned me a part.[2] My maid has orders to open my letters. If one comes from the Comédie-Française, she will let me know immediately, and no one will be inconvenienced, so I needn't worry about it for now.

[Addressed] For Victor.

Letter 12

Rennes,[a] Monday afternoon, half past 2:00 *[4 August 1834]*

My dear Victor,

I am writing you this letter on the chance that you may read it, but with the sad prescience that you will not. However, probably this won't be the last letter I'll write until the time when you'll no longer have the right to refuse to read them.

My beloved Victor, I love you more than ever. I can't do without you. I'd be willing to die for you. Yet I cannot accept your devotion, which, if taken word for word, would compromise your health and your life. I had to flee from you, and I did it. It pained me to resist when I saw you plead with me, to resist your eyes full of anger and hatred. Oh yes, it really pained me, and now at the moment that I write this, I wouldn't resist either your pleas, which were so sweet, or your anger, which was so terrible. I am very unhappy. I'm suffering. I love you and I bless you.

Juliette

Some of your wishes have been granted—I have already suffered greatly in body and soul. To that you can add all the vexations inflicted by the stupid authorities, who wish to find in a woman without a passport an object for all the vexation that their idiocy creates.

I have been at Rennes for half an hour. It's half past two. I'm leaving for Brest tomorrow morning at eight, I'll be arriving on Thursday afternoon at five.

My Victor, I love you. I'm capable of anything. I love you. Have pity on me! I love you.

Letter 13

Rennes, quarter past 2:00 in the morning, 5 August *[1834]*

Victor, I love you, Victor, I'm dying far away from you like this, you are necessary to me for me to live. Since the moment when I finished speaking to you, especially from the moment when my eyes were no longer able to look into yours, it has been as though my veins are open and my life flowing away without my having the power to stop it. I feel that I am dying and that I love you more with every pang.

My Victor, can you forgive me? Do you still love me? Is it true that you hate me, that I'm odious to you, that you despise me, that you would fling me face down on the ground if I were to press my lips to your feet in a plea for mercy? Oh, if you still love me and you can still respect me, if you can forgive everything, say so, and I'll do everything you want, I'll do everything, my God! Tell me, do you still want me?

I am very ill.

[Addressed] For Monsieur Victor H . . .[1]

Letter 14

Les Metz,[1] Sunday afternoon, half past 3:00 *[September–October 1834]*

My beloved Victor, I'm losing hope of seeing you today because it's already quite late. It's very sad for me as I had counted on this as my reward for the long and tiring job that I've finally finished—as far as it was possible to, since I'll have to have the actual bills and their details to compare and add up. In any case, I've done all I could do. I finished it today at two. I was happy to have made a start on the thing that's going to give me to you *entirely*, bind me to you for life, inlay me in your heart forever. I was very happy to have started on my deliverance. I was hoping you'd come and help me share my happiness, which is too heavy for me to bear alone. Naughty Toto, you stayed away! Why? For whom? This is what I don't know, and it adds to the sorrow of not seeing you. Come quickly, my beloved Toto, come quickly! You'll see how I love you. You'll see if I'm happy at the prospect of belonging to you forever. You'll see if I have faith in the future. You'll see *how beautifully I smile at the promised life, and how hideously I grimace at my past.*

Come, come, my love! I desire you, I love you, I admire you, I respect you, I bless you.

So come, come, come! You promised you would hear my voice when it came from the heart. So come, because I love you!

Juliette

I hope very much that you will come tomorrow.

Letter 15

Wednesday evening, quarter to 11:00 *[November 1834]*

My dear beloved, here's a letter very short in form but long in content, because it contains all my feelings and all my heart. I love you, I love you, I love you, I love you, and there you have it. It's not tiring for the mind and it's very sweet for the heart—I *love you!*

My love, you made me very happy this afternoon; doubly happy, in fact, because you shared my happiness. However, I have a feeling of sadness and anxiety that never leaves me, that I'd like to hide from you, but tonight, since it's overflowing, I have to let you see it. I'm afraid of being forever *a poor girl*. I'm afraid that this inaction in which I've been living for a year will complete the ruin already started with the failure of *Marie Tudor*.[1] I'm afraid that your apparent lack of concern for my dramatic career is as good as a formal avowal that I can't hope to aspire to a future in my art.

Your position and mine render these fears of mine real torments that obsess me day and night, that change the nature of my character, that destroy my courage, and that rob me of all confidence in the durability of our happiness. I'd like to be sure that my fears are only fears, and then I'd grasp my joy and resignation with both hands. But . . . who will tell me the truth on this subject? Do *you* dare to? I beg you on my knees to tell me the truth, nothing but the truth, whatever it may be, so that at least I may know where I am as far as the future is concerned, so that I may know for sure what you think of me. I ask you to give me your opinion in good conscience. I ask it of you with my hands clasped in prayer. I prefer the certainty of my ruin to doubt. So don't spare me!

"*Here's a letter very short in form,*" I said as I began, because my intention was to confine it to "*I love you.*" But I got carried away by the need to open my heart to you and release the sorrow and discouragement that have been devouring it for a long time. Forgive me my weakness! I ought to have waited until you were less busy, but I couldn't do it. Forgive me on account of the love I have for you!

My fear arises from a most passionate and delicate love. That is the truth.

Juliette

Letter 16

Tuesday evening *[1834? 1835?]*

I started my day, suffering. I finish it, suffering a thousand times more than this morning, for I now have the conviction that all is finished between us. God only knows what I've done during this whole painful day. Aside from suffering, I don't remember anything.

Ah, yes I do! I disobeyed you! Forgive me for today, forgive me forever, for I'll never be able to help disobeying you.

You can guess what this disobedience was. I went to your place. There was no light except in the dining room. I didn't dare to inquire whether you were at home. I waited for an hour, then I went by the rue Saint Antoine and the embankments as far as the rue de Seine.[1] There I waited again. Finally, not seeing what I was looking for with so much despair, I went back home at half past midnight. I've been writing to you for a few minutes. As I do so, the memory of things and times comes back to me. Here's another thing I did: I picked out a letter from the ones you'd left with me, I took the one that speaks to me most of you—in fact I *took them all*. Next, I bundled up my bedsheets. On my knees and in prayer, I folded them up, and when I had finished, I wrote on top:

"*This is my shroud.*"

I'll tell you the rest tomorrow. Tears are choking me. I think I am going to die.

Don't forget me!
Farewell!

Juliette

Letter 17

Tuesday, midnight, 28 April 1835
One hour after the triumph of *Angelo*.[a]

I had a fine old time indulging myself shouting out, "Bravo!" "Bravo!!" "Bravo!!!" "Bravo!!!!" "Bravo!!!!!" "Bravo !!!!!!" It was the first time that I could admire you at my ease. You weren't there to stop me.

Thank-you, my beloved, thank-you on my behalf—you make me a thousand times grateful for every second of my life! Thanks also on behalf of the whole crowd that was there, who admired you, listened to you, understood you.

I saw everything, heard everything, and I carry it all to you—although if the applause, the enthusiasm, and the frenzy had a weight, it would be a heavy burden.

Tomorrow I'll give you the details of the entire performance. For I don't expect to see you tonight. That would be too much happiness in one day; besides, you don't want me to go mad with joy.

So see you tomorrow! If only you knew how nicely I applauded Mme Dorval,[1] you'd be careful not to do or say anything tonight that could wound my poor heart, already a little pained by the thought that someone other than I has been allowed to interpret your most noble thoughts. Anyway, see how I'm becoming sad and troubled despite myself, just knowing you're near this woman!

Good-night, my beloved, sleep well, my great poet, if the uproar doesn't stop you sleeping. To your laurels I add tenderness, caresses, and a thousand kisses.

Juliette

Mme Pierceau is here.[2] She's too much in love with you this evening. But as I'm sleeping with her, I'm not worried.

Letter 18

Monday evening, 7 o'clock *[13 July 1835]*

You didn't come to see me, my dear little vagabond, and you think I'm not sad about that? You're wrong! It requires all the trust I have in you not to go and inquire personally what has become of you. I don't feel very reassured here in my corner. Besides, the law of chastity that you've been observing with me so rigorously for several months makes me fear all sorts of misfortunes. Look out for yourself first and foremost, my man! Given that my numerous knives are freshly sharpened, there could be an atrocious carnage of your dear little person if I were to discover the least infraction in the fidelity that you owe me. I advise you not to mess[a] with them. I'm talking about my instruments of death. As for me, I couldn't ask for better than that you mess with me in whatever way you want!

I didn't want to have dinner before writing to you because I wouldn't have been able to eat, and then I think that if you want to see *Jacques II*[1] you'll come to get me early and I'll have to be ready. So I kiss your hands, your feet . . . and what else? All your pretty little body.

Juliette

I've sent for the jeweler; he hasn't come yet.

Letter 19

Les Metz,[a] Monday evening, quarter to 8:00
[9 September–13 October 1835]

You will see,[1] my dear little man, from the look of my paper that you will have lost nothing by waiting and that I'm disposed to give you the story of my heart since yesterday evening, up and down, as well, perhaps, as crosswise. Here's my beginning: I love you, my Victor, I love you, my Toto, I adore you, my little man. I have no other thought than that of you, no other desire than that of seeing you, no other coquetry than that of pleasing you.

After I wrote to you last night, as I've already told you, I spent the evening singing and almost dancing. I went to bed at half past ten. I fell asleep thinking about you. I woke up twice or thrice in the night, and then, finally, at about six o'clock in the morning, I was woken by a dear little lover who slid into bed beside me and to whom I was charitable enough to give the best welcome that I could. This poor little dear, who hadn't been to bed that night, was nevertheless a very *sprightly lover*. But why tell you things you know as well as I do? I prefer to tell you things you don't know—such as that this same charming little bedfellow gave me a letter before leaving, which I read all alone with cries of joy, loving kisses on every line, and adoration at every word.

Since then I've done nothing except love him, think of him, and love him again as I work.

My dear little Toto, after I left you, I came back by the way we planned, without meeting anyone until I reached the first houses of Les Metz. Once I got back, I had a quick wash. Then I made a fire to warm myself up, as I had become chilled through without a hat or shawl. Since then I have eaten, I have reread your wonderful little letter—which I have beside me as I write back to you—and I have told you all that's most tender, sweet, and sincere in my heart:

that I love you.

I finish my letter in the hope that you're going to come in a few minutes. I'm praying that there will be no hitch to your plans and that we'll spend at least this night together. But whatever happens, I'll love you and be your very faithful Juliette.

Letter 20

Friday morning, 10 o'clock, 29 January *[1836]*

Good morning, my dear little beloved, good morning! How are your little insides doing? It really upsets me to know you insist on working every night despite them. I slept like a log, which didn't stop me from thinking about you and loving you with all my soul.

I'm going to get up as soon as I've written to you, do the housework, make my stew, and be ready in case you come for me. Manière[1] hasn't sent word yet, but it's still very early. Do you know that your log didn't go out the least little bit and that this morning it was still burning bright as ever! This is how we burn the candle at both ends, even while we're trying to economize!

My dear little Toto, I love you. I'd like to become a great *actress,* first so that I could perform all *your roles,* and then so as to earn a lot of *money,* and then to make you *rich,* which would be quite *wonderful.*[a] These are the reasons that make me want to *be* someone. They are reasons of love, of jealousy, of tenderness. I beg you, my dear little beloved, to do your utmost if you can see any way to advance me a little.[2] You would do me a big favor and make me very happy at the same time. I love you so, my darling. I would be so proud and happy to advance because of you and relieve you of the burden that you've taken on without consideration of your strength and resources, that you can certainly forgive me my ambition, which arises only from love.

I kiss you on your lips, which are fresh and perfumed like a bouquet.

Juliette

Letter 21

Saturday morning, 10 o'clock, 27 February *[1836]*

Good morning, dear pet, good morning, my beloved! How was your night? I'm still a bit sick and I'm thinking more than ever about the possibility of a pretty little baby, and it's just too bad for you![1]

I spent the night thinking about that idea, and I must say it helped me more than a little to put up with my nausea. This morning I still feel very ill, but I hope that it'll pass during the day.

Good morning, you bad boy, you who gallivant around from balls to rehearsals to meetings to bars, good morning! I love you, although I really shouldn't. But I do love you, I can't help it, and in fact—if you want the whole truth—I adore you.

Dear little darling man, I'd so much like what *occupies* me to be a reality. The joy that I'd have from it would, I think, cure me instantly. You don't know what happiness this other little *you* would create in my life. You don't know what joy, what bliss it would be for me if I had a little *double* of you for my very own. Even just thinking about it fills my heart with joy as though it were a fact.

I love you my Victor. I love you, that's all I can say. The totality of what I feel is: I love you.

Juliette

Letter 22

Monday evening, half past 8:00, 14 March *[1836]*

You are a great man, you are a great Toto. The way in which you've arranged our room[1] this evening will suffice to bar the Academy[a] to you for the rest of your days. Do you know something? I love you. I'm a bit *devastated* by this afternoon's rehearsal.[2] And I hope you made yourself inaccessible to the seductive charms of those more or less *sirenic* ladies. I am very juju tonight, and you, are you very toto? Will you come here soon and will you be very charming and very amorous????? and more besides?

To please you I'm going to make the curtain very soon. You see, my dear little Toto, that I'm very nice and that I love you with all my heart. *It's devilishly fine in this place of ours. I'm drooling all over it from my whiskers to my claws.*

I can't believe that henceforth—with such a room and a love to match it—we can . . . . *[sic]* without hindrance.

Letter 23

Thursday evening, 10 minutes to 9:00, 7 April *[1836]*

Without a doubt the greatest happiness I can have when you're not here with me, my darling, is to write to you, but I'd much rather have *you* and never write you a single word—that's my real preference. *Oh, get angry if you want!*

Yes, my dear little Toto, instead of scribbling about love *with my head in my inkpot and my ass in the air,* I'd much rather be *tumbling around with you.* But what's the point of *my* desires, tastes, and preferences? Don't I have to wait for *your* spare time, which never comes until as late as possible and goes away as soon as it is come? And you have the nerve to say you love me more than I love you! Well, anyway . . .

I love you, do you hear, I love you? And I'm proud of it. You can do what you want and say all the silly things that come to mind, but the fact is: I love you. I wish that at this moment you felt one *speck* of my all-consuming desire to see you arrive a little sooner and that we were able to love one another *enough and to spare.* I would be very happy and gay, and you would give me all kinds of good caresses, and I would tell you all sorts of things, each one sweeter than the last. But you have to be there.

Juju

Letter 24

Saturday evening, 7 o'clock, 14 May *[1836]*

Dear beloved, now the time at which I could have hoped to see you has passed. It's very true that I've got next to my heart and in my thoughts your good, your adorable, your enchanting letter of today,[1] and I never *have* been able to merge in the same moment the happiness of reading you and seeing you. So I was almost certain I wouldn't see you tonight. Poor dear, I know you're working, I know what an effort you had to make to give me a mark of your love, so it's just as precious to my heart as your presence itself would have been. Before leaving *the other one,* I reread it and kissed it will all my strength. It cost me to part from it.[a] I'd like to keep all your letters on me, just as I keep the memory of them in my heart.

Dear soul, come as soon as you can, for it's life, it's light, it's the sun itself you bring with you. But whatever work you have and whatever the time you're forced to spend away from me, be sure I'll wait for you with resignation and with love, my mind and spirit always fixed on you. Dear beloved angel, I wanted to write you several letters at once, but I have pity on your poor eyes. You won't lose anything anyway, for I'm going to put all my soul in this single phrase—*"I love you"*—and I put all my heart in this kiss here:

◯

Juliette

Letter 25

Sunday evening, quarter past 5:00, 13 November *[1836]*

I thank you, my poor angel, for I know how much trouble you had to get the seats you've given me.[1] I'd be very happy if you could come to see me *tomorrow night* in my fourth-tier box, on this condition: I consent not to see your opera from *a bird's-eye view*.[2] You know I have little respect for all *ascensions* in general. I like them only *in your case*, when they don't go beyond the first floor.

I've just sent the tickets to Mlle François. I wrote about tomorrow to Mme Krafft and Mme Pierceau.[a] Now I'm going to take care of *myself*. I still feel quite sick, I wish tomorrow were already over so I could *relax*, and also so as to have at least a little chance of seeing you a bit more than a quarter of an hour each day. I'm beginning to take a dislike to *operas*. I don't like poets who sing so well on stage and so poorly to their mistress, you understand? I'm very bored. I never see your dicky bird[b] anymore. It isn't funny. But patience! As soon as your cacophony is over, like it or not I'll take possession of your instrument, which has been played much too much at my expense these last few days!

I'd like to know, now you have your *seats*, your *opera* is *rehearsed*, your *libretto printed*, what stops you from coming to dinner or supper with me this evening?

If you knew my impatience and need to see you, you would drop everything to please me on this point. Ah! I didn't used to have to express this desire to have it gratified immediately. Now it's useless to beg, cry, scream, even sing, I get nothing . . . except a *fourth-tier box*. It's a bitter pill. But I love you and swallow the pain, though not without groaning.

Juliette

Letter 26

Saturday evening, quarter to 9:00, 22 July *[1837]*

Fat chance that you are going to come back right away! You take me as too much of a *tart* to do that. Plus you wrote me such a nice, good letter[1] that you insist on making me pay for it by coming as late as possible. However, it's very good to see you and even better to hold you in *my power*. If ever I become queen of something, the first act of tyranny I'll exercise will apply to you. I'll have you tied up and bound, not too tightly, to my bed. Ha, ha! I'm not a *tart*. Anyway, reread Racine and put an everlasting flower in the buttonhole of Sir

Viennet,² who deserves it in every respect.ª One of my friends, Viscount Droüet, proposes to give him an Anacreontic banquet, with a calf suckling on its thumb. The fatso will sing a pastoral melody. Each guest will get his oats.ᵇ 'Night 'pa, 'night 'ma.ᶜ Your soul is as tough as your skin is soft. When I tell you yet again I love you, you'll not be much better off. It's not off nasty paper written with a goose quill and mind ditto that you must pluck that fruit. It's only good eaten fresh, which is to say, mouth to mouth. Otherwise, without having your grace and your spirit, my great poet, it's all pretty tasteless. In any case, I love you with all my soul.

Juliette

Letter 27

Wednesday morning, half past 9:00, 25 October *[1837]*

Good morning, my dear little beloved! When I say you're very nice, I'm not mistaken, I hope, especially if you come to have lunch with me this morning, as you promised me just a little while ago. I feel my headache getting better at the mere thought of it. It's entirely up to you that it should no longer be a question an hour from now. I love you, my beloved Victor, I love you more than you can imagine, even supposing that you suppose infinity. Only *I* understand how I love you. I love you, I love you!

I come back again to the subjectª of our dear little valley and our delightful woods. I'd like to make a trip there. Your beautiful poetry has heightened this desire of mine yet further, and I would be very happy to make another tour of the place with you. I'm sure I'd be better than you at finding all the places where we were so happy.¹ Today would have been a very fine day for such an expedition, the sun is beautiful and warm, what a pity you don't want to go. I promise you, however, we would have fared well in this country spot.

You are a *beast!* Pooh! Pooh! I broke off my letter here to buy some beautiful grapes for you, and the hope that you are going to come and eat with me is growing stronger and stronger. In any case you can take some grapes back to your little pets, because they're very good. 'Lo 'pa.ᵇ I think you didn't kiss me much this morning because I was too ugly. But that shouldn't be a reason for you, and I resent the fact that you didn't go beyond my ugliness and kiss me with all your might. As far as I'm concerned, your beauty is so dazzling I wouldn't be stopped, and I'd caress you from head to toe without the slightest scruple—there's the difference. Dare to say after that you love me more than I love you! But it doesn't prevent me from forgiving you and loving you with all my soul.

Juliette

Letter 28

Tuesday evening, quarter to 6:00, 7 August *[1838]*

Another day lost for me, my beloved, since you didn't come. I'm not grumbling, but I'd like to kiss your beautiful mouth, which has the color and scent of a rose. I love you, my love, more than any word or any term can express. All that you can imagine, all that you can desire, can't come close to the reality. I wish, for all sorts of good reasons, that your fine play was finished—because I'd know it in its entirety, because I could admire it at my leisure, because you'd have the time perhaps to love me a bit, and then because we could perhaps set sail for a nice little voyage in a big steamboat.[1] This would be such a big joy for me that I dare not hope for it. However, I've done some magnificent drawings for you that would make our so-called great artists blush with shame and die with envy.

I laugh, but I'm worried. I'm afraid that, despite this letter, you'll go to the Théâtre-Français without me.[2] Why don't you come here for a little while just long enough to reassure me? That would be so nice and kind. I've been waiting for you for such a long time.

Juliette

Letter 29

Wednesday evening, quarter to 7:00, 8 August *[1838]*

Thank-you, beloved, thank-you for your kindness! The article is charming and I hope *M.P.* will be very grateful for it.[1] I saw with pleasure, my love, that you had taken note of the delightful *discovery* we made the day before yesterday. All you have to do is make use of it several times a day for this to be the most triumphant discovery anyone has made since the days of Adam. You went away much too soon this afternoon, my Toto. How do you expect me to have the courage to get through the whole evening if you don't give me a bit of happiness in the daytime? So what if I did draw a steamboat without paddle wheels? In fact my absentmindedness is rather epigrammatic, since our cherished little annual trip has neither foot, nor paw, nor wheel this year. If only we had the carriage of *Yure* or *Pierre* with the famous *favorite* or the hideous *hag*, there would be nothing but happiness and joy for us. But we make no more of these delightful trips—and carriages, landscapes, happiness, all of that is now only a picture, as you can see above.[2]

Juliette

Letter 30

Tuesday evening, 6 o'clock, 14 August *[1838]*

I'm still very sick, my beloved, and I'm even more eager and impatient to see you.

Mme Krafft sent her manservant with a package containing a shawl for the trip[a] and a matching dress of woolen muslin: it seems she particularly wanted to give me a dress made of this fabric;[b] plus a faded hat with *feathers*. I sent it back, not because it was faded, but because I can't ride on the top of a coach wearing a hat with feathers without looking like *Mme Fat Guts*. The feathers aside, the hat had to be fastened by a knot of assorted ribbons, and I have neither the time nor the talent for that. This package was accompanied by a letter, which I didn't open. The manservant who brought it asked for a box, without any further explanation. I wrote a letter to Mme Krafft to inform her I hadn't seen you and I didn't know when I would. Anyway, my poor beloved, I don't have what would much oblige me—some kind of hat. We must buy one, unless she has another thought, for I have to send Suzette to ask if she has a corset that laces in front. I write all these things to you because I know you wish to hear them, even though they aren't very interesting. It seems you don't want to take me to Mme Pierceau's. I knew very well asking you to do it gave you a reason not to. Try at least to take me out, for I'm very ill and staying indoors all the time is killing me!

I love you, as you well know.

Juliette

Letter 31

Wednesday evening, quarter to 10:00, 15 August *[1838]*

My dear little man, I love you, you are my beloved. I'd like to be already on the top of our coach, galloping, galloping, far, so far, so as to take a long time to return!

Since you've given me a glimpse of the possibility of performing in your delightful play,[1] I've been like a poor sleepwalker who has been given a lot of champagne to drink. I see double; I see glory, happiness, love, and adoration, and all of it on a gigantic and impossible scale.

I say "impossible," because I know well you cannot love me as I love you and that I can never, whatever my talent, reach the heights of your sublime poetry. It's not modesty on my part, for I don't believe there is in the world man or woman capable of playing the roles such as your wonderful mind envisioned them.

I love you, my Toto, I adore you, my little man. You are my sunshine and my life. You are my love and my soul. You are everything and much more besides. I adore you!

Juliette

Letter 32

Wednesday morning, quarter to 10:00, 29 August *[1838]*

The *kiss* has been replaced by *"good morning,"* happiness by the letter, sunshine by bad weather, joy in the heart by tears in the eyes.[1] I am alone and sad. I feel that happiness and joy are dead forever for me. I feel nothing alive in me anymore except my love. I love you more than ever, but with the painful conviction that our happiness is over. Perhaps my poor heart is just duped by a sad illusion—I wish it were so, but I have no hope that it is.

Poor friend, you also have already shouldered your yoke of drudgery. But when this yoke touches *you*, it becomes a necklace of diamonds and glory. You may in vain wish yourself a man like all other hideous humans, your divine nature always penetrates. Only your feet touch the earth, your head stays always in the heavens. For you happiness is discovering new stars or creating new ones finer and more luminous than those of God Himself. As for me, I have no other happiness than to love you and to see you. That's why I'm so often sad and discouraged, while you, on the other hand, are happy and victorious.

I don't expect you this morning, my dear beloved, I know how much you have to do. But I desire you with all my soul.

Juliette

Letter 33

Saturday afternoon, 2 o'clock, 1 September *[1838]*

My dear little *lover*, I've just finished my accounts and found there a discrepancy to *my advantage* of *eight francs, thirteen and a half sous*! I could have profited from it and put it in my moneybag, but I am honest and *poor*. Besides, you brought me a bouquet that's worth more than that, and so I have only done my duty.

I love you, my little man! You don't seem to believe it, but it's true. I spend my life wanting you when you're not there and adoring you when you are.

In short, I'm a poor old Juju, lost and preserved in her love like the toad in the bottle of the apothecary at la Ferté.[1] 'Lo 'pa, 'lo 'to,[a] you have to laugh. Look, there isn't much joy when you're not here, and if wasn't for the hope of a nice little night tonight, I'd be bellowing horribly. Papa was very stiff[b] with me just now, and that worries me. I don't like you being stiff when there's a rehearsal going on. I'm going to sharpen my big knife, and then we'll see. In the meantime, I lick your feet like the poor faithful dog that I am.

J.

Letter 34

Tuesday afternoon, half past 2:00, 4 September *[1838]*

I am ready, my beloved, but *you* are not. M. Manière[a] still hasn't come, and I fear he won't, as is his usual wonderful way. I'm sad, my dear beloved, I'm mourning a fine and wonderful role that has died for me forever. Never will *Marie de Neubourg* live *through me* and *for me*. My sorrow is greater than you can imagine; this last hope lost has been a terrible blow. I'm demoralized to the point that I wouldn't dare to perform, no matter what the role or whose play it was. I'm really very unhappy. However, my good angel, I realize it's not your fault and that you did everything you could to fight my jinx.[1] But it served only to highlight your perseverance and devotion. I'm very discouraged. My God, what's to become of me?

It's at this time particularly that you must be kind and indulgent, for I am really suffering. Love me, love me, love me, if you want me to live! *I* love you too much. Unfortunately, it's true, and you know it as well as I. But love you any less—that I cannot do. I need to love you as I need to breathe.

Juliette

Letter 35

Saturday afternoon, 3 o'clock, 29 September *[1838]*

Yes, you must be very tired, my love, yes! You "kissed"[a] me nine times, *that's tremendous!* Yes, you're my delightful little joker that I love and adore, yes, yes, yes! What more do you want, tell me?

I've just written to Faussier *[?]* asking him to send me some better wine or send me none at all, because the last lot was undrinkable. At the same time, I'm writing to Mlle François about my shawl—five or six months later it's getting a little ludicrous. Anyway, I'll have her reduce what I owe her if she turns out to have lost it or worn it out.

I love you my little o! I adore you my dear little o! You have too much "kissed"... my hand, my big 'to. I beg you henceforth to handle me more gently. 'Lo 'to:[b] it seems that tomfoolery is the order of the day? Alright, so I'll go along with it and joke like a native who intends her jokes *seriously*.

I love my Toto, I adore my Toto!

Juliette

Letter 36

Monday, noon, 4 November *[1839]*

Good morning, dear beloved! Good morning, my darling! It's midday by my clock, which is fast by I don't know how many hours *[sic]*, but it's already a while since I got up. I got done with my daughter's outfit, and now she's practicing the piano. I thought a lot all night about everything you said to me last night, my beloved. There's one luminous and shining phrase in particular that warms my soul. Perhaps it slipped out only as one of those compliments you feel compelled to pay to the woman who loves you? I don't know. But what is certain is that I've transformed the assurance you gave me of never having *really* loved *anyone but me* into something sanctified and sacred and of the highest truth. As for myself, I adore you, and I never felt even a *semblance* of love for anyone before you. I love you, I adore you, and I will love you and adore you forever, because my body, my heart, my life, and my soul are made of love. Believe me, my beloved, for it's God's truth!

As for the fears you have about seeing me go back to my career in the theater, they'll disappear when you see my virtuous and upright conduct—I hope, indeed, I'm sure of it. You have nothing to fear concerning me, wherever I might be or whatever I might be doing. I adore you and venerate you. If I could grant you your wish that I give up the theater, that is to say, the only chance for the future that still remains to me, I would do it without hesitating and even without your asking, just because you wanted it. But, my beloved, I think it would be easier for me to give up my life for you than to renounce the hope of repaying my creditors and earning my own living. If by some remote possibility I were to renounce it, I'm sure my despair would bring about an irreparable catastrophe that would weigh down my entire life.

My beloved, don't turn me away from the one thing that can bring me tranquillity and make me believe in your love! Help me and don't leave me unless I give you grounds to do so! In other words, spend your life loving me in exchange for an admiration and adoration without bounds. Give me your two little hands to kiss, and quickly bring me your two little jewels of feet, for I have a very pretty pair of *boots* to give them, which arrived this morning while I was still sleeping.

Kiss me, my little man! I love you.

Juliette

Letter 37

Monday morning, quarter to 11:00, 18 November *[1839]*

May you never regret what you did last night, my beloved![1] May you be happy! Henceforth this is my only care, my only ambition, my only glory, my only happiness. As long as you are happy, I'll be happy. May your generosity never be a burden or a duty to you, but a joy and security, and I will bless the night of *17 November 1839*.

That our *marriage* should lack for nothing, I had all the emotions that accompany the first day: unspeakable happiness, heavenly ecstasy, insomnia, astonishment—which would have been anxiety, if it weren't for the fact I know the divine goodness of your soul. I felt all of this last night, and I slept scarcely a few hours even though I stayed in bed very late. Anyway, my poor beloved, *almost my husband*, my prayers and my rising this morning were those of a *newlywed bride*. Oh, yes! I'm your wife, aren't I, my beloved? You can acknowledge me without blushing. Yet my first title, the one that I want to keep among and above all the others, is that of your *mistress*, your passionate, ardent, devoted mistress, counting only on your glance to live, on your smile to be happy.

I bless you, my generous little man, for having thought about my daughter, my poor daughter, who now becomes yours also and who will love you with a part of my love, the love that venerates you, admires you, and blesses you day and night. Thank-you for her, thank-you for me, for *us*, for we shall be happy I hope—you by your benevolence, I by my love.

Juliette

Letter 38

Monday evening, 5 o'clock, 18 November *[1839]*

I'm ready, my pet, and in honor of our marriage I've put on the beautiful new dress from Lyon.[1] I'm only afraid you might take me too late to old Mme Pierceau's,[a] and that there will be nothing left to *munch*, which wouldn't suit me very well as I had hardly anything to eat for lunch. Joy took away my appetite, happiness brings it back to me, and I feel I could do justice to a *nuptial* feast this evening if there were one. Résisieux has been here and is leaving.[2] She said I look *"very beautiful,"* I replied, *"Very happy."* She didn't understand the meaning of my reply, but *I* understand it and I'm surprised I don't have a *halo* around my head like the *blessed*. I'm so happy, so joyous, so much in love, that it's enough to make God envious. As long as you never regret the step you took last night! As long as you regard it always as a victory and a joy, then I have nothing to regret, nothing to desire. Poor beloved, your beautiful little lips are all feverish, and I'd like to make them better with my kisses. I hardly saw you this afternoon, and when you come to get me, I'll hardly have the time to tell you I love you. I feel like staying at home in my *fine attire* to keep you and caress you without losing a drop. If only you knew how much I love you! You know it, don't you, you know it and are happy? I kiss your little feet.

Juliette

Letter 39

Thursday afternoon, quarter past 1:00, 12 December *[1839]*

I'm late writing to you, my dear little beloved, but it's not quite all my fault because I wanted to make your tea and wash my face so I'd be all ready in case you should come, which I don't expect you will. Let's face it, you prefer to stay put, and you're right to do so, it's just that you're wrong to leave me so long without seeing you.

It's still very nasty weather, my beloved, but I wouldn't notice it if I were with you. I'm so happy, my Toto, when I see you, that everything appears beautiful and good to me, for I see everything in your eyes and in your soul. "Kiss"[a] me, my poor love, and think of me in spite of the candidature.[1] Be ready to buy me my wardrobe, for I intend and aspire not to give you credit for a single hour. Ah, you are a candidate! Ah, you put yourself in the running for a mean worthless armchair where these stupid old men have left their snivel on the arms and their poops on the seat! Well, *I* want a wardrobe in which to lock up your mind, for you seem to have lost it, or at least let it wander, the day that you allowed yourself to be seduced by the candidate's hat, which doesn't suit you at all. "Kiss" me and let's laugh, let's laugh together at all these old Academicians who dribble into their wigs and take enemas all the time! And above all let's not make visits,[2] and let's save the money for our wardrobe. I love you.

Juliette

Letter 40

Wednesday evening, 4 o'clock, 18 December *[1839]*

Oh, upon my word, my Toto, that was an abominable trick you just played on me, looking all the while as though butter wouldn't melt! You have me get dressed, have me turn myself inside out to get ready in time for you, and then you leave me waiting here! Toto, Toto, your cheek is asking to be scratched, my love, and I've a great desire to scratch it for you with a big kiss embellished with claws and teeth. I'm furious with you! It's very naughty of you to trick a poor trusting woman who has never done you wrong. Tut-tut!

You must come devilishly quickly to seek forgiveness for the fiasco just now. Also, you are not going to be elected tomorrow—Casimir will be.[1] That's good, and I'm sticking my tongue out at you as you can see.[2] We look very similar, although somewhat idealized. Monster that you are, you weren't ashamed to misuse a poor, wretched, innocent woman as she rose from her bed. Tut-tut, you should blush right into the depths of your fine overcoat! I shall tell everybody you have a barrel organ in your shirt that plays melodies all by itself. I shall say so, I shall say so, depend upon it! Henceforth you'll be represented only in the form of Boreas, god *of winds*. That'll teach you to make me perform useless feats! Never mind, you'll lose more from it than you'll gain, and all the winds in the world won't be able to fill the sails of the image of charming young man that you've so unworthily assumed. "Kiss" me, "kiss"[a] me again and again, and you'll only half succeed in disarming my hatred and my fury! Now it's dark, and I'm hurrying to finish this letter.

Notes

Notes in **boldface** represent additions by the translator.

Letter 1

    a. This hypothetical date is based on the supposition that this letter was written on the day preceding the night that Drouet and Hugo first slept together, and that that date was 16 February. However, there is some doubt as to whether the date was actually the sixteenth or the nineteenth of this month (see above, Introduction, pp. 10–11 and n. 45) [T].

    1. Mme Krafft was a friend of Juliette's (**see Glossary [T]**).

Letter 2

    a. *Les Feuilles d'automne* (*The Leaves of Autumn*) is a collection of poems by Hugo (see Glossary) in which he evokes the charms of children, childhood, and domesticity and also expresses sadness at the passing of time (although he was only twenty-nine in 1831 when they were published). Drouet's

letter is almost an accusation of hypocrisy: she contrasts Hugo's fictional sadness about "the leaves of autumn," written amid (in her perception) actual domestic happiness, with her real unhappiness, in the context of a real autumn [T].

Letter 4

1. Claire, the daughter of Juliette Drouet and the sculptor James Pradier, was at boarding school in Saumur in an establishment run by a Mlle Watteville. She was seven years old at the time. **The school was originally in Paris but was moved to Saumur (on the Loire river about 190 miles southwest of Paris) after 1834 (Siler, *Correspondance*, 1:162, n. 1) [T].**

2. Jourdain was an upholsterer and one of Juliette Drouet's creditors. According to the evidence of her account book, after her engagement at the Comédie-Française (February 1834) the actress would "almost [share her salary] with Jourdain" (Souchon, *Inspiratrice*, 40–2). **For more information on Jourdain, see *VS*, 4:50–5 [T].**

Letter 6

1. On 16 December 1833, the newspaper *Brid'oison* would carry this item: "The suit brought against Mlle Juliette, actress at the Porte-Saint-Martin, has fallen through; the court declared that the charges were not substantiated and ordered Mme Ribou, the plaintiff, to pay costs." Nevertheless, Juliette's account book contains the entry: "Debts in January 1834, fictitious or in interest: Ribot, Fr 8000 capital" (Souchon, *Inspiratrice*, 42).

Letter 7

1. The lovers had taken a short excursion to the Vallée de la Bièvre **(a beauty spot a two-hour carriage journey away from Paris). They had taken the carriage from Paris the morning before and spent the night at the inn in the village of Jouy-en-Josas near Bièvres – see Paul Souchon, *Olympio et Juliette: Lettres inédites de Juliette Drouet à Victor Hugo* (Paris: Albin Michel, 1940), 22, 40 [T].** Hugo would remind Juliette of the promise in this letter on the occasion of her flight a month later. See *LJD*, 54, 60. **Enchanted by this area, Drouet and Hugo would return to it for a more extended stay in September of this year— see below, L. 14 and n. 1 [T].**

Letter 8

1. *Claude Gueux* **(a story by Hugo, see Glossary [T])** appeared in *La Revue de Paris* on 6 July 1834. The exactness of this quotation, as well as the allusions to Albin, the friend of Claude Gueux, suggest a recent reading of the text. **Albin shares his bread with Claude Gueux until the head warder spitefully separates the two prisoners. The line quoted by Drouet (*OC*, 5:244) occurs in the context of a description of the lightheartedness that overcame Gueux once he had made a decision to kill this warder: as an amusing prank he extinguishes a candle with the breath from his nostrils [T].**

2. Response by Gilbert, *Marie Tudor*, I, 3. **In this drama by Hugo (see Glossary), Gilbert, a poor craftsman, has brought up Jane as his adopted daughter and now wishes to marry her.** The quoted words occur in the context of a speech in which Gilbert expresses to Jane his violent feelings toward the rich and handsome noblemen for whom he crafts weaponry and toward whom he fears that Jane is attracted. When Jane begins to remonstrate with his expression of violence, he replies, "Pardon, Jane. N'est-ce pas, l'amour rend bien méchant?" ("I beg your pardon, Jane. Doesn't love make us spiteful?") [T].

Letter 9

1. "Victor Hugo in front of Notre-Dame at Reims" (Maison de Victor Hugo, inv. 253), by Jean Alaux (1786–1864). This miniature, which was painted during Hugo's trip to Reims in May 1825 for the coronation of Charles X, was given by the painter to Mme Victor Hugo, before coming into the possession of Juliette Drouet. The poet then wrote on the back of the portrait: "These eyes whose light you are, these ears ... all that makes a head that would cut itself off for you."

2. On 20 July Juliette moved into 4 bis, rue du Paradis **from her expensive apartment at 35 bis, rue de l'Echiquier, where she could no longer afford to live [T].**

Letter 10

1. Saint Victor's day falls on 21 July. One would expect then the date of "Sunday, 20 July 1834" (which would be correct), but "18" is quite clearly legible.

Letter 11

1. Juliette's flight to Saint-Renan, to her sister's, was the culmination of an emotional and financial crisis. Hugo would go to bring back Juliette, and their return journey would be their first big trip. See *LJD*, 54ff. **Saint-Renan is about eight miles from Brest, in Brittany, a long journey from Paris by horse-drawn coach of about 360 miles. This was Drouet's first return to Brittany after leaving it some twenty years before. It was also the first time that she had met her sister, Renée's, family, the Kochs (see Koch family, Glossary). Hugo would travel out to meet Drouet in Brest on 8 August, and they would then travel together for three weeks [T].**

2. Juliette, who had been engaged as a *pensionnaire* on 13 February, would never be assigned any role in this theater.

Letter 12

a. **Drouet stopped at Rennes, in Brittany, about two hundred miles west of Paris, before continuing on to Brest and Saint-Renan, another 160 miles or so away [T].**

Letter 13

1. This letter to Victor Hugo was enclosed with a letter sent by Juliette to her maid:

[5 August, 1834]

Here is a letter for M. Victor H. If he doesn't come to get it at the house, try to find a clever way of letting him know that there is a letter for him at 4 bis, rue du Paradis, from M. Krafft. I think that if he is still in Paris he will understand the information and will either send for, or come himself to get, my letter. In any case, write to me by return post how M. Victor H. is, if you have seen him, what he said to you, if he is at Paris, or if he is no longer there. In short, tell me everything that you know about him.

I am writing to you from Rennes, where I arrived very sick and my daughter also. However, I'm hoping to set off again tomorrow for my sister's, where you can write to me at this address: Mme Drouet c/o M. Louis *Kock* [sic] at Saint-Renan near Brest.

Once again, I ask that you take care of my house.

J. Droüet

[Addressed] Mme Droüet for Madame Marie
4 bis, rue du Paradis
Le Marais, *Paris*
[Postmarks]
Rennes, 5 August 1834
7 August 1834

Letter 14

1. On 1 September Hugo installed Juliette at Les Metz, two and a half miles from the Bertin house **(see Bertin family, Glossary [T])**, where he was to spend two months with his family. The lovers would meet in the forest and left letters in the trunk of a chestnut tree (cf. *LJD*, 63). Juliette would spend six weeks there again in the autumn of 1835.

Letter 15

1. Juliette played the role of Jane in *Marie Tudor* only once: at the premiere on 6 November 1833. She was panned by the critics and replaced in the second performance by Ida Ferrier, who was to become Mme Alexandre Dumas. **On Hugo's play *Marie Tudor*, see Glossary and above, Introduction, pp. 12–13. Pouchain (*JDD*, 139) points out that the premiere had to be delayed until 7 November [T].**

Letter 16

1. The elder Bertin, editor of the *Journal des débats*, lived at the time on the first floor of the old residence of Queen Margot, at the end of the rue de Seine.

Letter 17

    a. **On Hugo's play** *Angelo*, **see Glossary [T].**

    1. Marie Dorval acted the part of Catarina. Juliette was jealous of her. **Catarina is the wife of Angelo, the governor of Brescia, in** *Angelo*. **On Marie Dorval, see above, Introduction, p. 6, and Glossary [T].**

    2. Juliette often refers to this friend in her letters before the period of exile. **On Mathilde Pierceau, see Glossary [T].**

Letter 18

    a. **I have translated "frotter" ("to rub") as "mess." The word "frotter" has an obscene meaning in the expression "frotter le lard"—see below, L. 26, n. c [T].**

    1. *Jacques II*, a historic prose drama by Vanderburch, was performed Monday, 13 July 1835 at the Théâtre-Français. There were only ten performances; the first was the only one that took place on a "Monday evening" at a time when Hugo was in Paris.

Letter 19

    a. **This is the second time Drouet and Hugo have stayed at Les Metz. Hugo installs Drouet on 9 September in the same house in which she had stayed the previous year (Souchon,** *Olympio*, **83), while he and his family stay as in the previous year with the Bertins at their country house nearby [T].**

    1. This letter was doubtless written the same day as Hugo's—see *LJD*, 75.

Letter 20

    1. Juliette Drouet's lawyer, who was often delegated to deal with her creditors (see Souchon, *Inspiratrice*, 41–3).

    a. **The words for "actress" and "wonderful" are "acteuse" (rather than "actrice") and "phame" (rather than "fameux"), both invented words [T].**

    2. No doubt Juliette refers to the Comédie-Française, where she has still not performed **(see above, Introduction, p. 13 [T]).**

Letter 21

    1. This hoped-for pregnancy, like the others, would not materialize. Cf. below, L. 43.

Letter 22

    1. On 8 March 1836, Juliette moved **(from 50 rue des Tournelles [T])** to 14 rue Saint-Anastase, near the place Royale (now the place des Vosges), where Hugo lived.

a. See below, L. 39 and n. 1 [T].

2. *Angelo* was to be revived at the Théâtre-Français on 26 March 1836. **On Hugo's play *Angelo*, see Glossary [T].**

Letter 24

1. Cf. *LJD*, 85.

a. In his letter (***LJD*, 85) to which Drouet is replying, Hugo says, "This letter will replace the other one that you are carrying next to your heart"** [T].

Letter 25

1. *La Esmeralda*, an opera by Louise Bertin with a libretto by Victor Hugo inspired by *Notre-Dame de Paris*, made its debut at the Opéra de Paris on 14 November 1836. **On Louise Bertin, see Bertin family, Glossary [T].**

2. An allusion to "Paris à vol d'oiseau" ("A Bird's-Eye View of Paris"), a famous chapter in Hugo's novel. **There is a pun here on the two meanings of "à vol d'oiseau" that cannot be conveyed in English. Although Drouet's box is so high, she promises not to watch the opera only "superficially"** (cf. Littré, s.v. "vol," [1]) [T].

a. **On Laure Krafft and Mathilde Pierceau, see Glossary [T].**

b. **The French says "vot moigneau," which could be "votre moineau" disguised in a "funny" accent (possibly baby talk?). "Sparrow" could be coarse slang for "penis"—John S. Farmer, ed., *Vocabula Amatoria. A French-English Glossary of Words, Phrases, and Allusions Occurring in the Works of Rabelais, Voltaire, Molière, Rousseau, Béranger, Zola, and Others* (New York: University Books of America, 1966), s.v. "moineau" [T].**

Letter 26

1. See *LJD*, 94. **This letter is an apology on Hugo's part for having hurt Drouet—perhaps by accusing her of being a "cocotte"? [T].**

2. Viennet (1777–1868) had been one of the most resolute adversaries of Hugo and of Romanticism. He was a member of the Académie française from 1830 and *pair de France* from 1836. **The "Peers of France" dated back to the time of Charlemagne but had been subsequently abolished and reinstituted more than once. Peers of France existed between the Restoration (1814) and the revolution of 1848 and were created by the King. Viennet wrote, among other things, fables in the style of Aesop where the protagonists are usually animals—see his *Fables nouvelles suivies de deux épîtres* (Paris: Amyot, 1851)—which may be part of the joke here about the calf and the cows. He initially opposed Hugo's admission to the Académie française. Hugo had indicted Viennet's "long and pale" tragedy, *Clovis*, in an article in *Le Conservateur***

littéraire, describing it as a work that "makes one yawn incessantly" (*OC*, 1:738–42) [T].

 a. The "everlasting flower" is "une immortelle" and is perhaps a reference to the feminine form of "un immortel," a term for a member of the Académie française, as well as, possibly, to "une immortelle" in the sense of one of the Olympian goddesses (a Muse?). "Buttonhole" may possibly have a vulgar meaning in this context. The reference to Racine (1639–1699) is presumably an illusion to his status as chief exemplar of French classicism (to which school Viennet aspired to belong) [T].

 b. Anacreon was an ancient Greek poet, whose extant poems are mainly celebrations of love, wine, and revelry and who is mentioned by Hugo in his poetry. This letter is replete with obscene double meanings not all of which can now be reconstructed. "Le lard," translated here as "the fatso," but also meaning "bacon," may be a reference to the expression "frotter le lard" ("rubbing the lard [or the fat]")— an obscene expression for copulating—see Farmer, *Vocabula Amatoria*, s.v. "frotter." I have translated as "oats" the expression "picot teint," which seems to be a pun on "browned fish" (dab) and "picotin" as in "ration of oats," with its obscene meaning, see ibid., s.v. "picotin." The "rance des vaches" literally means "the smell of cows" (whores), but is no doubt a play on "ranz des vaches" meaning "pastoral melody." There is no way to translate this phrase and preserve both meanings at the same time [T].

 c. The French says "Soir pa, soir man," which seems to be a (meaningless?) play on "Bonsoir papa, bonsoir maman" ("Goodnight papa, goodnight mama") [T].

Letter 27

 a. The French involves a pun on the expression "revenir à mes moutons" ("to come back to my sheep") meaning "to come back to the subject": "I come back again, not to my sheep, but to our dear little valley and our delightful woods." This pun cannot be successfully rendered in English [T].

 1. "Tristesse d'Olympio" (*Les Rayons et les ombres*, XXXIV—a collection of poetry by Hugo, see Glossary [T]) was inspired by a pilgrimage made by Victor Hugo alone into the Vallée de la Bièvre, 15 October 1837. The poem is dated the twenty-first. He evokes the irrevocable alteration of the countryside where the lovers had been so happy in 1834 and 1835 (see above, L. 14 and n. 1). Juliette's attitude is a priori very opposed to this "sadness" ("tristesse").

 b. The French—"Jour pa"—seems to be a (meaningless?) play on "bonjour papa" ("hello papa"), which I have tried to mimic in English with "'lo 'pa." Cf. above, L. 26 and n. d [T].

Letter 28

 1. Juliette has drawn here a steamboat with passengers, the captain who rings a big bell (for departure?), and some puffs of smoke across the whole page. Between the

time of finishing *Ruy Blas* and reading it to the actors, Hugo was able to offer Juliette only ten days in Champagne **(an area in northeastern France [T])**, from 18–28 August. **On *Ruy Blas*, a play by Hugo, see Glossary [T].**

2. The first of six revivals of *Angelo*, in the season of 1838-1839, took place on the evening of 7 August. **On *Angelo*, a play by Hugo, see Glossary [T].**

Letter 29

1. We do not know what text is involved here. This would not be the first time that Hugo had intervened on behalf of Pradier (see Sheila Gaudon, "James Pradier, Victor Hugo et l'Arc de Triomphe de l'Etoile," *Revue de l'histoire littéraire de la France*, September–October 1968, 713–25). When the sculptor did not pay the school fees for his daughter Claire, Hugo subsidized them. His fatherly role toward Juliette's child would grow stronger over time. **On James Pradier, see Glossary and above, Introduction, pp. 2ff. [T].**

2. Juliette has drawn in her letter a two-wheeled horse-drawn carriage that is passing between trees. A man and a woman sit on either side of the driver.

Letter 30

a. **This is the trip to Champagne from 18–28 August, see above, L. 28, n. 1 [T].**

b. **"Mousseline de laine" is described by C. Willett Cunnington, *English Women's Clothing in the Nineteenth Century* (1937; New York: Dover Publications, 1990), 433, as "a fine, light, woollen cloth, of a muslin-like texture, and often 'figured in gay patterns like a calico print'" [T].**

Letter 31

1. Juliette was to play the role of Maria de Neubourg, **the queen of Spain in Hugo's play *Ruy Blas* [T]**. Mme Hugo, however, interceded with Joly, the director of the Théâtre de la Renaissance, to remind him of the "opinion which is, rightly or wrongly, unfavorable toward the talent of Mlle Juliette." She wrote: "Nothing could be more appropriate than that my husband, who has an interest in this lady, should support her admission to your theater; but that this should go as far as jeopardizing the success of one of the finest things in existence, I cannot accept" (*OC*, 6:1135). The role went to Mlle Beaudoin, who was at that time the mistress of Frédérick Lemaître **(on whom, see Glossary [T])**.

Letter 32

1. Their little jaunt had finished the day before. Juliette seems to sense already that she will not perform in *Ruy Blas*.

Letter 33

1. Juliette and Hugo had passed through la Ferté-sous-Jouarre on 19 August and again on the twenty-eighth.

a. The French says "jour pa, jour To," probably a (meaningless?) play on "hello papa, hello Toto"—cf. above, L. 27 and n. b [T].

b. The French is "i," which I have translated as "stiff and upright" on the assumption that it is a reference to the expression "droit comme un i" ("stiff as a poker"). Drouet suspects that Hugo's interest in actresses in the play he is rehearsing is causing a change in attitude toward her [T].

Letter 34

a. See above, L. 20 and n. 1 [T].

1. It is not certain that Hugo "did everything" for Juliette to obtain the coveted role (see above, L. 31 and n. 1) [T]. According to a letter from Anténor Joly, director of the Théâtre de la Renaissance, to Frédérick Lemaître, director of *Ruy Blas*, Hugo admitted the possibility of a different casting for the part of the Queen, from the time when he returned from his trip: "Last night I saw Hugo; he was making his way here hastily, thinking that we were going to rehearse today. We talked for a long time about the casting of the female parts. There is an important female role in the work; whether it would suit Mlle Beaudoin, you and she shall judge; please bring her with you tomorrow [to the reading of the play]." (Letter of 29 August 1838, cited by A. Ubersfeld, *Le Roi et le Buffon* [Paris: Corti, 1974], 334).

Letter 35

a. While "baiser," as a literary word, can be used politely to mean "kiss," it can also be used vulgarly in an obscene sense. There is no doubt that Drouet sometimes intended the obscene sense of the word, as in her letter of 27 October 1841 ("Baisez-moi dans toute l'acception du mot" [" 'kiss' me in the full meaning of the word"], *CL*, 16) and as here, where both meanings are intended [T].

b. The French says "jour To"—cf. above, L. 33, and n. a [T].

Letter 37

1. On the night of 17–18 November, Hugo and Juliette allied themselves in what has been erroneously called a "mystic marriage": in exchange for her promise never to return to the theater, Hugo promised he would never abandon either Juliette or her daughter.

Letter 38

1. During their trip in 1839 Hugo and Juliette twice passed through Lyon: on the night of 25–6 September and on the afternoon and evening of 16 October. It was at the time of this second stop that the purchase of a dress could have occurred. In Hugo's account book, beyond the expenses for a meal and hotel, there is the cryptic comment: "At Lyon—R—72 f." (*OC*, 6:700). *R* could stand for "robe" ("dress") [T].

a. On Mme Pierceau, see Glossary. Given that she was only two years older than Drouet, she hardly deserved to be called "la mère Pierceau" ("old Mme Pierceau") [T].

2. Résisieux Besancenot, the child of neighbors and sister of little Jonas mentioned below, L. 43 and 46.

Letter 39

a. On this "kiss" and the one below in this letter, see above, L. 35, n. a [T].

1. Hugo is a candidate for the Académie française for the third time. **The Académie française was founded originally in the sixteenth century and continues to this day, with a membership limited to forty. Its original purpose was to maintain standards of literary taste and establish rules of acceptability for the French language [T].**

2. Four days previously Juliette had written: "I have just bought a foot warmer so that you can take me with you without fear or regret when you make your visits. I very much want you not to make them without me" (Bibliothèque nationale, Cabinet des manuscrits, nouvelles acquisitions françaises, 16.340, f° 135). **The visits are those made by a candidate to members of the Académie seeking support for his candidature [T].**

Letter 40

1. The election to the Académie scheduled for the day after will be adjourned—after seven rounds—to a date three months later. Victor Hugo will beat Casimir Bonjour by only a few votes. **The voting continued through as many rounds as were needed for one candidate to obtain an absolute majority. Casimir Bonjour (1795–1856) was a dramatist. Some of his successful plays performed at the Comédie-Française were *La Mère rivale* (1821), *L'Education ou les deux cousines* (1823), *Mari à bonnes fortunes* (1824) [T].**

2. Juliette has drawn here a woman who is sticking out her tongue to a man dressed in a top hat and overcoat.

a. See above, L. 35, n. a [T].

1840s

Letter 41

Saturday evening, quarter to 7:00, 18 July *[1840]*

I'm dismayed, my beloved, by the daguerreotype taken of me! I'm demoralized, *seriously*, for it's not that it hurts my pride in my appearance or still less my self-respect, but it kills my confidence in your love. I'm aching and sick, I would like to die. If I didn't have my poor daughter, I think I'd hasten the moment, such is my shame and such my fear of not surviving a second after the extinction of your love. I feel true despair. I really am a monster of ugliness! What frightful portraits, including the *successful* one! And I can suffer from no illusions, for yours—although they are not as handsome as yourself—are charming. So it is in fact I, *I* who am ugly and frightful! It's very sad, my God, for *in my soul I am beautiful*.[1] This is the first time that this line has struck me as one of the most true and poignant expressions of the pain of the poor monster you created.

If you have pity for me and if you care about your love and my life, you'll erase all these hideous images that multiply me and, as it were, double my ugly carcass. I'll beg you so earnestly to do so that you'll have to consent. Meanwhile, I think you've left for Saint-Prix.[2] My head is on fire and I would kill myself with pleasure, such is my suffering in body and soul. I love you too much—that's what makes me so ugly.

Juliette

Letter 42

Friday afternoon, half past 4:00, 28 August *[1840]*

All my money people have come, my love. In the meantime I've finished putting aside what we are going to take,[1] and I've written various farewell letters that you'll see and that I'll have Suzanne[a] deliver as soon as we leave. I've also written to Mme Krafft but *by the mail* in order not to double the expenses of the carrier, in case Mme Pierc22 has already been to Mme Krafft's and has sent me a shawl. Besides there was sufficient time for the mail, and we don't risk the indiscretions of the porter. Today is the last time for two months that I'll be writing to you, my beloved. I can't say I'm vexed about it, far from it—I'm delighted, and tired and exhausted as I am, I yell my war cry joyfully: *"What happiness!!!!!!"* I'm jolly well going to take my fill of happiness and love for two months. All the humps, terrestrial, animal, and otherwise will be nothing compared with the heaps of fun[2] I'm going to indulge in all along the way. Hills, mountains, the humps of camels, dromedaries, and others—all will be but a pimple beside the heaps of *my* fun.

If the dress was still at Cologne,³ we could pick it up as we passed, which would be something quite original and not unappealing, since the dress could come to the aid of the one I have on my back, which is not very ravishing. But I'm afraid that we might not find it there, or in such a state of degradation it would no longer be good for anything. But whatever happens, the important thing is to love each other and be happy. We *do* love each other and we *are* happy, aren't we, my beloved?

Juliette

Letter 43

Thursday evening, half past 6:00, 5 November *[1840]*

You see, my beloved, I was quite right when I said this morning I wouldn't see you again until midnight. Alas! When it comes to your absence, I have sad premonitions that don't deceive me.

I saw Mme Triger and gave her the two glasses, one for her and one for Mme Pierceau, as she was going to see her this evening. I got through as quickly as possible the job of giving her the two glasses, which are nothing marvelous in themselves. To give them a little something special and to thank these two ladies for having attended the prize-giving in my absence, I presented them with our two purses, saying Claire had made them for them. Besides, we'll lose nothing by it, because our Clairon will make us more, and they'll be more useful and prettier, because they'll be better made.

My darling Toto, I love you with all my soul, and I'd like to have a little *Jonas*¹ with you. It's my dearest wish, but one that will never be granted, like everything that one desires with all one's heart. For example, since this afternoon I have ardently wished to kiss you *immediately*, and yet it's only too certain I won't have this happiness before midnight. Look, I tell you you're a rascal! Be quiet and come, that would be best, or I'll *dirty all your combs*. Mm, mm,ª old pig, they're clean when they're out of your hands! You're a beast, and I am too, but I love you.

Juliette

Letter 44

Saturday, noon, 7 November *[1840]*

You've acquired a very bad habit, my little man—that of not coming back to the house before midnight.¹ I warn you, if you persist in this absurd system, I'll go out gallivanting from noon till midnight to teach you to be on your guard.

Be quiet, or I'll reveal all your frightful failings! I'll cry from the rooftops that your shirt and pants and other things are full of poops. Be quiet and do your duty, or otherwise I'll *tell everything*. "Kiss"[a] me, you rascal, and make me a little Jonas immediately! I'd give ten million to have one no bigger than my little finger. Alas, I'm not destined for this happiness, and I have no little Jonases except for those of your imagination, but the illusion's no substitute for having a real little child of flesh and blood by you. It's sad when one loves the way I love you. Be quiet! Once more, you're a beast, and that's all!

I haven't received any news about my poor father;[2] he's probably ill. I'll ask Lanvin[3] to inquire in person, if I don't receive any letter from him or about him within a few days.

I love you, my beloved Toto. I love you, my darling Toto. I adore you, my handsome and noble little man!

Juliette

Letter 45

Saturday evening, quarter past 4:00, 28 November *[1840]*

Hardly had you left, my darling Toto, when I had an unpleasant visit, or rather an unpleasant message. This is what it was: the maid of Mme Ribot, the moneylender, brought a letter from her mistress that you'll read soon.[1] I had to open it to find out what it was about. The maid was told I was sick in bed, and not well enough to make any reply at the moment. I think I did the right thing. But the awakening of this old monster has caused me inexpressible sadness that I could well have done without. I foresee a renewal of the pursuit, scandal, and annoyance, and my heart feels as though it is being tightened in a vise. Anyway, by the grace of God and if you still love me, I'll soon find my courage again.

All of this has not prevented me from being ready on time, but you, rascal, will probably not be so and will no doubt arrive at some ungodly hour! While I wait for you, if I have the time, I'll write to poor Claire and perhaps to the landlord also, for the coal is running short. 'Lo Toto. 'Lo, my little beloved, 'lo, oh, 'lo. I certainly *have* hidden my comb and my little brushes, and you'll be very clever if you can find them. Mm, mm, mm,[a] Toto is a pig. Toto is a filthy animal with whom my combs and brushes are a sorry sight. Be quiet, you old dirty, and don't use my things! Brr, brr, it's pretty cold waiting for you! You're really ridiculous to have me get myself ready for battle two hours in advance. I dare not relight the fire, in case you suddenly arrive and we have to leave. I tell you you're a beast! *Yes, sir? Yes, yes, madam, yes, sir, he is under arms.*[b] "'Kiss'[c] me," she says to you,[d] and come immediately!

Juliette

Letter 46

Monday evening, half past 8:00, 21 December *[1840]*

You know, my dear beloved, that my clock is exactly one hour fast? As a result it's really half past seven. I have Résisieux with me, who is flipping through the pictures in *La France pittoresque*.[1] Mme Besancenot just came up to show me *Jonas*, but hardly had the little rascal come in than he began to yell so frightfully he had to be taken back down home again immediately. Anyway, I ate, I washed my face, I put my place in order, and I'm all ready to *start again*. I'm counting on you not to break your promise, even though you're not very accustomed to exactitude.

Well this is nice, Résisieux is beautifying my scribble by dragging her book across the ink while it's still wet! It's really a pity, for I'm writing well, even though I say it myself. However, I will *copy*[a] the notes in a little while and I'm going to really apply myself.

I'm delighted with your idea, Toto, of putting your deerskin on the bed.[2] I like the idea of preserving the memory of our charming little trip across the Black Forest. Everything that reminds me of time spent with you becomes sacred for me. That's why, my beloved, I insist so much on bringing back from the various stages of our trip little souvenirs which can later on become relics of our past happiness. I love you, my Toto, I love you, my beloved. I would like to give my life for you. Believe it, my Victor, for it's the most sacred and sincere truth! I kiss your dear little feet. I kiss your hands, your hair, and all your dear, adorable, little person.

Juliette

Letter 47

Thursday morning, quarter to 10:00, 31 December *[1840]*

Good morning, my beloved little Toto, good morning, my dear little man! I kiss you inside and outside, everywhere that you are hot or cold. I hope that you're still asleep, my poor adorable swot. I thank you for coming last night in that terrible weather. There's no one but you with courageous tenderness like this, and so I thank you for it and love you with all my soul.

While you were dining in town, I was repairing my *only* dress. I stress this word: *"only."* I don't want to lose my effective words like *Madame Magloire*.[1] I worked until eleven o'clock and then I went to bed, which is why you found me asleep when you arrived last night. A little tiredness, the warmth of the bed, being horizontal, all of those are so many invitations to sleep, which to my great annoyance I can't always resist. Tonight I'll fight against it if I can, so as to learn not to be an old, sleepy, bleary-eyed Juju like Madame Guérard. I must, however, say this for myself, that I didn't give in to sleep until after midnight. But that was still too early, because you hadn't come, and that deprived me of the happiness of having a bit more time with you. I'm definitely an old dormouse. By the way, I'm doing *well*. We'll see how it turns out, but I would have very much liked to finish and begin the year with a *fine deed*. Unfortunately, I need your *collaboration* for that, and that doesn't seem possible in view of what you said to me yesterday. I'll comply with it, for better or worse. It won't be the first time I've done that, like it or not.

'Lo, Toto, 'lo, my little *o*. I love you despite my *venomous* allusions. I love you despite my big insults. I'm too happy that you let me love you even for *nothing* in return. "Kiss"[a] me, and smile right away if you love me!

Letter 48

Thursday evening, quarter to 4:00, 31 December *[1840]*

May the devil take you and confound you, little pig, who put my toothbrush in your washbowl with all your dirty water so that it was thrown out with the water into the *pisspot* and from there into the gutter, from where it was brought back to me in a *fine state!* I don't know any pig more piggy than you. Really, you finish the year as you'll start the next, by an unspeakable piggery! And that's not to mention the snot you have the nerve to wear on your frightful overcoat, which looks like a dead dog! If you think it's cute, then you're completely mistaken. Mm, mm,[a] you're very sweet, and I advise old Mme Briché to compliment you on it. I'm starting to think you'll soon be appointed to the Cacademy.[b] You have all the *requisite* qualifications for it. It's impossible to look more dirty, I mean more of a cacademician, than you right now. "Kiss" me, filthy old pig! "Kiss"[c] me, old bandit, and try to love me a bit under your filth!

I'd like it to be tomorrow already so I could have your dear little New Year's missive to kiss, to admire, and to adore.[1] Just thinking about it makes me crazy with impatience and joy. The time from now till then is going to seem eternal. There's only one way to prevent it from seeming too long, and that's for you to come and spend the time with me. Tomorrow I won't have anybody with me except my daughter, but she won't bother us. The day after tomorrow I have all my scatterbrains[d] and my father[e] coming, and although that doesn't prevent you from coming to *dine*, it'll still force us to get up early. I love you, Toto. I adore you, my dear, darling, little man!

Juliette

Letter 49

Thursday afternoon, half past 5:00, 3 June *[1841]*

Where shall I start, my love—with your divine feet or with your celestial forehead? What shall I tell you about first, my beloved? Shall it be the admiration or the adoration that fill my heart and overflow it just as much as your sublime genius surpasses all the mediocre intellects who listened[1] to you without understanding you, and who looked at you without falling on their knees? Oh, let me mix and meld together these two emotions that dazzle my spirit and fire my heart! I love you, I admire you, I adore you! Oh, you are really beautiful, noble, and sublime, my poet, my beloved, the light of my eyes, the flame of my soul, the life of my life! Poor adored beloved, when I saw you coming in so pale and moved, I felt as though I were dying, and if M. Démousseaux and Mme Pierceau had not supported me, I would have fallen to the floor.[a] Luckily nobody noticed my emotion, and when I recovered and saw your sweet smile answering mine and reassuring me, I had the impression I was emerging from the sleep of a long and painful dream, whereas in fact no more than a minute had passed. Thank-you, my beloved, thank-you for thinking of the poor woman who loves you at a moment so serious—indeed I could say *supreme*—if the people who were there had not been for the most part hideous cretins and vile knaves. Thank-you, my good angel, thank-you, my sublime Victor, my *illustrious child!* I saw them all, my dear little ones: enchanting Didine, charming Charlot, and my dear little *Toto, like the other one*,[2] who looked so pale and suffering. I kissed them all from my soul as I did their divine father. I love you!

Juliette

Letter 50

Wednesday morning, 9 o'clock, 15 February *[1843]*

I have been praying to God during the last hour for you, for your family, and for your dear little beloved daughter,[1] my Toto; I hope my prayers will be united with yours at this moment that is so decisive and solemn in the life of your dear child.

I think I hardly slept two hours all night, so agitated was I by the thought of your child and you, my beloved. I thought how sad you were going to be after this day of celebration, and I regretted not being sufficiently *everything* to you to fill the void that the absence of your daughter is going to make in your life.

There are no events or incidents in your life, the most insignificant as well as the most important, that do not remind me how little I am for you and how everything you are to me. Today, more than ever, this sad truth is shown.

I do not hold it against you, my beloved, I realize that it cannot be otherwise, and it doesn't prevent me from loving you with all my soul.

I don't dare to hope you'll find a minute to come here this morning. It would mean a great deal, and I'd be very happy if you were able to come to me for a moment on this day. I'll try, my Toto, to accept the inevitable, but that won't stop me from finding the time very long. Think of me if you can, my Toto, pity me and love me, I well deserve it!

It's fine weather; it's a good omen for the happiness of this dear little *Madame*. I would have given anything to see her in her *bridal* gown. But, alas! I didn't even dare to tell you of this desire, certain as I was it would be refused, which would have added a sorrow to a deprivation. I renounced my desire and contented myself with praying to God for her with the fervor and the heart of a mother.

I love you.

Juliette

Letter 51

Saturday morning, quarter to 12:00, 18 March *[1843]*

Good morning, my darling Toto, good morning, my beloved! How are you, my dear little man, this morning? How are your poor eyes, my Toto? Did you get some rest last night? You should really consult an oculist, my dear beloved, so you can find out what's wrong with your eyes and what to do to cure them. It seems to me, darling Toto, that no matter what you may be busy with and interested in at the moment, your eyes ought to come before everything. Perhaps there's nothing much you can do to soothe them, but even that you should know, and for that reason, my beloved Toto, I beg you to consult M. Louis or a doctor that specializes in this type of ailment.

I love you, my Victor. I'm exasperated when I see stupid cretins and vile scoundrels attacking you.[1] And at what a moment, my God!—at the moment when you were the greatest, the most sublime, and the divinest of poets! It is an act of audacity as revolting as it is ridiculous and one for which one cannot have enough anger and contempt. I'd like to get hold of them all and rub their noses in . . . although it's less stinking and stupid than they are. I came back furious and indignant last night. I dreamed about it all night. I don't know if that's what has given me a headache, but I can't see this morning. If you add to that the frightful Cocotte[a] making frightful earsplitting shrieks, an imbecile of a servant who has just broken one of the fanciful ceramic lions you gave me nearly a year ago, plus the atrocious necessity of *sharpening four quills*, you will have some idea of what I must be suffering at the moment. This would be the time to put me *face to face with your enemies*. I can tell you they would see some funny stuff. *Juju, whirlwind of claws,* would show them her expertise in this area.

The doorbell has just rung for a collection on behalf of orphans. Suzanne said I wasn't available, and she did well. Besides, what with the swindlers and thieves who are around, one can't trust this kind of request. However, if they come back and if you think it necessary, I'll give what you want. In the meantime, my dear beloved, I give you my thoughts, my life, my heart, my soul.

I love you, I wait for you, and I desire you. Try to find a little moment in the day to come and kiss me! It would cure my headache and put some joy and happiness in my heart. Bring me the letter from Didine if you can. I'll take good care of it and put it with the two others. I'll be the monster, the dragon, who guards your treasure. I can hardly be anything else at the moment. You must bring me this letter and all those you receive from now on, you understand, my dear little one, and then you must love me a little—for I love you with all my soul.

Juliette

Letter 52

Sunday morning, half past 9:00, 9 July *[1843]*

I saw you leave almost with pleasure, my dear beloved, with the thought that your absence was the result of a joy awaited and desired for almost three years now.[1] But hardly had you turned the corner of my street than my courage turned to sadness. From that moment onward I've been counting the minutes and the hours with painful impatience. Hurry to return, my beloved, for nothing is worth as much as a look from you, a word from you, a kiss from your beautiful mouth! Your letters are wonderful, but *you* are worth still more, because you are happiness incarnate. However, if you could have seen me kissing each of your words and dancing with joy when I received your little letter[2] just now in my *red room* amid all my *birds embroidered* and *real,* you would have thought I was the happiest of women, alas! God knows that after this first moment of wonderment and delight had passed, I plunged once again into my impatience and sadness. What I want is you. What I desire is you. What I love and adore is you, always you. In thoughts, in words, in actions, you, you, and again you!

I took a bath yesterday before dinner. I snuffed out the candle at half past eleven. I woke up more than twenty times in the night. There was even one time when I thought I heard a noise, and I threw myself to the bottom of my bed, yelling out the famous question, "Who is there?" I lay down again, feeling sheepish. I pray to God that tonight will be less solitary than last night, for I don't know how I'm going to get through it calmly. I kiss your feet, I think about you, I wait for you, I desire you, I adore you!

Juliette

Letter 53

Wednesday afternoon, quarter past 4:00, 13 September *[1843]*

Where are you, what are you doing, my poor beloved? In what state is your family,[1] in what state are you yourself, my God, and what will come of all our despair if God does not take pity on us? Since you left me, I have had my heart and mind fixed on your arrival at your house. I see all that has happened: the cries of despair of your family, the explosion of your own frightful despair, so long and cruelly contained. All these tears, all these griefs rebound on my heart and break it. I can take no more. My poor head is on fire, and my hands burn like hot coals. I want to pray to God, and yet I cannot, all my faculties and all my being is turned toward you. I would give my life to spare you some pain. I would have given it in this world and the other to save your adored child. My God, my God, what is to become of me if you delay even longer coming here, when I have had so much difficulty reaching even this point without sending for news of you? I asked Mme Lanvin to come here this evening and to bring her husband,[2] so that if, as I fear, I haven't seen you by then, he can go and inquire about you in the name of M. Saint-Hilaire. My heart is broken, my beloved, as I think about all that you are suffering. I feel I won't be able to bear not seeing you any longer. I will do something foolish if you don't come to my aid. I have exhausted all my strength and all my courage with this frightful journey and with the experience of last night and today. My God, I can't endure your absence any longer. I imagine your wife is ill, that you are, also—in fact so extreme are my anxiety and sorrow that I am like a madwoman. I make every effort to occupy myself with mechanical tasks to make the time pass until the moment comes when I'll see you, but all my efforts cannot prevent every minute's wait from seeming like a century and all the fears my heart foresees and dreads from being frightful realities in the face of which I'm powerless. My beloved Victor, whatever the degree of your despair, mine is yet greater, for I feel it through my love, which magnifies it a hundredfold and multiplies it beyond human strength. Never has a man been loved by a poor woman as you are by me, and the poor angel we all weep for knows it and sees it right now, as God also knows it and sees it, and she pardons me as He also does, I'm sure. I think of her, poor beloved, only as a poor angel in Heaven. It is to her I will address my prayers, so that she can give you the strength and the courage you need to bear her absence. It is her I will ask for you to love me still. And it is again her I will ask at the hour of my death that God might take me with you all into His paradise.

My beloved Victor, it's past five o'clock and you are still not come. What am I to do, what am I to think, or rather, what am I to dread? We are in a time of terrible misfortune, and God only knows when it will stop.

My Victor, before abandoning yourself to your despair, think of mine! Remember I love you more than my life!

Juliette

Letter 54

Thursday afternoon, half past 5:00, 14 September *[1843]*

It is very late, my dear love, and you have still not come. My heart is very heavy and very sad. When shall I see you, my God, and how shall I see you? As long as you are not ill?

What suffocating weather! I'm afraid for your poor head; you must take good care of yourself. You know how the blood rushes violently to your head—you must take some care, don't stay shut up indoors for a long time. Especially—if my God it's possible—you shouldn't absorb yourself, destroy yourself as you do, poor father, in your pain and despair. If you love me, my beloved, my life, my soul, my God, my everything, you must take it upon yourself to go out, to walk, to come and see me. I'll love you so much, so much, you will perhaps find some consolation and sweetness in it. Why don't you come? What's holding you back, if you love me and if you don't wish to make me despair? My beloved Victor, my beloved, my Toto, don't leave me to long for you, or torment me any longer! I'm suffering, Toto. If you could feel my hands at the moment they would burn you. My head is all awhirl. I hardly know what I'm writing to you. I know that I love you and that you are my life. I know that I am suffering and dying far from you, that is all. So come quickly, my enchanting Toto, to calm me and give me strength and courage!

I have had my daughter with me since just a short time ago.[1] I was also very tormented by her lateness, fearing her ill. Finally the poor child is here. Old Mme Lanvin[a] had taken her time, that was all. I kiss her, thinking of you, my poor beloved, and of all your dear children, whom I love as though they were my own flesh and blood. I want you to kiss them for me and hold them close to your heart, thinking of me.

My God how much I would like to see you! I'd give years of my life without thinking twice if I could see you right now. I don't know whether it's a premonition, but I've never been more eager to see you than at present. I have the constant feeling that I will be leaving you for a long time and that I must hasten to stock up on provisions of love for when we're separated. Forgive me, my Victor, forgive me, I don't know what I'm saying! I'm sad and distressed, and my heart is full of blackness and mourning, but I want to live to serve you, to kiss your feet, and to adore you. My God how I love you, my Victor!

Juliette

Letter 55

Monday evening, quarter to 7:00, 3 June *[1844]*

My beloved, my beloved, my heart is inundated with love, with gratitude, with happiness, and with joy! I'd like to kiss your dear little feet. Poor angel of God—in the middle of the night, overwhelmed with fatigue, and despite your poor irritated eyes—you found the time, the strength, and the courage to write me this sweet and enchanting letter.[1] Oh, among all of them, this one will be the star in the heaven of my love! Forgive me my exaltation, my beloved, I can only love you like this and know no other way! I cannot love you as a man, I love you as something divine and worthy of adoration. Here you are!

Quarter past 8:00

You always come to surprise me, rascal, just when I'm confiding to you my dearest thoughts! It's very indiscrete of you, and I didn't think you capable of it! Another time I'll be on my (national!) guard. In the meantime I order you to have a sore throat no longer, or I'll end up getting downright angry. Personally I don't *need* a man who is sick as a dog, it's already enough with my poor servant. I want you to be well immediately! I *need* your health to live. Yes, my poor beloved, I love you and I don't want you to be ill, do you understand? For that reason you must protect yourself well against the cold tonight, my dear little man. You must come and *warm yourself up* at my place. I'll read you some *good* sugary magazines and you'll be delighted with them—not to mention the nice little caresses I'll give you.

Juliette

Letter 56

Monday evening, half past 9:00, 1 July *[1844]*

My dear little Toto, I really kicked myself the day I insinuated you were guilty of *coquetry*. But on the other hand, who would have ever believed you would acquire a taste for these kinds of airs, unworthy of a man like you? I'm furious that I succeeded so well. Oh, if only I could give you back your good old fingernails, your simple suspenders, your tousled hair, and your crocodile teeth, I'd certainly do it. And it would be well done! For you don't use, you *abuse*, my lessons. Take care I don't discover the true reason for this frenetic coquetry![1]

On top of all this, I haven't seen you. You only came to make use of my hands as models for your gloves.[2] You must agree I'm good-natured to lend myself to this ridiculous research. Mm, mm,[a] look out for yourself, rascal, or I'll give you some blows with the *gloves off!*

Will I see you tonight, my beloved? I'm much afraid I won't. It would be very naughty of you, if you have a minute during which you're not working, not to give it to me, the one who desires you so much and loves you with all her soul. To make you come, I kiss your little feet!

Juliette

Letter 57

Saturday morning, half past 10:00, 5 July *[1845]*

Good morning, my beloved Toto, good morning, my darling little Toto, good morning, my love! How are you today? Do you love me? You stayed very little time last night even though I was wide awake. You must have been unable to stay any longer, my Toto, because you seemed very preoccupied.[1] You have been so for some time now, which shortens yet further the already short moments you give me. I don't even have the hope it will soon be over, since you say that after the *session*[2] you must *work*. So I don't know what's going to become of me. I'll try to be courageous and not add to the fatigue of your work by perpetual moaning.

Dear beloved, I'm writing late because I want to make your tea early to give it the time to cool, and then we're going to take advantage of the fire to make lunch right away. I don't need to resort to my scrawl to think of you and love you. All my thoughts are with you, my whole life and all my love belong to you. Whether asleep or awake, I think of you. Last night I didn't leave you... *in my dreams*. Why did I wake up?... My darling Victor, I'm waiting for you. Try to come very soon and not be sad, as you have been these last few days. I desire you, I kiss you, I wait for you, I adore you!

Juliette

Letter 58

Sunday morning, quarter to 10:00, 20 July *[1845]*

Good morning, my beloved and adored Toto, how is your dear little arm? I can't wait to know whether this placebo has given you some relief or whether it's just a mystification. On the question of mystification, I have just received a letter from my brother-in-law, who asks whether there is any truth in the rumors circulating about you in Lorient and Brest. It seems, as far as I can tell through his reserve, that it has to do with the stupid story of Mlle Plessy.[1] I'm going to reply to him right away and tell him to calm himself and not give credence to any of the stories it pleases people to make up about you. As these poor people are very worried, I'm going to write to them immediately. I really don't understand people who invent stories as unlikely as that. The taste for lying must be strong if no amount of implausibility can suppress it.

I don't know what God and you have in store for me, but I know I would never be able to bear any betrayal on your part and that your indifference would kill me. My beloved Victor, you know very well that I have given you my whole life without reserve. You know also that no woman can ever love you as I do. You are completely certain of it, aren't you? I adore you!

Juliette

Letter 59

Sunday afternoon, 4 o'clock, 7 September *[1845]*

My dear little darling man, I think you're taking me in, and that you've made off while seeming to say *you didn't know yet!* This would be very absurd of you because you would have prevented me from going to see poor Clairette just when we have a holiday.[1] If I'm wrong, prove it to me by coming to see me—if you don't, I'll be even more sure that you have left. Oh, no, my little beloved, I *don't* think that you have! I'm *afraid* that you have, but that's all. I know you are incapable of lying to me, because *I* always tell *you* the truth. It's just I fear you might have received a letter when you went back home that obliged you to go away today[2] without having the time to kiss me. I hope you won't have left without writing to me, so I'm waiting for a letter from you. A hundred million times better would be *you* yourself, even though your letters are wonderful from the first word to the last. In any case, I'll make your hops[3] tonight. It's the last packet, so it would make things very difficult for me if you were not to use them tonight, because I don't know how to purchase them and what dosage should be in each packet, and because I think that once they're made up they must ferment and spoil overnight. You see, my little beloved, you don't have the right to go away without letting me know first, especially not without having kissed me and provided me with provisions of love and courage for two days! In the meantime, I'm waiting for you and loving you with overflowing heart.

Juliette

Letter 60

Saturday morning, 8 o'clock, 27 September *[1845]*

Good morning, my dear beloved, good morning, my soul, good morning, my life, good morning, my adored Victor, how are you? Yesterday's trip didn't tire you I hope?[1] I didn't think about it until you told me you had been told not to walk for long periods of time. But it won't have done you any harm, will it, my darling Victor? Personally, I didn't feel tired—I felt as though I had wings! I would have liked to set foot on all the pathways we followed together eleven years ago, to kiss all the stones on the road, to greet all the leaves on the trees, to pick all the flowers in the woods, so much did they seem to me to be the same ones that saw us go by together before. I looked at you, my beloved Victor, and I found you just as young, just as handsome—even more handsome in fact—than you were eleven years ago. I looked into my heart, and I found it full of ecstasy and adoration just as on the first day that I loved you. Nothing had changed in us and around us. It was the same love, passionate, devoted, sweet, and sad in our hearts. It was the same autumn sun and the same sky over our heads. It was the same picture in the same frame. Nothing about it had changed in eleven years. I would have given ten years of my life to be ten minutes alone in this house that for eleven years has so piously preserved our memory. I would have liked to carry away the ashes from the hearth and the dust from the floor. I would have liked to pray and weep there where I had prayed and wept. I would have liked to die of love in the spot where so many times I have received your soul in a kiss. I had to make a superhuman effort not to do silly things in front of the girl who so indifferently showed us this house that I would have gladly bought for the price of half the rest of my life. Anyway, thanks to the fact that she knew nothing at all about us, she suspected nothing, and we were each able to carry away a little relic of our past happiness. When I die, I want to have them buried with me.

Dear beloved, did you work a long time last night? That would have been very imprudent after the fatigue of the day. Today you must be very careful and not walk too much. I'll be very fierce today: my passion as an *antiquarian*[2] won't make me forget, as I did yesterday, that you are still convalescent and that you must do almost no walking. And you will obey me, for Totos must always obey Jujus, you know that! Kiss me, my beloved Victor, and God bless you for all the happiness you give me!

Letter 61

Saturday afternoon, quarter to 1:00, 27 September *[1845]*

I owe you this little letter since the night before last, my beloved. I didn't give it to you last night, because my heart was overextended with too many things. The soul has aches and pains like the body, and mine yesterday succumbed to the weight of the emotions I had just experienced in seeing again this dear little house and all the immense and delightful landscape that had witnessed our love. I went to bed as soon as you were gone, and I fell asleep thinking about you and our memories of the past eleven years. This morning I wrote you a long, rambling letter about yesterday. I was still in the mood of happiness mingled with melancholy and regret I experienced yesterday when I found those beautiful places just as if we had left them only the day before. What a day, my Victor! In the space of a few hours I relived the total of four months we spent together at two different times. I felt the same beating of my heart, the same birdsong, the same ecstasies, and the same sun, as well as the same loyal, faithful, and devoted love. Our hearts were like the sky and, like nature, they were unchanged.

I don't know the financial situation of Pernot's heirs,[a] but whatever it might be, I confess I have the selfishness to hope they don't succeed in either renting or selling our dear little house until I die. It is perhaps a very bad wish to have, and to modify its malice a bit *I wish myself* to have the means to buy it before anyone can profane it. In the meantime, dear beloved, I very much want you to come. It's already a quarter past one and you're still not here. Hurry up!

Juliette

Here you are, right now! What happiness!!!

Letter 62

Saturday evening, 9 o'clock, 2 May *[1846]*

I cannot get used to the idea that I won't see you this evening, my sweet adorable beloved, and yet, alas, it's only too true. For the first time in fourteen years I'm sleeping in a room that doesn't belong to you, and so I'm sad and desolate in my soul.[1] Everything fills me with despair. This afternoon when I left you, I would have liked to die. All the tears I was holding back flowed into my heart like molten lead. God knows what I suffered! If this life of anxiety about my poor daughter and separation from you were to last for long, I think I wouldn't have the strength to bear it. I'm tired of, and disgusted with, the infamies I see around me. I'm ashamed and indignant that I cannot escape them, no matter what I do.[a] And then at the same time I think about you, so generous, so loyal, so great, so good, and so indulgent, and I feel all my bitterness disappearing, and I am left with nothing but admiration, recognition, and love for your whole divine and enchanting person.

When I got back,[b] I found my daughter suffering from a tremendous fever. I renewed her compresses, and she has been sleeping for a little while. May God will that she should do so all night and that the change of ideas, of place, and of air should have a beneficial effect on her health. I will then less bitterly regret the deprivations that have been imposed on me toward this end.

In the meantime I am prey to the most atrocious anxiety, and I suffer all that one can suffer in the absence of what one loves the most in the world, much more than life, much more than duty, much more than everything in fact.

Good night, beloved, think of me, sleep well and love me![2]

Juliette

Letter 63

Saturday morning, half past 10:00, 16 May *[1846]*

Good morning, my dear adorable beloved, good morning, my thrice-blessed Victor, good morning, my life! All my thoughts and all my soul belong to you. I wanted to write to you last night, after I received your dear little, *too little* letter,[1] but I was afraid of waking my poor daughter. From eight o'clock to ten she had an attack of coughing and vomiting and struggling to vomit a bit of bile. I went to bed immediately so as not to make any noise. This morning she had another attack, almost as long, that tired her horribly. Her poor little face is extremely drawn, and her cheeks are redder than ever. My heart is full of anxiety and painful premonitions. I fear that M. Chomel saw only too clearly the state of the unfortunate child. All my hope is disappearing from day to day along with the poor child's strength. If you saw her today, you would think as I do and you would be full of sadness and discouragement. My heart is broken, and I have hardly the strength to conceal my despair from her. If M. Triger[a] does not come today, I will send for his locum, M. Lemoine. The disease has made such visible progress since yesterday evening that I can't wait until tomorrow for a doctor's opinion. Even today my anxieties are such that, if her father's doctor were to hand, I would consult him out of desperation.

I write to you with my mind on the danger my poor daughter is in, my adored and beloved Victor, forcing myself not to cry, so as not to alarm the dear child. But I am suffering horribly, and I don't know what will become of me if you can't come to see me this evening. To see you is to find new strength, courage, and hope. My soul is refreshed by one of your kisses, and I go home less tormented and desperate.

Her father has still not come. I think he is very embarrassed and irritated by this incident, but I don't have the courage to laugh about it, given the too real and alarming suffering of my daughter. What I feel is a deep disgust and inexpressible contempt for this boastful and disloyal character. I had promised myself never to talk to you about him again, but despite myself I find myself compelled by the behavior of the man to return to the subject. I ask your forgiveness, my beloved, as though for wrongdoing, for I assure you, much as I would prefer not to, *[that this man]* has some hideous depravities that your noble and generous nature could not even suspect. I kiss your feet with respect, your hands with admiration, your mouth with passion, and all your sublime and divine personage with adoration!

Juliette

Letter 64

Tuesday morning, half past 9:00, 23 June *[1846]*

I want my first letter to be for you, my sweet beloved, I want to consecrate the first action I have undertaken serenely since the death of my poor angel by dedicating it to you.[1] I am trying to find in myself strength and courage, and I will succeed, I hope, by virtue of love. I went to mass this morning at the time when you must also have been at church yourself.[2] There I prayed a lot, cried a lot, and loved a lot. I came back calmer. I felt that prayer had brought me closer to my child and that she had made the love between you and me yet more holy and sacred. My love is far from diminished or strained by the frightful unhappiness with which I am stricken, but is rather augmented and purified with gratitude. As long as something of myself survives, I will piously preserve the memory of the ineffable kindness you have shown me throughout this long and painful illness.

Dear beloved, I still feel very troubled. My poor head rejects all thoughts except those that concern my poor daughter. I feel my heart overflowing with love but cannot voice it in words, so much does pain intercept every expression of tenderness. However, I wanted to write to you. I wanted the first action I undertook to be for you, without worrying about the difficulty I might encounter in performing it. It's the first time in my life I've written to you with this kind of paralysis of thought. I don't apologize for it, because I feel my heart is not to blame. I'm obeying you by making efforts to shake off the painful torpor that besets me. I'm looking forward impatiently to the time when I will see you. The days seem to be never-ending. It isn't the first occasion on which I've noticed this while away from you, but this time it seems they are longer than ever. I don't know how we'll get back from Auteuil. Here is M. Rivière, who has undertaken to come and see what's happening in this sad house.[3] I'd much like to be back in mine to be close to you, my sweet beloved. I hope nothing will happen to prevent it tomorrow.

Juliette

Letter 65

Saturday, noon, 11 July *[1846]*

You were right, my beloved, to foresee yesterday that today's[1] sad ceremony would go on until very late. I fear you must have left home without having eaten anything and that you are suffering as a consequence.

Nobody from here has come back yet. As for me, I went to church from half past nine until eleven o'clock, thinking I would find everybody back at my place and hoping to see you. If I had known otherwise, I would have stayed until now. In any case, everything becomes altar and temple for the heart that loves, suffers, and prays. I feel this to be so today more than ever. Just as long as this painful ceremony hasn't done you any harm? In the last few minutes anxiety has started to mingle with my sadness and is making it sharper and more bitter than ever. I'm anxious to know you are back, I need to see you. I would like to know where I could meet you and go and run there. I am so unhappy, in fact, that everything scares me. However, if pious and saintly action is to protect the man one loves, then that is what you are engaged in at this very moment, my beloved, and my poor dear daughter can only bring you happiness, as long as the soul is not a mockery and God the most ferocious of beings. Oh, I wish you were back and I had kissed you so I would know for sure my fears are absurd. I love you too much and have too sad a heart not to be alarmed by your lateness.

Juliette

Letter 66

Monday morning, quarter to 12:00, 8 February *[1847]*

Good morning, my Toto, good morning, you, how could you write *"Je t'haïme,"* academician?[a] Do it again, scamp, and then you'll see me give your nose a good pull! I don't want anyone to be lacking in respect for me, do you understand? I don't want anyone to make fun of me, niggle at me, or rile me. I don't need to have anyone making a fool of me right in front of my nose—I'm quite against it. I'll scratch you handsomely, and then you'll see if it's funny!

You left me very early yesterday, my beloved Toto, even though this would have been a time for giving me good measure, since you weren't going to come back again at night. What did you do all evening? Were you very attentive, very nice, very charming, very flirtatious, and very gallant to some women in *low-cut dresses?* I put this question to you as a formality, since I know only too well all you did and could have done, and I'm neither prouder nor happier for all that—quite the contrary, but I don't want to grumble, I don't want to annoy you, I want to be gay and pleasant, even if it means attempting the impossible. Perhaps you, for your part, will take into account my goodwill just as though I really felt so.

I saw M. Vilain[1] for a moment yesterday. I told him what you thought about the prince's visit. He asked me to thank you very much on his behalf. As for myself, I torment you to the point of satiety, but the reason is so good I'm sure you don't resent it. Aren't I right? It's because you are so really good, so really generous, that it would be hard to find the limit to those qualities. So in this respect I'm happy. I'd like to be equally so with respect to *tableaux vivants*[2] and lithographs in action or delivered to the home.[b] Then I wouldn't be so often sulky and so often tormented. Unfortunately, you're not as *well behaved* as you are good, far from it. Be quiet, scoundrel, you know very well what I'm saying is true! But what you don't know well enough is that I'll kill you outright like Dominus! "Kiss"[c] me, and tremble!

Juliette

Letter 67

Wednesday morning, quarter to 10:00, 31 March *[1847]*

Good morning, most monstrous of men, good morning, you that one cannot help loving, "Good morning," she says to you!^a Oh, how I wish I could hate you! With what pleasure I'd give back to you all the pain you give me! What happiness it would be for me to pay you back in irritation, in vexation, in anger, and in fury everything you make me suffer by your *fancy envelopes*, by your *aristocratic laughter*, by your *airs of the conquering and Spontinian*[1] *academician*, by your *encounters on the omnibus*,^b by your frequent visits to the town hall and to Chaumontel, by Charles' service in the National Guard, by his number 24 *which is not as simple* as one thinks,[2] by your *labors*, which are not *Herculean*, by all that is most hideous, most annoying, most irritating, most titillating, most vexing, most infuriating, most exasperating, most aggravating, and most cringe-making! With what fierce joy would I seize any opportunity to pay you back annoyance for annoyance, anger for anger, jealousy for jealousy, fury for fury, and *air for aria*. Doing it would require only that I extricate my heart from your clutches. But that's not an easy job, and it's only too probable that you'd give it back to me dead. The sooner the better, alas, if you no longer love me enough to sacrifice for me the duchesses you pick up and your taste in luxurious stationery!

Juliette

Letter 68

Thursday morning, half past 10:00, 3 February *[1848]*

Good morning, my sweet adorable beloved, good morning, my saintly, my great, my sublime poet! Good morning, I kiss your forehead, your hands, and your feet as a sign of respect, of admiration, and of adoration! How are you this morning? Did the reading tire you too much?[1] It seems to me you must feel all the frightful pains you describe with so much truth and poignant poetry. As for myself, I had all the trouble in the world trying to sleep, and this morning my heart is still wrung. Much as I might try to think of something else, I cannot escape from this lugubrious and terrible courtroom. I see everything, as though I were there. I feel all the frightful torture of poor *Jean Tréjean*, and I can't help crying over the fate of this poor martyr. I could even say of *all these poor martyrs*, for I don't know anything more harrowing than poor Fantine or more painful than this poor, brutalized creature, *Champmathieu*. I'm living with all these characters and sharing their suffering as if they were real flesh-and-blood people, so *true to life* have you made them. I don't know how to express this to you, but I do know that all my intelligence, heart, and soul are taken by the sublime book you so justly call *Les Misères*. I am sure everyone who reads it will experience the same thing as I, not to mention its literary merit, which I do not have the competence to judge. I adore you.

Juliette

Letter 69

Thursday morning, 8 o'clock, 2 March *[1848]*

Good morning, my sweet adored one, good morning, my beloved, good morning, my joy, good morning! May God watch over you and all those you love!

How are you, my beloved? Always be careful, not with the cowardly carefulness that risks honor to avoid danger—I do not mean that kind, and it would be in poor taste if I did, because you wouldn't listen to such advice or you would laugh at it, and rightly so. But I beg you to keep your position quite clear, quite pure, quite resolute. You can no longer take part in public affairs except officially.[1] My God, I must certainly count on your indulgence and kindness to allow me to talk to you in this way! It is because, in fact, I'm so sure of your heart that I reveal myself to you without restraint and without preoccupying myself besides with the fact that I must be making myself slightly ridiculous. I am so sure that I love you and that it's only out of an excess of love that I venture into offering advice on matters above my intelligence that I don't mind at all. But I found your attitude during recent events so completely noble and dignified that I would fear to see you deviate from it, bearing in mind the thought that "the best is the enemy of the good."[a] If what I say is silly, which is entirely possible, *smile at me* and *bear with me*. I'll repay you later when I'm less on edge and my legs are less wobbly.

Juliette

Letter 70

Wednesday morning, 9 o'clock, 26 April *[1848]*

Good morning, my beloved, good morning, my heart's *Elect*, good morning![1] I proclaim you the first citizen of my republic, and I put you at the head of my permanent government. If that doesn't compensate you for your lack of success among the *Montagnards*,[a] then you are difficult to satisfy and ferociously ambitious! But I think I'm well enough acquainted with you to know that the honor of serving me will suffice for you and that you'll not bitterly regret your *unelection* by the fine people of Paris, *capital* of civilization and of the arts. Mm, mm!ᵇ That said, I would like to know the result of the voting so as to know who the lucky representatives are who've been invited to have their *mugs* and even their jaws smashed by the friends of our good M. Blanqui.[2] I must admit I'm waiting impatiently for the announcement of these wonderful representatives and of the slaps, blows, and other punchesᶜ delivered by the state in the service of liberty, equality, and fraternity. Long live the Republic!!!!!! Nor would I have anything against a bit of sun and much less rheumatism, as I had a lousy night that is still with me this morning. Which doesn't stop me from loving you—on the contrary.

Juliette

Letter 71

Tuesday morning, 8 o'clock, 2 May *[1848]*

Good morning, my little man, good morning, the best, the sweetest, the greatest, and the most charming of men, but the least loving . . . of me, good morning!

If I'm to believe Ninon de l' Enclos,[1] you must be very close to hating me, if as she says, *"the man who gives his time to his mistress gives proof of his love"* . . . from which one must conclude that he who *doesn't* give it gives proof of . . . nothing at all. And from indifference to hatred there's only a step. So, you must be very close to detesting me. I'd just like to be quite sure of it, so I could disencumber you of me as soon as possible. It's not by imposing oneself that one obtains love, and I'd prefer death a thousand times to living without your love.

Now that this declaration of principles has been clearly enunciated, I beg you not to be embarrassed, but to say it straightforwardly and simply, since I can more than half guess it without your saying anything.

I don't know whether it's the influence of the new moon, the beautiful sunshine, or the birds and the flowers that make your indifference seem more melancholy this morning, but I'm sad and discouraged as if I were sure you no longer love me.

Juliette

Letter 72

Wednesday morning, 8 o'clock, 3 May *[1848]*

Good morning, you, good morning, good morning to all that is most hideous and loathsome under the sun! I detest you, I abominate you, and I abhor you! I'm furious! You can tell that from my paper,[1] and if I had you here I'd make you spend a bad quarter of an hour . . . without a mattress. When are you hoping not to return? Forever, probably. But because that would be too convenient, I'm going to go and fetch you right now. You're going to see it happen, and you're going to be amazed. Ah, you rascal, that's how you treat a Juju who's too soft! But don't worry! *I'm finally waking up.* It's not been bad for the last fifteen years or more, but you know what an unbridled Juju is like. In the meantime, have a long lie in! I agree to it on the condition that I can be your nightmare.

Frightful monster, the more I think about it, the less resigned I am to your squalid conduct! Rascal, Peer of France, Academician, all the infamies of nature!

Letter 73

Wednesday afternoon, half past 12:00, 3 May *[1848]*

So you persist with the same system, it seems? You find yourself amusing in fact, but to *me* you're very annoying. I wouldn't mind if you could vary the aggravations a little! In the meantime I rage, I fume, and I drink water. Anyway, I'm perfectly indifferent to this last vexation, and if I talk about it, it's only to humble you. Aside from all of that, I have a little job that I must absolutely get done. I have very seriously ordered six chemises from old Mme Sauva *[sic—torn paper]*, who is to deliver them this week or the beginning of next. Beat me if you want, but don't let me go around with my ass bare and my arms the same!

Now that I've just announced my price, my face is all red and my nose shines like a ruby, but that doesn't matter as long as you don't scold me and you let me do what I want with my *own affairs.* Is it anything to you? Does it concern you?

"Kiss"[a] me, be quiet! Besides I find it rather strange that you meddle in my affairs, when you abandon me every day like a mangy dog. "Be quiet," she says to you.[b]

Juliette

Letter 74

Thursday afternoon, half past 12:00, 4 May *[1848]*

What a very beautiful day, my Toto! So far everything seems very calm, and probably nothing will trouble the Parisians' tranquillity.[1] I hope very much I'm right, for nothing aggravates me more than these riots in which you have a mania for getting involved. Let the devil wring the rioters' necks once and for all, and let there be no more question of them! Provided there are no more revolutions, evolutions, or mystifications, I give my support to this government.

Apart from all of that, "kiss" me, you, and try to attend regular sessions of *my chamber!* You are my representative with my unanimous support, and I beg you to perform your functions regularly and to do honor to the trust that I've invested in you. Don't allow the hour of pardon to pass if you don't wish to hear the hour of justice toll!

You can see I'm equal to the situation, and that the republicans of yesterday have nothing to teach me. I could even teach those of tomorrow a thing or two if I wanted, but I don't. I want you to "kiss"[a] me to death, that's all. I don't think that's too hard. Try it and you'll see!

Juliette

Letter 75

Friday morning, 8 o'clock, 26 May *[1848]*

Good morning, my dear little beloved, good morning, my adorable Toto, good morning! I love you!

I don't like telling you this, but I can find nothing else in me except love from head to foot. The longer I go on, the more I'm invaded by this emotion. Soon there won't be anything left of the original Juju, love of you will have absorbed everything, including the marrow of my bones.

I waited for you yesterday until past eleven o'clock, but without great hope of seeing you. You were too handsome, you smelled too good, and you had much too much white piqué waistcoat to think about coming back to your poor old Juju. So I was under no illusion about the possibility of your returning, and if I waited for you, it was only out of habit and so as not to have to admit to myself immediately the sad and harsh truth to which I have so much trouble getting accustomed. Finally, tired of putting up a fight, I went to bed wishing you much success... politically I mean.

I dreamed about you all night, and this morning, still hardly awake, I'm scribbling you a pile of nonsense before getting as slowly as possible to the point, which is: I adore you.

Juliette

Letter 76

Friday morning, 8 o'clock, 2 June *[1848]*

Good morning, my poor scribbler, good morning, my poor, swotting slave, good morning! I love you and I kiss your dear little cajoling mouth. I think I'm a stupid creature, which won't surprise you, or me either. I should have immediately accepted yesterday the copies of your declaration of principles[1] that you were offering me. It went without saying I would find a way to distribute them, it required only that I should give it some thought, something I'm not used to evidently. Anyway, the night brings counsel as you can see, and if I had known how to reach you at home, I would have sent for as many circulars as possible this morning. I intend to write to M. Cacheux about this first of all, plus I'm sure to distribute many to advantage among the members of *my entourage*. Unfortunately, I must wait for you to come back, and perhaps between now and then you'll have given them all away. This annoys me more than I can say. Without a doubt, I'm a much too stupid creature,[a] but I adore you.

Juliette

Letter 77

Sunday morning, 8 o'clock, 4 June *[1848]*

Good morning, my sweet beloved, good morning! May God give you every consolation and every joy, as He has given you every glory and every tribulation. I think about you with adoration, and I pray to God with all the pure and ardent faith in my heart for all those you love. I hope God will grant my prayers again this time and that you will have no new sorrow in your dear family. In the meantime, your poor life is overloaded with all kinds of heavy and onerous duties, and it terrifies me to see you are about to add to them the most difficult and painful of all.[1] I hope that, with the help of God and the electorate, you will not be elected. The more I think about it, the more impossible it is for me to want you to be elected to this assembly, because I foresee that all your courage, all your devotion, and all your genius will not succeed in preventing the next catastrophe that must unseat it and carry it away. In the interest of everybody, it is better that you should find yourself all in one piece and with all your power intact at the moment of regeneration.

I beg your pardon for daring to talk politics with you—God knows I do so unwillingly and that I'd rather talk sex, travel, love, and sweet leisure than election, republic, riot, and revolution.

Juliette

Notes

Letter 41

1. "Dans mon âme/Je suis beau!" (Quasimodo's song, *La Esmeralda*, IV, 2). **This is the song of Quasimodo, the ugly hunchback, whose spiritual beauty is his love for the gypsy girl, Esmeralda, in the opera *La Esmeralda* (see Glossary) [T].**

2. Mme Hugo was taking her vacation with her father and her children at Saint-Prix, near Montmorency, **in the Val d'Oise department, ten miles or so north of Paris [T]**. She had been there since the beginning of May.

Letter 42

1. The next day, 29 August, Victor Hugo and Juliette Drouet would leave by mailcoach for the Rhine.

   a. **On Suzanne, Drouet's servant, see Glossary, s.v. Blanchard [T]**.

2. "Se faire une bosse" or "se donner une bosse" means, in popular idiom, "to make good cheer" or to indulge in a pleasure trip or orgy. **The pun on the word "bosse," meaning "hump," "hunch," "lump," etc., cannot be satisfactorily translated into English. I have tried to convey it with the parallel between "hump" and "heap" [T]**.

3. A stay at Cologne had been planned in the trip in the autumn of 1839; Hugo's first letter to his wife asked that she write to him *"at Cologne, poste restante"* (*OC*, 6:744). It was the bad weather, apparently, that caused Juliette and Hugo to change their route.

Letter 43

1. Juliette gives this fantasy child the name of the neighbors' baby: see below, L. 46. She would never have any child besides Claire. **Mme Triger was the wife of the doctor who delivered Mme Pierceau's children (*VS*, 4:74) and who would also administer to Drouet's daughter, Claire, during her illness—see below, L. 63, and on Mme. Pierceau, see Glossary [T]**.

   a. **The French says "voime, voime" which I have translated as "mm, mm," following Evelyn Blewer's suggestion that "voime" "is an untranslatable, onomatopoetic expression of satisfaction" (personal communication, 24 October 2002) [T]**.

Letter 44

1. Mme Hugo and the children were still at Saint-Prix when the lovers came back from their trip to the Rhine, and for some time Hugo will spend his days with his family and his nights with Juliette.

   a. **See above, L. 35, n. a [T]**.

2. Juliette's father died when she was still a child; she called "father" the uncle who had brought her up, Lieutenant René-Henry Drouet **(see Glossary [T])**, whose name she adopted.

3. Lanvin, a printer, would play a big role in Hugo's life. It was under his name and with his passport that Hugo left for Belgium after the coup d'état of 2 December 1851. The last love affair Hugo had was with Blanche, his adopted daughter. **On the Lanvins, see Lanvin family, Glossary [T]**.

Letter 45

    1. See above, L. 6, n. 1.

    a. See above, L. 43, n. a [T].

    b. The French says "Oui fir? Ia, ia, monsire, matame, il est sos sarmes." This is a private joke the meaning of which is not fully clear. Drouet uses military imagery along with "accent" in other letters—cf. *LVH*, 78, 81 [T].

    c. See above, L. 35 and n. a [T].

    d. The phrase "qu'on vous dit" (literally, "that one says to you"—translated here by "she says to you") seems not to make any sense unless it is a play on words with the obscene meaning "con vous dit," "con" being a vulgar word for the female genitals.

Letter 46

    1. *La France pittoresque, ou description pittoresque, topographique et statistique des départements et colonies de la France*, by Abel Hugo, 3 vols. (Paris: Delloye, 1833–1835). Victor Hugo took this work by his older brother on his travels of 1838 and 1840, and it became one of the important bibliographical sources for *Le Rhin*. Cf. Evelyn Blewer, "Abel et Victor, les frères amis," *Europe*, March 1985, 104–15 and *Le Rhin: lettres à un ami*, ed. Jean Gaudon, 2 vols. (Paris: Imprimerie nationale, 1985). **On *Le Rhin*, see Glossary. Résisieux is the name of Jonas's sister (see above, L. 43, n. 1). Drouet says unkind things about Mme Besancenot in a letter dated 15 December 1840 (*MUL*, 198): "Now she's finally gone, thank God, for she really is too stupid and too vulgar" [T].**

    a. The French says "copire," a word that Drouet invented to mean "copy" [T].

    2. See on this subject the preface of Jean Gaudon, above, pp. xiii–xiv.

Letter 47

    1. This would be the name eventually given to the servant of Monseigneur Myriel in *Les Misérables*. **On *Les Misérables*, the novel by Hugo, see Glossary. Mme Magloire is an elderly, plump, talkative, and somewhat officious servant of the bishop, who sometimes finds herself at a loss for words at his saintly acts of self-abnegation [T].**

    a. See above, L. 35, n. a. The "fine deed" to which Drouet refers is probably a request for sex from an unwilling Hugo, given the similarity of this letter to many others she wrote at this time—see *VS*, fasc. 4 [T].

Letter 48

    a. See above, L. 43, n. a [T].

    b. A pun on "caca" ("poop") and Academy [T].

c. See above, L. 35, n. a [T].

1. See *LJD*, 112.

d. Drouet uses this word jokingly to refer to her daughter and here, it seems, also to her daughters' friends (cf. *MUL*, 258, 304) [T].

e. Actually her uncle. See above, L. 44 and n. 2 [T].

Letter 49

1. Having been elected to the Académie française in January, Hugo gave his reception speech on this day.

a. On Mme Pierceau and Félicité Desmousseaux, her lover, see Glossary, s.v. Pierceau, and *VS*, 4:73–4 [T].

2. Three of Hugo's four children: Léopoldine (born in 1824), Charles (born in 1826), François-Victor (born in 1828). Juliette does not mention Adèle (born in 1830), but she quotes her with the words "like the other one." For more on Hugo's children, see Glossary. On the basis of another letter of Drouet's, dated 1 January 1855 (*LVH*, 219), it is clear that "like the other one" was an expression of Hugo's daughter Adèle that she had used in a context now unknown to us and that had amused both Hugo and Drouet. "Like the other one" may mean here that the young Toto (François-Victor) looked "like the other" Toto, his father. [T].

Letter 50

1. It was at this very moment that the marriage of Léopoldine Hugo and Charles Vacquerie was being celebrated at the church of Saint-Paul-Saint-Louis. On Charles, see Vacquerie family, Glossary [T].

Letter 51

1. *Les Burgraves* has been playing at the Comédie-Française since 7 March. The reception has been bad, not only on the part of the public, but also on the part of the critics. On *Les Burgraves*, a play by Hugo, see Glossary [T].

a. "Cocotte" is the name of Drouet's pet parrot—see *MUL*, 267 [T].

Letter 52

1. Victor Hugo had left Paris on 7 July to make a quick visit to Léopoldine and her family, who were staying at Le Havre. On his return he was to leave again with Juliette Drouet for Spain, the first trip since the one to the Rhine in 1840.

2. See *LJD*, 127. The words in italics that follow are a response to Hugo's letter. Hugo says in his letter: "At this very moment, even if you think I'm absent, my eye is on you and sees you in your red and gold room, surrounded by the beautiful peacocks embroidered on the tapestry, cultivating your flowers, chattering with your pretty little green bird, and thinking of me" [T].

Letter 53

1. On 4 September Léopoldine, her husband, and two of his relatives drowned in the Seine in a boating accident. Victor Hugo learned the news five days later when he opened up a newspaper at Rochefort. After a hasty return to Paris, he rejoined his family on the evening of 12 September. See the account of these terrible days that Juliette made a month later, collected in Victor Hugo, *Choses vues: Souvenirs, journaux, cahiers*, ed. Hubert Juin, 3 vols. (Paris: Gallimard, 1972), 1:256–72.

2. For Lanvin, see above, L. 44 and n. 3.

Letter 54

1. Since 1836 Claire had been in a pension at Saint-Mandé run by Mmes Marre and Hureau. **Saint-Mandé is (now) a suburb of southeastern Paris, near the Bois de Vincennes [T].**

a. **Mme Lanvin was hardly "old," being only two years older than Drouet (see Lanvin family, Glossary)! The Lanvins frequently chaperoned Claire, Drouet's daughter, to and from her pension [T].**

Letter 55

1. See *LJD*, 130. **In this letter Hugo says: "I want your poor heart to calm itself and be reassured. Never have you been more beautiful to my eyes; never have you been more charming and more tender; never have you had more devotion, resignation, and virtue. I love you as a ravishing woman, I love you as a poor angel!" [T].**

Letter 56

1. It seems that the relationship between Victor Hugo and Léonie Biard dated precisely from the spring of 1844—but Juliette would not know about it for a long time yet. **On Léonie Biard, see Glossary and above, Introduction, pp. 17–19 [T].**

2. The sketch of a large hand extends across these lines.

a. **See above, L. 43, n. a [T].**

Letter 57

1. According to the traditional chronology, it was on this night that Hugo was arrested in flagrante delicto with Léonie Biard.

2. The session of Parliament. Since 13 April Hugo had been a *pair de France*, **see above, L. 26, n. 2. Hugo's election to the Académie française had made him eligible for this honor—cf. *MUL*, 200 [T].**

Letter 58

1. The matter of being caught in flagrante delicto with Léonie Biard had been reported, more or less obliquely, by *Le National* on 10 July and *La Quotidienne* on 11

July. On 12 July the actress Jeanne-Sylvanie Plessy fled Paris with the writer Auguste Arnould, producing quite a stir in theater circles. This event actually had nothing to do with Hugo.

Letter 59

1. Claire is still at the pension at Saint-Mandé, where she has been acting for a short time now in the capacity of assistant schoolmistress.

2. This remark is perplexing. Victor Hugo had informed his wife that he would be away from Monday, 8 September to Wednesday, 10 September; two letters to Juliette from the eighth and ninth confirm this trip (see *LJD*, 147–9). It is not impossible that Léonie Biard accompanied Hugo on this mysterious trip.

3. Hops were believed to have purifying benefits for the stomach.

Letter 60

1. Victor Hugo and Juliette Drouet had returned the previous day to the house at Les Metz, now up for sale, where she had stayed in 1834 and 1835 (see above, L. 14, 19, and *LJD*, 63). Hugo had already gone back there in October 1837; from this trip arose "Tristesse d'Olympio" (*Les Rayons et les ombres*, XXXIV). This letter is, in a way, a negation of the poem, **in the sense that whereas Hugo's poem stresses how much nature had erased the memory of their presence there ("How little time suffices to change everything! / Serene-browed Nature, how you forget! / And how you break with your metamorphoses the mysterious bonds with which our hearts were bound!"), Drouet emphasizes in this letter that nothing has changed and that nature has preserved their memory [T]**.

2. Hugo, also, often describes himself as an antiquarian (see, in particular, the preface of *Le Rhin*).

Letter 61

a. The house belonged to the Pernot family, who did succeed in selling the house in June 1846—Souchon, *Olympio*, 37 [T].

Letter 62

1. Claire's condition—she was suffering from tuberculosis—had abruptly worsened since March. At first she had been installed with Juliette in the rue Saint-Anastase. Pradier insisted she should be transported to a villa in Auteuil.

a. This is probably a reference to the behavior of Claire's father, Pradier, with whom Drouet was particularly disgusted during Claire's illness. While he has shown very little affection for, or interest in, her up until this time, Pradier suddenly takes it upon himself to show officious solicitousness toward his daughter, insisting that Drouet move her to what turned out to be a not-very-nice apartment that he had rented outside Paris in Auteuil. In a letter dated 1 May 1846 (*MUL*, 323) Drouet comments to Hugo: "Besides, nothing is more suspect than this fine sentiment that has waited until now to

show itself with ridiculous bluster. Nothing is more revolting to me than exaggeration, and arm waving, and big words. I may be mistaken. But until I get honest and sincere proof of the sincerity of M. Pradier, I believe myself unfortunately only too right to doubt it" [T].

b. According to Souchon (*MUL*, 323), Drouet accompanied Hugo to the omnibus by which he returned home after visiting her in Auteuil [T].

2. See the letters from Hugo in the following days, *LJD*, 152ff.

Letter 63

1. See *LJD*, 156. In this letter Hugo warns Drouet that he may not be able to come to see her this evening, in which case he will see her tomorrow. The letter includes the words: "Oh beloved, if only you knew how you are my joy, how I need to see you, how your conversation is my music, how your presence is my sun!" [T]. During the entire period of Claire's illness, Hugo was very present and attentive (see *LJD*, 152–64).

a. On M. Triger, see above, L. 43, n. 1 [T].

Letter 64

1. Claire died on 21 June.

2. A very exceptional piece of evidence, for Hugo seems to have frequented churches very little. Is it a pure coincidence that, the day before, Hugo had put into verse some verses from the Book of Jeremiah?

3. It was on this day that Claire was buried at the cemetery in Auteuil.

Letter 65

1. A new burial of Claire's corpse took place on this morning in the cemetery at Saint-Mandé, to comply with the girl's last wishes. Hugo followed the hearse on foot, side by side with Pradier, from Auteuil to Saint-Mandé. It was following this ceremony that he composed the poem in *Les Contemplations* (IV, 11), dated "11 July 1846, on coming back from the cemetery." **On *Les Contemplations*, see Glossary [T].**

Letter 66

a. The "good morning, you" contains in French ("bonjour, vous, bonjour, toi") a play on the two different words for "you," the one formal, the other familiar, which cannot be rendered into English. "Je t'haïme" instead of, more correctly, "je t'haïs," ("I hated you") [T].

1. Victor Vilain (1813–1899), a sculptor, had made some busts of Claire and her mother in 1846 and had remained a friend. The "prince's visit" that Juliette talks of here was doubtless that of the duc d'Aumale, the fourth son of Louis-Philippe, who was having a bust of himself made by Vilain at this time. See for the date of 7 January the account by Victor Hugo in *Journal de ce que j'apprends chaque jour (juillet 1846–février 1848)*, ed. René Journet and Guy Robert (Paris: Flammarion, 1965), 49–50. **On Vilain, see Glossary [T].**

2. *Tableaux vivants* were very much in fashion at this time. The account of the sitting by the duc d'Aumale for Vilain describes them at length (see on this subject the notes by Journet and Robert, *Journal*, 132). **Hugo describes how, during a session of posing in Vilain's studio, the duc d'Aumale made jokes about the "tableaux vivants," "poses plastiques," and nude women that were to be seen at that time performing at the Porte-Saint-Martin, the Cirque, the Palais-Royal, and the Vaudeville [T].**

b. ". . . des lithographies en action et à domicile"—so translated by Robb, *VH*, 258. Robb interprets these, as well as the *tableaux vivants*, as part of the "menu of sexual sports available to a man with spare time and influence in mid-nineteenth-century Paris" that he finds listed in this letter and the next [T].

c. See above, L. 35, n. a [T].

Letter 67

a. For the phrase "qu'on vous dit," see above, L. 45, n. d [T].

1. Gaspare-Luigi-Pacifico Spontini (1774–1851), an Italian composer and, at the time, famous composer of *La Vestale* (1807), asked Victor Hugo in April 1839 for a libretto. Hugo designated Théophile Gautier in his place. See the exchange of letters in Hugo, *OC*, 5:1142. **Robb, *VH*, 259, pace Blewer, notes: "The word 'spontinian' has been interpreted, inexplicably, as an allusion to the composer, Spontini; Hugo's later notes show that it was his code word for ejaculation." See *HS*, 95, on this code word. However, the whole point of Hugo's code words was to prevent Drouet from finding out about his infidelities. Therefore, it is unlikely that Drouet would have known the secret meaning assigned to this word by Hugo. Robb interprets "your *airs of the conquering and Spontinian academician*" as a reference to Hugo's "telltale demeanour" evident to Drouet as a sign of the life of flirtation and (unknown to Drouet) sexual infidelity he led behind her back. By this interpretation, the frequent visits to the town hall, to Chaumontel, and possibly even the negotiations for Charles' replacement in the military, were all used as "excuses and alibis" (*VH*, 259) [T].**

b. Arsène Houssaye talks about Hugo's fondness for taking omnibus rides—*Confessions*, 5:292 [T].

2. Three days previously Hugo had signed a contract with a certain Grangé to substitute for his son Charles in military service. See Journet and Robert, *Journal*, 62.

Letter 68

1. It seems that Victor Hugo had read to Juliette a large part of what is called here *Les Misères*, which would become *Les Misérables*. **Jean Tréjean was the original name for Jean Valjean, the reformed convict and central character of *Les Misérables*. Fantine is a beautiful young woman and unmarried mother of Cosette, who is forced by poverty into prostitution—cf. below, L. 131, n. 1. Champmathieu is an ex-convict rearrested on a second charge and falsely**

identified as Jean Valjean, whose acquittal Valjean obtains by admitting to his true identity [T].

Letter 69

1. On 24 February, at the time when the popular uprising was growing, Victor Hugo had attempted to proclaim a Regency headed by the duchesse d'Orléans. The following day, after the formation of a provisional government, Lamartine tried to appoint Hugo mayor of his district, but Hugo refused. **The revolution of 1848 began on 22 February 1848 as a result of long-term popular grievances against the king, Louis-Philippe, caused by food shortages and his failure to make democratic reforms. Louis-Philippe was forced to abdicate and went into exile in England. As a result the Second Republic came into being, which lasted officially until December 1852 (and the accession to power of Napoleon III)** [T].

   a. A proverb, "le mieux est l'ennemi du bien," roughly equivalent to "a bird in hand is worth two in the bush" [T].

Letter 70

1. Although he was not a candidate, Victor Hugo garnered 59,446 votes in the election for the Assemblée constituante **(so called because it was charged to frame a constitution for the new Second Republic [T])** of 23 April. He was not elected.

   a. **A designation revived after the 1848 revolution in reminiscence of the extreme revolutionary party in the Convention nationale during the French revolution** [T].

   b. See above, L. 43, n. a [T].

   2. Louis-Auguste Blanqui (1805–1881), leader of the left wing of the French socialist movement. Fearing a conservative reaction after the events of February, he announced the adjournment of the elections in order to enlighten public opinion, and participated in the organization of two popular demonstrations. The first, on 17 March, brought about an adjournment of some weeks; the second, on 16 April, encountered the National Guard in front of the Hôtel de Ville and failed. See the remarks about Blanqui that Hugo recorded in his diary in 1848—*OC*, 7:1148–50.

   c. I follow the text as emended by Blewer (*LVH*, 113 and n. 3) from "des gibbeux, des borgnes et autres gourmardes nationales" to "des giffes, des beugnes et autres gourmades nationales" [T].

Letter 71

1. Anne de Lenclos, also known as Ninon de Lenclos (1620–1705), renowned for her wit and many liaisons with famous men, moved in aristocratic, artistic, and intellectual circles and maintained a salon attended by writers such as Boileau, La Fontaine, Molière, and Racine. She wrote *La Coquette vengée* (*The Coquette Avenged*) (1659) [T].

Letter 72

    1. Juliette has begun this letter on the back of the second page of a folded sheet of paper.

Letter 73

    a. See above, L. 35 and n. a [T].

    b. See above, L. 45, n. d [T].

Letter 74

    1. The Assemblée constituante met for the first time on this day.

    a. On the meaning of "baiser" used twice in this letter, see above, L. 35 and n. a [T].

Letter 76

    1. Electoral profession of principals, written 22 May, made public on the twenty-sixth in view of the complementary elections for the Assemblée constituante. See *Victor Hugo à ses concitoyens* in Hugo, *OC*, 7:134–5.

    a. In the French, "je suis une bête beaucoup trop bête," there is a play on the word "bête," meaning "beast, creature" and also "stupid," which cannot be rendered in English [T].

Letter 77

    1. It was on this day that the complementary elections for the Assemblée constituante took place. Victor Hugo was elected as a Paris representative, but the outcome was probably not known until the sixth.

1850s

Letter 78

Saturday morning, 8 o'clock, 6 April *[1850]*

Good morning, my all-beloved, good morning, my poor sublime beloved, good morning! How are you? Was last night better than the others? You weren't too tired and tense to sleep?

When I think about that wonderful speech, so religious, so noble, so devout, and so conciliatory that you delivered yesterday at the risk of your health, and when I think of the stupid uproar it provoked, of the inept and violent heckling it aroused, I have not enough hatred, contempt, or disgust for politics.[1] I find it revolting that a man like you could be the butt of the baseness of political factions. I find it odious, abominable, and vile that wretches without talent, heart, or soul should dare to battle with you and be listened to attentively, while you are being covered with imprecations of all kinds. Really, my poor beloved, the more I see what a life in politics is, the more I miss the time when you were only the *poet* Victor Hugo, my sublime beloved, my radiant and divine lover.

I admire your courage, your self-sacrifice, and your devotion, but I suffer in the most tender, respectful, and sensitive part of myself when I see you offered up to these beasts of the political arena, who are a thousand times more ferocious and a thousand times more stupid than those of ancient Rome. So, my beloved Victor, I have conceived a revulsion not only for your antagonists, but also for the form of government that is imposing on you this Sisyphean existence. If I had the power to change it, I assure you I wouldn't hesitate, even if I had to deprive you forever of your rights as *citizen.*

Unfortunately, I can do nothing except cordially detest all those who constitute an obstacle to the work of courage, devotion, and mercy that you have undertaken, as well as pity you, bless you, admire you, and love you with all my soul.

Juliette

Letter 79

Sunday morning, half past 8:00, *[2]* 8 July *[1850]*

Good morning, old crafty one, good morning, you! How well you did to send me to your play yesterday![1] Mm, mm,[a] charming! Besides, you probably did well from the point of view of your own personal satisfaction too, for you would have been disagreeably surprised to see your Don César de Bazan[b] dolled up like Nigaudème, more stupid than a Fool at Les Funambules and more hideous than a traitor at the Petit-Lazary.[2] It was revolting to see! That didn't impede, however, the comic success of the fourth act, so true is it that your wonderful poetry triumphs over the most ridiculous obstacles and the most absurd interpretations.

I didn't think Frédérick[c] was on top form. Apart from a few shining moments, the role was more mumbled than spoken, more extinguished than illuminated. In short, it was a wonderful performance from the point of view of attendance, for the house was full, from the point of view of the respect and admiration for the poet and his masterpiece *[word obliterated]* the fools and the cretins were on the stage, the intelligent and educated in the house. That was a situation of great originality, and from this point of view, I repeat, yesterday's performance was epoch-making and must take its place among your greatest literary successes.

After that I had my young men bring me home, but I didn't find that very satisfying.

Juliette

Letter 80

Mardi Gras morning, 9 o'clock, 4 March *[1851]*

Good morning, my beloved, good morning, my sweet adored one, good morning! *Remember!* It is eighteen years ago today that we had our first night of love.[1] When I look around me, it seems it was eighteen centuries ago, to such an extent the relics of my happiness have dispersed and disappeared. But when I look into my heart, I feel that I am still on the brink of this first night of enchantment and ecstasy. Happiness grows tired and dies, love survives and grows and roots itself to the point of absorbing the heart in its entirety. I don't complain, because it is the natural law of this species of vegetation. I complain all the less given that I can live without happiness but I could not live without love.

I would have liked to celebrate this anniversary with you, but I resign myself to the impossibility of your leaving your family on a day like this when it's traditional to assemble rather than separate. So I'll resign myself to going and eating the pancakes and sacramental pastries of my good denizens of Sablonville. I'll go especially because they're sad and sick, the husband, in particular, with an attack of sciatica that is worse than ever. I was asked to invite Vilain,[2] but he must have several invitations of this kind and with tarts more diverting than those one meets in these honest and respectable parts. So I would be very astonished if he were to privilege us. Soon I'm going to convey the message to him, but I wanted to give you the firstfruits of my pen along with those of my mind and heart. I'm sure you are *flattered*. Mm, mm,[a] you have no time for my *firstfruits*, you prefer young fruits and primroses to all the flowers of my rhetoric. I know you, my good man, I know all your weak spots, but alas, I don't know your strong ones! This topography is completely foreign to me, and you're too discrete and too prudent to show me the way. Thus I remain on the road watching the shadows turn at my feet,[b] a melancholy occupation if ever there was one.

Juliette

Letter 81

Saturday morning, 8 o'clock, 28 June *[1851]*

Good morning, my good little man, good morning! Well, how did your whole day go yesterday?[a] Did you enjoy yourself, was there good grub, lots of pretty women, and all the *rest*?[b] What time did you come back yesterday? I passed your door at half past ten, but I didn't see a single light. I simply went to bed and dreamed about you the whole time that I was able to sleep. This morning I'm already overwhelmed by the heat; but far from complaining, I'm glad of it on account of you, my beloved. What happiness! What happiness! What happiness! At ten o'clock this morning I intend to send you all the undamaged strawberries I have been able to save.[1] I'll have Suzanne say they should be put in sugar right away, because that's the way they keep without spoiling. I'm sending them to you in the dish you so horribly ruined for me in one of your hideous *washings*. It will be left in your house so you can't forget it. The least you could do is compensate me for the damage you do to my poor crocks, not to mention the frightful uproar you cause in the whole of my small household. Be quiet, pay up, you can talk later if it amuses you! As for me, I'm not finished yet and I must kiss you.

Juliette

Letter 82

Saturday morning, quarter past 10:00, 28 June *[1851]*

I'm hurrying to write to you while Suzanne is away at your house, because I must comb my hair and have a thorough wash today, which is bound to take a long time especially in this sizzling heat. When I think about the fact that I won't see you again tomorrow, I feel very dismayed. And yet, at bottom, I feel it'll do you good. So go to the country as often as you can, my beloved, and try to take me there sometimes. As far as tomorrow is concerned, I've decided to stay at home, because I have no taste for going out unless it's with you and because, even supposing that Julie were free, it would be impossible for me to incur the expense of an excursion somewhere. I wrote to her yesterday to tell her she was entirely free for the day.

Suzanne is back from your place. She gave the strawberries to your servant, but as I had told her to insist on having them put in sugar immediately, it was the first thing she didn't do, with that contradictory instinct that's typical of her. So probably you'll wait until this evening to give them this little preparation, by which time they will no longer be edible. Lucky that you have your dish to console you! Kiss me, my little man, get better, and enjoy yourself! As long as you're completely faithful to me and love me, I permit you everything.[a]

Juliette

Letter 83

Wednesday morning, 11 o'clock, 2 July 1851

How are you, my dear beloved? You're coming to the end of your trial—at least on my side—my poor, great, reckless man, since, whatever happens now, you can expect from me only forgiveness, kindness, gratitude, and love.[1]

You are still free, my beloved. I don't want to be too hasty in accepting your offer of happiness, which you may make at the expense of your own.

Far from weakening me, the blow that should have killed me has given me superhuman strength, and I consider without dizziness and without pusillanimity the different eventualities that smile or frown upon me at this moment. As long as you're happy, that's all I want. I need your happiness like a bird its wings. I can't live without your happiness. All that isn't *that* is hateful to me. So act without fear and without scruple and as though I were dead.

If you knew how true it is I love you, how my love flies above all the miseries and all the pains of this life, you wouldn't fear to let me see the human side of your love. You are no longer a man for me, you are the soul of my soul.

I would like to make out of all the days of life that remain to me as many years of happiness, joy, elation, and glory for you, even if to accomplish that I had to undergo again all the trials and all the acts of martyrdom I have already experienced. My Victor, my Victor, believe what I'm telling you as though God himself were saying it to you! Don't fear to make me suffer, if my suffering can give you true happiness in this world! My turn will come and that will be for eternity, for I'll have nothing to fear from a contest for the most beautiful soul and the greatest love when you see my soul and my love disrobed of all that conceals and disfigures them in this poor body that is so little worthy of them.

Juliette

Letter 84

Saturday morning, half past 7:00, 5 July *[1851]*

Good morning, my much-beloved, good morning! All my soul is in that ray of sun that will be coming to caress your soft hair.

How are you this morning, my dear beloved? Did you sleep well? I hope you didn't get up at five o'clock, because then you would not have had time to rest. Try to stay asleep and don't wake up until the sun itself is completely awake!

You gave me a very nice surprise yesterday when you put a packet of your letters among the newspapers. It took me back to the good old days when you used to involve me in your whole life without restriction. Thank-you, my beloved, thank-you for having resumed this nice habit again at this moment. I need to think I'm returning into your love and into your life by all entrances at once. I need to think you've been returned to me in your entirety and that I'm regaining possession of all my rights and all my privileges as a loved woman. So whatever appears to me to be a proof of that, however indirect, becomes dear and precious to me. That's why I welcomed with tears of faith and gratitude these letters come from I know not where and saying I know not what, just because it was one of your habits in the past when you loved only me. Thank-you, my beloved, thank-you, you are good, I love you! Think of me! I desire you with all my strength, and I kiss you with all my soul. I love you, I love you.

Juliette

Letter 85

Sunday morning, half past 7:00, 13 July 1851

Good morning, my beloved Victor, good and *fine* morning; good morning with all that health, joy, and happiness give, good morning! If you knew what sweet joy I promise myself in spending a part of this day alone with you, you would understand to what degree you are my life, my breath, my soul.

Poor dear beloved, I do not mistrust you, but I fear that you are mistaken about the true state of your heart. I fear you take the interest and the devotion I inspire in you for a more tender emotion, and that you sacrifice yourself, without yet being conscious of it, to a sort of mirage of love that I can no longer actually inspire in you. The trial, or rather the *trials,* that will soon take place will enlighten you more concerning your true feelings than will this dubious light of pity. Until they have shed light on the state of your heart, it is impossible for me to give myself up completely to the joy of having you back in your entirety. Let us wait until reconciliations and renewed relations have passed and passed again across your life, as though over a suspension bridge whose solidity we are testing. God willing, the weight will not break my hope halfway across! I await with painful anxiety the outcome of these trials that are so decisive for everybody. Whatever the trials may be, I submit to them and accept them, putting, in advance, all my courage, all my strength, and all my resignation at the service of your happiness.

As for the other hypothesis, I only hazard my thoughts there tremblingly, as though it might collapse under them like a plank too frail to support so much happiness.

If it is I whom you prefer, if it is really I whom you love, my Victor, I will not have enough time left to live to show my gratitude for it to God, not enough joy, not enough kisses, not enough blessings to thank you!

Juliette

Letter 86

Monday afternoon, quarter to 1:00, 28 July 1851

Here is the time when I must start to wait for you, my Victor. Each second that passes by with the slowness of an eternity of impatience carries away with it all my hopes as soon as I conceive them. What is to become of me during this whole frightful day if I cannot see you? Oh, I believed myself to be stronger, more courageous, and more resigned, but I feel that I have consumed all my energy in the horrible struggle I've been having with my despair for the past month! My God, what is to become of me, here alone, locked up with this horrific date: *28 June 1851?*[1] How to defend myself against its horrible grip that makes me dizzy? What way to escape the intoxication of suicide, the desperate pleasure of death? My God, my God, my God, how I suffer! Oh, I beg you, do not leave me here alone tod . . .[a]

Midnight

This letter, which was begun in a paroxysm of fever and jealous madness, I finish—thanks to you, my ineffable beloved—in the happy tranquillity of trust and with all the sacred joys of mutual love. Be blessed, my Victor, as much as you are respected, venerated, admired, and adored by me, and you will have nothing to desire in this world and in the next!

Juliette

Letter 87

Tuesday evening, 8 o'clock, 9 September 1851

Happier than the person who wrote to you yesterday, my beloved, I recognize no right over you, and the nineteen years you have *taken from the very heart of my life* do not weigh an atom in the scales of your repose, your consideration, and your happiness. Hence I hope you will behave toward me like a man free of obligation of any kind, and conduct yourself toward me without false delicacy, without exaggerated generosity, and without offensive pity. I put all that I have in the way of courage, strength, self-abnegation, and love at the service of your happiness. Make use of it unsparingly and fearlessly, for I have no ulterior motive and no hope except for the life hereafter, to which I am already so close, thank God.

I thank you for your trust, I thank you for your loyalty, I thank you for your kindness, I thank you for your patience and your indulgence. I thank you for them with a grateful heart, I thank you for them with sincere and passionate devotion, I thank you for them with tears and joy, I thank you for them with love and pity!

Juliette

Letter 88

Friday afternoon, half past 2:00, 12 September 1851

O God, inspire me with trust, since you cannot take away my love![1] Make me believe in him, since I cannot cease to love him. Conceal from me the past that kills me, and show me a radiant future. God, have pity on him and on me, for I know his heart suffers from my despair. God, give him happiness, and restore my peace of mind. God, let him not tire of my tears before they have ceased to flow. God, if you cannot make me more happy, make me strong, courageous, resigned, and generous!

God, God, forgive him and forgive me, for it is neither his fault nor mine if we are reduced to this cruel extreme of distrusting one another.

You know, God, whether I love him and whether I wish to impose myself on him. You know what I say to You alone, O God, with all the tears in my eyes, all the tenderness of my heart, all the adoration of my soul. Make him be happy with no matter whom, no matter how—so long as he is—and do with me as you wish. Extinguish the hideous jealousy in me, and reignite his love if such a miracle is possible!

Half past 10:00

My beloved, my beloved, be calm, be happy, for I love you, I trust you, I adore you, I'm happy. All is forgotten, I remember now only your love. I bless you!

Juliette

Letter 89

Monday morning, 8 o'clock, 29 September 1851

Good morning, my Victor, health, glory, and happiness to you, good morning!

Out of caution I should stop here and limit myself to these three wishes of my soul to avoid the risks of saying anything further. But since you don't wish me to, I obey you, my beloved, by asking your pardon in advance for all the crazy, unjust, and sad things I might say to you today. I assure you it's not my fault, for I'm more determined than ever to leave you entirely master of your actions, your liberty, and your love. I want you to be happy, my Victor, and I feel I have the courage to make any kind of sacrifice to reach this end. I give you the greatest and most difficult proof of it today by consenting to your seeing this lady again.[1]

I don't deceive myself as to the danger there is for me in these relations, but I don't recoil—on the contrary—because your *true* happiness is my life's only ambition. For *that* I'll joyfully live or die and bless you at the same time.

Go, arrange everything as is best! I ask only your unrestricted trust, loyal and complete, worthy of the unlimited love I have for you. Tell me everything, for I intuit everything and am resigned to everything—except betrayal. Your happiness mustn't cause you remorse, my poor beloved. So you must hide nothing from me! Your honesty will be the ladder that will bring me back, little by little, from the summit to which my love had taken me. Your betrayal, on the other hand, would make me fall off it headlong. Out of respect for yourself and gratitude for our early happiness, you can't commit the evil deed of deceiving me. I'm sure of this, Victor, and I trust entirely in you.

Now, my Victor, I await my fate with resignation. May the test not last too long, for mental strength, like physical strength, has its limits—only love and devotion have none. I love you, I bless you, I adore you.

Juliette

Letter 90

Monday morning, half past 10:00, 10 November 1851

I have just written you some very silly and very sad things, my poor sweet beloved. It is a very bad way to recognize all you are doing to calm me and make me happy. I blame myself and excuse myself for it all at the same time, for it pains me to respond so badly to your generous efforts, and yet it is not my fault. I know all that you are doing, and I am touched by it to the depths of my poor sick soul. But frightful jealousy undoes all the good as you do it. I tell myself that this prolonged illness, and the solicitude so strongly and justly awakened by it, cannot fail to reignite a love that was not completely extinguished.[1] It is impossible that your heart should not be more tenderly interested in the beautiful and intelligent young woman that you used to adore, than in a poor woman consumed and devastated by passion who has nothing more to do in this world except die. I am so sure of this physical and mental phenomenon that I wonder why I wait for it to be realized to give up my place.

My adored Victor, my poor beloved, aren't I really insane and really nasty? But I'm unhappy and suffering even more so. My heart is in torment. No, no, no, it isn't true, I don't know what I'm saying! I trust you, I'm happy, I'm not suffering! I love you—that's happiness, that's life!

Juliette

Letter 91

Wednesday morning, half past 8:00, 12 November 1851

Good morning, my dear little man, good morning! Sleep! *I* have something else to do—to love you, which isn't a small job. I know I won't see you earlier than half past one at the soonest, which isn't funny, since I foresee that every day henceforth will be cut from the same cloth. I'll get at most a five-minute scrap for myself out of the twenty-four hours given to all and everything else. I'd like to appear not to notice it. But I have too much real love to be able to have a single grain of pride.

I take my happiness wherever I can find it: at every street corner and at every milestone; at noon as at midnight; I wheedle and beg for it in every possible way and with the most lamentable perseverance; I extend my heart and hand for the meanest alms that your charity will give me, and I thank you for your pity in no matter what way it shows itself. My pride and arrogance consist in loving you more and better than anyone else in the world, and without wishing to boast, I think I've succeeded very well. My ambition would be to die for you. O my adored beloved, it's true that my most ardent wish is to devote myself to you until death! I believe that if I could be sure of giving you my life in exchange for sparing you a danger or a sorrow, I would already be the most happy of women. In the meantime, I am the most tenderly passionate. I adore you!

Juliette

Letter 92

Saturday morning, 10 o'clock, 15 November 1851

My dear beloved, I keep my ears pricked for all signs of a possible *coup d'état,* but thank God all seems peaceful so far. I hope, I might even say I'm sure—if premonition had the force of law—that there'll be no coup, at least not the one that has threatened you for so long.

The fear of a bloody struggle in the future with an unforeseeable outcome is already more than enough, my God. It's not for myself I fear, for the dream of my life would be to die devoting myself to you, but it's the thought of seeing you subjected to all the hazards and dangers of a terrible revolution. My adored Victor, my sublime beloved, my blessed lover, I feel capable of all kinds of courage except that of seeing you suffer. So it's for this reason I fear everything that can compromise your health and life. If I were sure that by giving you mine I could guarantee yours, I'd be the most happy of women, and nothing would cause disquiet to my solicitude or trouble my serenity.

But God doesn't always accept such bargains. That's why I fret as soon as there is a question of conflict and civil war.

My Victor, my happiness, my life, I'll serve you—you'll see—with what courage, what ardor, what devotion, what love, what happiness!

In the meantime, I adore you and bless you.

Juliette

Letter 93

Sunday morning, half past 8:00, 30 November 1851

Good morning, my good little man, good morning, my sweet beloved, good morning! I think you can look me straight in the eye this morning, for I hope you'll find there nothing except love and trust. It's up to you to put happiness and joy there.

Anyway, my dear little man, I know the reason why you didn't close your shutters was so as to have daylight sooner, which is brave. But I would prefer that you have lots of rest and sleep, especially after the agitation of the night before last.

Sleep, my beloved Victor, and don't wake up except to go to Labarne's [?],[a] even if it means not eating until you come back. I'm scared you won't find him home, and I can't wait to be calmed and cheered by knowing the outcome of your initiative, if by chance he *did* happen to be at home this morning.

Yesterday as I left you, I met the same patrol who was retracing his steps: it's probably the same strategy that made us think the other night that two had passed, one after another. In the three years I've lived in this district, and in the three months I've been going out with you at all hours of the night, I've never noticed or encountered these formidable patrols before. There must be some other reason to this than just to have these poor soldiers take a moonlight walk? As long as it's not the sign of a violent and absurd coup, I don't mind. As long as there's no shooting and your freedom is respected, they can double and triple the number of patrols in every direction, but it's hardly probable that these nocturnal ramblings are being taken for no reason or for a good reason— that's what troubles me. So I slept badly and very little last night. My beloved Victor, my life, my soul, I would like to serve you, keep you, and watch over you day and night.[1] I feel that everything threatens you when I'm separated from you and that my presence preserves you from every evil and every danger.

Juliette

Letter 94

Brussels,[1] 17 December 1851
Wednesday afternoon, quarter past 3:00

Don't worry about me, my poor beloved, for I never love you more and with more sense of security than when I know you're busy with your duties toward your family and concerned with ensuring the tranquillity and happiness of your wife and children. Devote yourself wholeheartedly to your courageous and worthy wife during her entire stay here! Don't stint her of any diversions that can soothe her after the cruel trials she has just undergone. Make out of my resignation and courage, my discretion and my devotion, a kind of soft and comfortable litter that will cushion the roughness of the road during all the time she spends with you. Give her all the consolations and joys you can. Shower on her all the respect and affection she deserves, and never fear that you are at the end of my trust and patience!

Dear beloved, here you are! Bless you!

Letter 95

Brussels, 20 December 1851[1]
Sunday morning, half past 8:00

Good morning, my poor tormented one, good morning, my sweet afflicted one, good morning!

All you want me to do in the interest of your dignity, trust, glory, and happiness, I will do. I have already told you so many times, my poor generous man, but I am ready to prove it when and as you like, however difficult or painful the sacrifice you ask from me.

I promise also, my ineffable beloved, not to indulge anymore in these bitter recriminations that wound you without soothing me. I want to be for you a sure, tender, and devoted friend, with all the courage of a man, all the solicitude of a mother, and all the disinterest of the dead.

You will see that I'll succeed, my poor beloved, for I want your happiness at whatever price. For your part, my dear beloved, you must tell me outright what you hope and expect from me. Draw me the boundary within which our external relationship must remain, and however constrained and narrow you make it, I promise in advance never to exceed it.[2] You must understand that, in the vague and rather free space in which I have lived until now, it has been quite difficult for me not to be tempted sometimes to open wide my soul's wings, and try to fly again in the beautiful sunlight of love whose last rays dazzle my eyes and burn my heart. I beg you, my Victor, put your plans on hold, specify clearly, without hesitation, without false delicacy, and without distrust the relationship I must keep with you!

I am ready for anything as long as it ensures your tranquillity and serves your present glory and the future of your children. I say this to you from the bottom of my heart and with all the most cordial, honest, and devout tenderness.

Juliette

Letter 96

Brussels, 28 December 1851
Sunday afternoon, 2 o'clock

I no longer know how I live, my sweet beloved, but I do know more than ever how I love you, and I feel into the very marrow of my bones that you are my life and my happiness.

Which is to say, I find the time very long, gloomy, and sad in this little room without you. However, I don't want to be ungrateful toward Providence and I try to make for myself a sort of drab happiness with all the gray joys of my new life. Besides, isn't this about as much light as I can reasonably hope for at the moment? My poor love has been so shaken up that it can never be put back on its feet. Try as I might, I cannot deceive or delude myself. In the depths of my soul there is something dead that will never revive. Try as I might, I cannot go back eight years in time. Fate pushes me and hurries me toward the end of everything. My heart says to me, *"Love!"* and my reason says to me, *"Die!"* What is the good of lingering in this life?

Here you are!

Tuesday morning, half past 8:00, 30 December 1851

Good morning,[1] my ineffable beloved, good morning! I'm happy because you love me. I smile at you, I bless you, I adore you. I want to resume my nice habit of daily scribbling about whatever happens. I won't fear being ridiculous any longer, since you love me. My Victor, I feel I'm starting over with a new life of love, of trust, of security, and of happiness. Bless you!

Juliette

Letter 97

Brussels, 13 January 1852
Tuesday afternoon, 2 o'clock

A month ago at this same time, my dear little man, I waited with inexpressible impatience for the moment when I would set out on my journey to join you. And although I was confident about you personally—since I knew you were no longer within reach of the claws of that wretched tiger cat with a parrot's beak[a]—I was nonetheless troubled by the immense responsibility of bringing to you all the treasures of your genius that you had accumulated and stored up during so many years.

Thanks to God I succeeded, and I always will succeed as long as there remains to me a breath of life. Yes, my adored beloved, as long as I live, your mind and body will be free, I'm very sure of it, as sure as I am that I love you as more than a man, as much as a god. My presentiment is that as long as [I] am of this world no irreparable misfortune will touch you, and I trust in this sort of intuition and second sight, which comes to me from God, as in a sacred promise that nothing can destroy.

What charming letters your dear children write, my Victor! Everything is there: the mind of mature men, the innocence of children, the sensitive and gracious tenderness of women. They love you, both these fine young men, with the expansive abandon of youth and with the strong and energetic virility of mature manhood. It is charming and powerful. I am never tired of rereading their letters, so much do they please me. As for your daughter, she is an angel, and I love her with a sort of respectful motherliness. I admire her and bless her.

Dear beloved, there is no joy without a sorrow. Mine came today in the unexpected arrival of Mme Esther Guimont,[1] who has just taken up residence at Mme Wilmen's. I foresee all the trouble and perturbation that this proximity is going to bring into our poor little establishment, and I'm all sad and unhappy about it in advance. I doubt you can find any solution other than our departure from Brussels before this lady's arrival. But then what a lot of trouble, worry, and expense!

Juliette

Letter 98

Brussels, 19 January 1852
Monday afternoon, 4 o'clock

I should immediately resume my *work* and let you rest your poor, beautiful, eagle eyes that you're good-natured enough to wear out reading this shapeless scribble. But I'm so happy when I have an opportunity to spout out my whole repertoire of ineptitudes and stupidities, of gobbledygook and nonsense that I can't let a single one go by.

You know, my dear little man, that I owe a tremendous "thank-you" to your town hall bells and quite a lot of gratitude to the racket and barbaric sounds that drove you from your bed into mine the other night. If I dared, I'd cast some spells so that this noise continued and increased to the point where you had no peace or respite except in my arms.

But I'm a better Juju than you think, and I don't want anything from you except voluntarily and without the least constraint from anyone or anything whatsoever. So, my good little man, since it's your pleasure to sleep in this Grand' Place, try to get used to the intemperate tolling of the big clock and to the yelling of the Flemish clowns and the Belgian women in their carnival costumes. Sleep well and be happy, since you can be so without me! Try above all not to be caught by M. Bonaparte's cutthroats. The locksmith still hasn't come. God willing he'll come tomorrow, and I'll send him to you right away. From now until then keep your door firmly closed and stay on your guard! My dear beloved, I'm very serious when I beg you to keep your ears open for the least sound around the door to your room. What despair if, out of unthinking trust, you should let yourself be abducted! Just thinking about it makes my heart stop.

Juliette

Letter 99

Brussels, Sunday afternoon, 1 March 1852[1]

I am still preoccupied with the difficulty of having your son Charles come here, for I see so many drawbacks as a consequence.[2] Moreover, my adored beloved, if dining here meant that your health and that of your son had to suffer from the bad cooking here, and if you wished to give preference to the dinners at your house, I would be ready to resign myself to eating alone at home every day. But on no condition would I risk being in the company of your son without being sure that he consents to it. I wouldn't be so formal if it were a question of serving him and devoting myself to him until death; but when it's a question of my personal happiness, I have the right to take a second look at it and consult my dignity and sensibility before attempting something so delicate.

I thank you for having thought of it, my adored beloved. It's already a great consolation to me to know you think of ways of being closer to me by having me enter as much as possible into your private life. They say *all things come to him that waits*. I have waited nineteen years for the acceptance to which the love and the boundless devotion I have for you and yours should have entitled me. It hasn't yet come. Will it ever? I doubt it. I will not, in any case, sacrifice your dear son to the process of making it happen more quickly.

It is my pride and glory to bear courageously and patiently the prejudice that has unjustly befallen me since the day I first loved you. Yes, since the day I first loved you, my beloved Victor, no woman has had the right to carry her head higher than mine, for from that day forward I have had complete modesty, honesty, and purity of body, and nothing but noble and generous feelings of the heart and soul. My love has become more than a duty, it has become the cult of my life. I have loved you as both man and god simultaneously. My lips touch your lips with ineffable pleasure, and, dazzled and ecstatic, I worship the majesty of your genius.

Juliette

Letter 100

Brussels, 11 March 1852
Thursday morning, half past 8:00

Good morning, my Victor, good morning! I hope your indisposition hasn't increased since yesterday. I hope also M. Yvan[1] will rid you of it as soon as possible. In the meantime, my dear friend, it appears you must double your chastity, which won't be difficult as far as I'm concerned, for you only have to continue the continence you have observed with me so scrupulously for what will soon be two months, although I could even say for what will soon be *eight years*.

You're often surprised at my sadness and unequal temper, and you attribute it perhaps to my character and bad upbringing. Well, most of the time you are mistaken, for the secret of my impatience and sorrow lies in my memories. Much as I would like to forget, I remember the time when you loved only me, and I remember also, my God, that the day when you used your health as pretext for a *physical* separation, you *adored* someone else. Hence, my poor beloved, a heartache that no homeopathy could cure; hence despair that no pity, no tenderness, no human respect, no duty, no recognition could calm. The more you shower these on me, the more I suffer in my love. My soul recoils with horror and disgust at the kind of compromise—humiliating for one's dignity, odious for one's soul—that consists in making two parts of oneself: one for physical pleasure, the other for affection. These subtle distinctions make me fume with indignation at the hypocritical contempt they conceal.

So have the courage, once and for all, of your physical and moral infidelity! What is a love that has a need for a third to satisfy it? What, you need several bodies for a single love, when mine would like two souls to love you better? What a profanation of love! How disgraceful all these miserable treacheries are that deceive no one and satisfy no one! It is time for us to be completely sincere toward each other, it is the only end worthy of us, worthy of this love that circulates in my veins along with my blood, that regulates the beating of my heart, that is the soul of my soul, that is more me than I myself, that is everything, that wants everything because it gives everything, that prefers nothing to something! Keep your generosity, your devotion, your pity, your gratitude, if you think you owe me them, which I deny, and let me die in peace far away from you—this is the only favor that I ask!

Juliette

Letter 101

Brussels, 18 July 1852
Sunday morning, 7 o'clock

Good morning, my Victor, good morning! I will do whatever you want. Given the impartiality of my heart, it little matters when or how my body is transported from Brussels to Jersey.[a] So, my Victor, I have no objection to leaving at the same time as you, since my poor heart would find it difficult to choose between the sorrow of a twenty-four-hour separation from you and the bitterness of being near you, like—and yet less than—a stranger. It is a simple matter to sacrifice myself to prejudice and respect the presence of your sons with this painful incognito. But I find it quite cruelly unjust and frightfully absurd to think that these sacrifices and signs of respect that are imposed upon my devotion, my fidelity, and my love were of no consequence and were held cheap and a matter for scandal when another woman was involved whose only virtue consisted in having none.[b]

To her, the bosom of the family was hospitable; for her, protective and deferential courtesy on the part of the sons was a duty; around her, the legitimate wife threw a mantle of consideration and accepted her as a friend, as a sister, and more. For her, indulgence, sympathy, affection! For me, the rigorous and pitiless application of all the penalties contained in the code of prejudice, hypocrisy, and immorality! Honor to the brazen vices of women of the world, infamy to the poor creatures guilty of crimes of honesty, devotion, and love! It's simple: society must be safeguarded with respect to what it holds most respectable and dear.

I will leave for Jersey when and as you want.

I am quite ready to do Charles' copying. I fear only that my bad handwriting will be more disagreeable to him than useful. However, I'll do my best and I'll try to have better pens than this one. But the manuscript should be sent to me as soon as possible.

Until then, my Victor, for that as for everything, I'm entirely at your disposal.

Juliette

Letter 102

Jersey, 3 December 1852
Sunday morning, 9 o'clock

Good morning, my life, good morning, my soul, good morning, my joy and my happiness, good morning!

Dear beloved, starting from yesterday until the fourteenth of this month, not a single day will go past without my remembering the dangers to which you were exposed a year ago and the terrors and inexpressible anguish I experienced during those ten frightful days.[a]

On this day in the morning at this same time you were in the faubourg Saint Antoine, confronting and challenging all alone a frenzied band of troops who no longer recognized or respected anything. I still see you, my poor beloved, haranguing the soldiers to recall them to their duty and to true honor, threatening the generals and blasting them with your contempt. You were fearsome and sublime; one might have described you as the genius of France witnessing, in the grips of bitter despair, the most cowardly and vile of crimes. It is a true miracle that you came out alive from that place, which you, all alone, filled with heroic fury. All those wretches must have felt the influence of your transfiguration, for at that moment you were no longer a man, you were the angel of the fatherland afflicted by a most painful indignation. Just thinking of it, I still feel completely awestruck and dazzled.

Juliette

Letter 103

Jersey, 6 January 1853
Thursday evening, 9 o'clock

If the soul had a form visible to the eyes, you would see mine leaning over you at this moment, my sweet beloved, smiling at you lovingly. If kisses had wings, you would feel them swoop down upon your dear little person in flocks, like joyful birds onto a beautiful tree in flower. Unfortunately, my soul and my kisses pass and pass again around you without your seeing them, and even perhaps without your sensing them. But that doesn't discourage me, and I'm drawn invincibly toward you by the need to live in your atmosphere. My thoughts sit boldly at your side wherever you are. Much as my melancholy personality allows itself to be tyrannized by the contempt and disdain of the world, so much the more does my love trust in its superiority and carry its heart high. Though you may leave my person at the door, my love enters boldly with you and doesn't leave you. Perhaps that isn't an act of refined delicacy, but it's one of a very passionate and loyal heart, and in any case, "we are on an island."[a]

Ah, I see you making eyes at your female neighbor on the left and communicating by submarine telegraphy with the woman sitting opposite! I want you to belong to me *body* and soul, and I claim the right to cede none of it to anyone. Accept it as beyond discussion, and content yourself with devouring the cosmopolitan cuisine of the Hungarian Lucullus![1] I permit you to eat like four Englishmen and drink like a Pole. The *rest* belongs by right to the young Victor and will help to console him.[b] In the meantime I won't take my eyes off you, and I watch all your movements. I find you laugh very frequently for a serious man who has such fine teeth. Well, here are the hands that are going to make the paws of female expatriates redden with spite and show the claws of jealousy![c] They are humiliated by the comparison. It serves them right—that'll teach them to give victuals to a man handsomer than they are and without asking my permission! Hold your tongue! Drink, turn my way at once, and stay like that!

Juliette

Letter 104

Jersey, Saturday, noon, 23 April 1853

I say, man in the big hat![a] Upon my word! My dear! You strike me as a real Norman when it comes to mercantile probity. If that's how you carry out *agreed* transactions, I don't compliment you on it, believe me! But I'll pay you back without spending a penny, you and your *hat*. You'll kick yourself for having missed the opportunity to squeeze four shillings out of me, but it'll be too late. From now until then I agree to give you some rope, such is my grandeur, my generosity, and my magnanimity! Be quiet, you *proper* scoundrel you, and come quickly so I can forgive you and clean you out!

In the meantime I'm inclined to think I should take advantage of the sunshine, if you share this opinion. It's quite a long time since I've done that, and I feel it would do some good to my old rheumatism. After that I'm going to hurry to patch up my blouse for tomorrow, Sunday—quite a dispiriting occupation, for nothing is more antipathetic to me than patching up of any kind. So I'm going to buy myself some blouses no later than next week. It's a great pity I can't buy some of your love. What a lot of it I'd store up and how I'd revel in it!

Juliette

Letter 105

> Jersey, 28 April 1853
> Thursday evening, 9 o'clock

I come to you, my dear beloved, because you cannot return to me tonight.

I come to you to tell you I love you above and beyond regrets about the past and fears about the future.

I come to you with a smile on my lips and a blessing in my soul.

I come to you with my hand on my mutilated heart and my eyes full of forgiveness.

I come to you washed pure and my soul redeemed by twenty years of fidelity and love. I come to you without delusions and radiating faith. I come to you without rancor and with the sustenance of divine hope.

I come to you with maternal devotion and the passionate tenderness of a lover.

I come to you with my mind full of veneration and admiration.

I come to you resigned and pious like a martyr before God, and I make you supreme and absolute master of my fate. Do with it as you wish in this world, even if I must understand your will only in the other! I lay my sufferings as homage and protection at the feet of your wife's virtue and your daughter's innocence, and I keep my tears, my indulgence, and my prayers for poor fallen women like myself.

Finally, my adored beloved, I give you my chance of paradise in exchange for your chances of hell, considering myself only too happy to have bought your eternal happiness by my eternal love.

Juliette

Letter 106

> Jersey, 14 September 1853.
> Wednesday afternoon, 1 o'clock

However little my sympathy for, and affinity with, *spirits*[1] may be, if your commerce with the other world is at all to continue, I'm going to be forced to join them so as to have a chance to see you sometimes. In any case, it's not a repellent or disturbing idea; this life is not so attractive to me that it would require great persuasion to make me leave it. In that, as in all things, it's only the first step that counts. Let me take the first step, and you'll see how easily I'll go the rest of the way.

As far as your witchcraft is concerned, *I* see a future more inconvenient than pleasurable, whatever *your* personal and collective convictions may be.

It's difficult to explain what I mean, but I feel that this pastime contains an element of risk for one's sanity if it's serious—which I don't doubt it is on your part —and an element of impiety if there's the least amount of insincerity involved. As for myself, I don't want to indulge in such bold curiosity. I have, in any case, enough troubles[a] here on earth without going to look for them among the ghosts.

Juliette

Letter 107

Jersey, 24 September 1853
Saturday afternoon, half past 2:00

How it inspires the imagination to live constantly between four walls, and what lively and varied incidents one gathers in this life of a squirrel in a cage! As far as I'm concerned, I'm so stuffed[a] with them I don't know where to start. Let's see, let's take them in order: my cat, which has been sleeping on its right ear since two o' clock, has now turned over onto its left.

M. J. P. Nicolle, leaving his plowing, informs that on Thursday, 29 September he will offer at auction three fat pigs, eight ditto with their mother, three yearling bulls, *one ditto rising two years old,* and other items, the enumeration of which would be too long and even more amusing.

Birth:

5 August. Blanche-Laura, daughter of M. Harper Richard *Hugo.*

The anniversary dinner of the Society will take place on the said day. Those who propose to take part in the dinner and those who propose to furnish fruit for dinner are earnestly requested to send in their names on or before the preceding Saturday.

What more do you want? Eleven pigs without counting the mother, three yearling bulls without counting the one that is *rising two,* one daughter *belonging to you,* and the right to invite yourself to a dinner of the *Society* and even to provide fruit for it! If all that doesn't charm you, doesn't appeal to your guts, and entice your gluttony, it means you're a lousy man when it comes to sensibility, paternity, and sensuality! In this case, go to bed and sleep and leave me alone, all the more since *I* don't have a helpful table that gives me *subjects* ready-made, chapter by chapter! Just think that I'm my own Dante, Aesop, and Shkspeare *[sic]!*[b] As for you others, you're fishing for the dead fish that the spirits of the other world attach to your lines—procedures already known in the Mediterranean long before the invention of tittle-tattling tables. With this, I tap to you my fondest regards.

Juliette

Letter 108

Jersey, 3 January 1854
Tuesday afternoon, 4 o'clock

    I struggle with courage, patience, and good humor, my sweet beloved, with the rain, the cold, and the dark sky. I deserve to be commended for it, especially because there's sadness in the depths of my soul at your absence and a sort of vague anxiety caused by the disclosures of the table. This kind of revelation has the double inconvenience of troubling one's sense of security, without inspiring one with enough confidence to take precautions against the dangers against which one is warned.[1]
    As for myself, my Victor, I don't feel that I'm a great enough acrobat to keep my balance in this kind of tightrope walking between the worlds of fantasy and reality. If I gave myself up for long to this dizzying exercise, I would soon have muddled in my poor head Heaven and earth, God and M. Bonaparte, fairies and tarts, day and night, good and evil, love and madness. So if you'll listen to me, you'll not involve me any further in this birchwood magic, and you'll leave me to love you on this earth until I go to adore you in Heaven!

Juliette

Letter 109

Jersey, Monday evening, 28 August 1854

    I write to you at the end of the day, my dear little man, although I've been up since half past six this morning. But the mending of your overcoat took the best and finest part of the day—if that is, there *is* any fine day for me when you're not on my horizon. In any case, my dear beloved, you'll have had, I hope, very good weather where you are and consequently a good crossing and fine walk on Sark.[a] Knowing this gives me the peace of mind I need to take your absence with courage and patience. If you knew how sad my heart is as soon as you're no longer there, you'd never take it upon your conscience to leave me. I hope—for my life passes in hoping for all sorts of happinesses that never happen—I hope, I say, that you'll come back tonight. Right now in fact there's your wife, all dressed up, with Vacquerie,[b] probably going on ahead of you! I compare this splendid *uniform* with my slattern's *livery*, and the advantage is not in my favor, alas! It's true, in fact, that while I do a little bit of everybody's work, I neglect to do my own, the virtue of which doesn't do me much good, to judge by my happiness.
    Well now I'm choking with tears, which isn't going to improve my beauty much. I was wrong to start this scribbling. I should have stuck to my tasks as

darner and slut. I'm more expert at that than at the fine style, and I can keep my composure better.

My Victor, I'm absurd, ugly, sad, old, dirty, and nasty, and I love you! That's more than enough to disgust you. So I permit your disgust and ask only your permission to go and die elsewhere.

Juliette

Letter 110

Jersey, 3 March 1855
Saturday evening, half past 5:00

By the light of the moon, Toto my friend, lend me your pen so I can write you a word! My candle isn't yet lit, so I write to you by the light of my soul and without the least inconvenience, since my love has neither inside nor outside (don't add—nor head nor tail!).

Apparently you continue your criminal conversations with the beautiful lady in the other world, and you find me too materialistic (read stupid) to confide in me your Sibylline dialogues with your familiar spirit?[a] Well, you're wrong, because everything you believe in, I believe in, everything that preoccupies you, interests me, but I'm jealous of, and worry about, all that you love beyond me and the limits of your family. So you see I should have as much right to know your secrets and penetrate your mysteries as those who are simply curious and indifferent.

Ah, here you are! So much the better, I prefer that to ghosts!

Letter 111

Jersey, 10 May 1855
Thursday afternoon, half past 3:00

I've just done something so monstrous and so against nature that I must be dangerously ill and on the point of dying—which would be no pity because then I wouldn't regret the frightful act of cowardice I've just committed against myself. I have just given . . . No, it's not true . . . Yes, it's I who *am* a liar. I have just stolen one of your drawings from myself! I don't know what stops me from carrying myself off to the asylum, without the assistance of any magistrate, like the thief and the good-for-nothing that I am. Can you imagine? Of course it wasn't really me, and some hideous pickpocket slipped into my skin while I was gallivanting after your heart! I am nonetheless to blame for it, and it wouldn't take much for me to hang myself as an example to Jujus now and in the future. People certainly have been hanged who desired it less than I do now. It's frightful! It's horrible! It's disgusting! I'll never forgive myself for it! Vengeance! Vengeance! Vengeance and death! That bear Charrassin[1] must have swallowed some potion of dried toad, and the *charm* worked on me by refraction, and that's how I found myself pushed despite myself to give him... Alas! To give him, oh, la la! To give him... Ah, my God! To give him... Oh, anger is suffocating me... To give him one of your drawings!!!!!

Letter 112

Guernsey,[a] 26 January 1856
Saturday afternoon, 3 o'clock

Dear beloved, one must have one's love firmly pegged in one's soul, as I do, if one is to feel it quivering in this horrible weather of frost, rain, wind, and gray sky without concern—not to mention your absence, which is still more gloomy, chilling, and saddening than all of that. But the strength of my love is such that I feel my scrawl has wings and that my kisses fly directly from the nib of my pen onto your beautiful mouth. However, this power of illusion mustn't prevent you from coming as soon as possible, for the slimmest reality is worth more than the fattest illusion. In the meantime I find you rather irreverent toward my Greek and Latin. In any case it probably comes from an ignoble and ugly feeling of jealousy. I pity you, I pity you, yes I pity you in my soul!

But what can be done about it? My erudition is like the sun and the Republic: blind are they who see it not.

"Kiss"[b] me anyway, and ask me for some lessons and some *roots*.[c] I'll give you as many as you can consume without impoverishing myself. Until then I adore you *proh pudor!* and I kiss you *in naturalibus* from your head, *caput*, to your feet, *pede, non claudo!!!!*[1]

Letter 113

Guernsey, 23 April 1856
Wednesday afternoon, 3 o'clock

The heavens are fine today, my dear little beloved, in honor of the appearance in this world of your wonderful book.[1] For my part, I'm counting on welcoming it this evening in the form of your dear little adorable person. In the meantime I'm impatient to have my own copy, so as to read with my eyes, my lips, and my soul all this sublime poetry that I already know by heart.

I was in the process of clucking to you my admiration and anticipated joy when you arrived so opportunely to interrupt me, but my *inspiration* did not stop so abruptly, and here it is continuing while you are being groomed by

Wideon.² Dear beloved, as from today, 23 April, there arises on earth in the minds of men and in Heaven among the spirits the name *Les Contemplations*, a new date and constellation for the almanac and for astronomers present and future.

What I say is quite irrelevant, but I love you enough to make God's mouth water. I adore you.

Juliette

Letter 114

Guernsey, 3 June 1856
Tuesday morning, 11 o'clock

Dear beloved, I never tire of gazing at the famous house of Tantalus, which seems to elude my hopes as fast as I bring my mind to bear on it. Let's suppose we succeeded in overcoming the reluctance of the owner to give up a part of his house, then I would be in the false position of a woman who had solicited and, in a sense, imposed her presence in the intimacy of this Guernsey home. Hence a dependence and embarrassment every day and at every moment for me personally as well as for Suzanne's service, which is not something as insignificant as you think for tranquillity and physical well-being. In order to have the chance of seeing you furtively from the little Lukout¹ *[sic]* once or twice a day, I would have to sacrifice the chance of seeing you with complete freedom and security at any moment of the day and night throughout the entire year, not to mention having to take into account the bigoted, Methodist, and stupidly meticulous prudery of these two good burghers.

Certainly, if I could concentrate all the requirements of material existence into this little Lukout *[sic]*, how much joy I'd have in concentrating all my heart and soul there, it would be delightful!—but given the impossibility of establishing my whole life there from the cellar to the barn, from my dignity and liberty to my happiness, I think it's better to give up the idea and see if there isn't a way to make do with the little house next door² while trying to appropriate the *Attic*, as they call it, for the functions of the *Lukout [sic]*.

In any case, it's you who will make the final decision. As long as I love you and you're happy, the rest will come in time.

Juliette

Letter 115

Guernsey, 21 July 1856
Monday evening, half past 7:00

It shall not be said that your beloved name with its dazzling and sublime nimbus passed before me¹ a single time without being saluted by my heart with

La Fallue (at the far end of the lane), Saint Peter Port, Guernsey: Juliette Drouet's home from 1856 to 1864. (Photo taken by the translator).

a triple salvo of love, O my sweet beloved, and without all the perfume of my heart emanating over your divine feet! Although I'm very tired and almost ill, I won't let this day finish without giving you the most tender, smiling, happy, flowery restitus[2] that I can. Others will give you bouquets and well-turned compliments, I will give you twenty-three years of tried and true fidelity, pure of all human sully. I have only that to offer you. It is very little, and yet it is everything. It is not for sale, but it counts among God's treasures, and that is where you'll find it when the goods of Heaven replace for us those of the earth.

In the meantime, and to show you that I am still of this world, I *give* you my beautiful violet dress embroidered with gold brocade,[3] but I prefer that it be part of the arrangement of your bedroom rather than that of the gallery.[4] However, if you prefer to use it somewhere else, I leave you completely free to do what you want with it, since more than anything I wish to give you pleasure. However, don't go and think my generosity is completely disinterested, for you'd be absolutely mistaken! I hope you won't want to remain *in arrears* with me and that you'll give me a little drawing *for your feast day*. That's my one desire. Now bring your two cheeks so I can kiss them without discretion, and behave yourself free of all coquetry this evening with the ladies when they wish you a *good and happy* one, and keep your heart completely entire and intact for me.

Juliette

Letter 116

Guernsey, 28 March 1857
Saturday afternoon, 3 o'clock

Yes, *manche* from Dieppe, yes, Chinese *mouffetard*, yes, Coromandel[a] from Nanterre, yes, yes, yes! For a big collector of bric-a-brac really you surprise me![b] If that's how you mix your furnishings, I'm no longer surprised at the cries of wonder uttered by the natives of Guernsey from the four corners of the universe, indeed in fact from five. When I think that I took my self-abnegation to the point of offering to disencumber you of this counterfeit of the celestial empire and that you had the unbelievable stupidity not to accept, I'm astounded.[c] Keep your thingamajig and be happy—you deserve it, you're such a connoisseur! Mm, mm,[d] antiquarian and collector of chinoiserie of the first rank! See for yourself![1] I'm still laughing, I'll be laughing for a long time, I'll be laughing forever!

Now I leave you to dream about your flyswatters, not to say flycatchers, and I return to my embroidery. Try not to come at impossible times if you can, and love me, if you dare, after all that you've done to me and not done!

Juliette

Letter 117

Guernsey, 14 April 1857
Tuesday afternoon, 3 o'clock

I scribble out my heart to you with a pen that isn't a pen, with ink that's water, and with paper that's merely a scrap. But all that won't prevent my love from frolicking with tender caresses, my joy from beaming, and my happiness from bursting forth. For I love you, for you have showered me with marvels,[1] for I'm happy to the very marrow of my bones. Now I can't wait to see all your masterpieces in place.

As for the house, it'll come when it wants and all the quicker if we don't wait for it to make our happiness. In fact, true richness is in love and not in bricks that only more or less belong to us.

There you are, my dear beloved! I'm not such an ass as to be working on style *down here* when I can be covering you with kisses *up there*. So I'm coming upstairs as fast as my legs can carry me and faster.

Juliette

Letter 118

Guernsey, 16 May 1857
Saturday evening, half past 7:00

I still don't know from what angle to handle my heart, my poor beloved, so bruised it is on all sides by my own blows. However, I need to extract a bit of what it contains, even if I hurt it by touching it with the tip of my pen.

I love you, my Victor, with all the modesty and chastity of a virgin. I love you as though death had already purified and consecrated my soul. I love you as the angels love God. I love you in every sense of this word in Heaven and on earth. So when your suspicions profane this love so sacred and so sublime, my whole being revolts as though at the most odious impiety. Confronted with this jealousy that has no excuse or foundation, my soul takes fright as though pursued by some evil bird of prey. Hence all these flapping wings of despair that surprise you more than they touch you. Hence all this tiredness and discouragement with life that seems exaggerated to you because you cannot understand how much I suffer.

Letter 119

Guernsey, 28 August 1857
Friday afternoon, half past 2:00

My heart runs after you, my adored beloved, even at the risk of getting out of breath on the way. If you see on your path a sweet bird looking at you, it's my heart; a butterfly dallying in the bushes with the little flowers, it's my heart; a cloud following you, it's my heart! If you smell a perfume that attracts you, it's my heart; a zephyr that caresses you, it's my heart; a ray that blesses you, it's my heart! It's my heart, it's my heart—always, everywhere, and in everything that can please your eyes, gladden your soul, and transport your being into the regions of happiness!

My sweet beloved, I don't expect you before the end of the evening. It's a very long time, but I won't complain if you use your time to be very happy and to love me a little. As for myself, I don't know how I could help thinking only of you, living only for you, being happy only through you, and loving only you with all my strength and all my soul.

Juliette

Letter 120

Guernsey, 23 April 1858
Friday afternoon, quarter to 5:00

I've just finished copying what I had of Charles' manuscript,[1] my dear little man, feeling ashamed of my clumsiness and sorry not to have copied the rest, not only to be obliging to your Charles, but also to know the end of this charming little novel that begins so well.

In the meantime I inform you that I'm entirely at your disposition, on horse or donkey, on foot, paw, wing, soul, or heart. If, at this very moment, it pleased you to climb the mountain,[a] I'd follow you joyfully. Unfortunately, you're not expected, nor is it likely you'll be back before six o'clock. Ah! There is Chougna's[2] barking, but it's getting more distant and disappearing in the direction of town, which doesn't encourage me to hope to see you immediately. Concerning *immediately*, you really should give me some of your own copying, so that I can get ahead with *my work* while the days are long and you are busy with other things. That way, by the time that Hetzel[b] is working at full throttle to publish *Les Petites Epopées*,[3] I'll have reached the end *with ease* and without too much loss of breath. Ah! There you are! What happiness! What happiness! What happiness!

I'll finish distilling my restitus while you read your newspapers. Listen, I love you, and I'm very happy about it! You've caught me![d]

Juliette

Letter 121

Guernsey, 16 July 1858
Friday morning, 11 o'clock

My beloved, my beloved, my beloved, what have we done to God that He would strike us so cruelly in your health[1] and in our love? Unless it's a crime to love you too much, I don't feel seriously guilty of anything. What am I to do, my God, what is to become of me with you sick and far from me? I fear as I write this that you hear my sobs and feel my despair in the cry of my pen and the form of my words.

I expected what is happening, I believed I was prepared for it, I feel it is necessary—imperatively so—that you stay at home, and yet my whole being rebels against this separation as against the greatest injustice from God, as against the greatest unhappiness of my life. Why? Why? Why am I like this, O God? However, I have courage, God, You know that? You know also whether I desire his prompt recovery and whether I love with a devoted and limitless love my beloved Victor? Why then this deep black despair that robs me of my strength and reason all at once? O God, do You hate me, have I, more than other creatures of my kind, offended You, that You punish me so pitilessly? Oh, how I suffer, oh how how *[sic]* I love you, my Victor, oh how unhappy I am!

Letter 122

Guernsey, 2 October 1858
Saturday morning, 8 o'clock

Good morning, my ineffable beloved; good morning, my sublime, divine, and long-suffering one, good morning! I smile upon you, I bless you, I adore you. Don't be sad, my beloved, for yesterday's incident was more a misspoken word than an unjust thought.[1] It's impossible that your children don't feel right into the very marrow of their bones the superhuman kindness of your heart toward them, just as much as they benefit from your ardent and unceasing devotion toward all their needs and pleasures. What saddened you yesterday was no more than the typical behavior of a spoiled child who assumes an air of impartiality toward his elders. I understand their hearts by understanding my own, and I therefore feel it's impossible that they don't admire you and adore you just as much for your kindness as for your genius. So I don't hesitate to act as guarantor for their love and gratitude, convinced as I am of their feelings of filial piety and of their adoration for you. My Victor, my beloved, my good, my honor, my joy, my virtue, my happiness, my faith, my God, I bless you!

I hope that yesterday's little unhappiness won't have prevented you from having a good night, my poor little man? You would be surpassingly good if you came and told me so this morning, as soon as you can. In the meantime I've been struggling since yesterday with stomach pains and an unending ferocious headache. But I love you, that's my panacea.

Letter 123

Guernsey, 31 December 1858
Friday evening, quarter to 10:00

Dear beloved,[1] I'll do for you what Muhammad did for the mountain. In my thoughts and with the help of my soul I'll go to your feet and kiss them. Enjoy yourself, my beloved, be happy in the midst of the joy of your whole family; benefit from this sweet and delightful relaxation of the body and mind between the last lap of this year that's finishing and the first lap of the one that's beginning! Don't refuse yourself any of the little happinesses that will come this evening to put a smile on your lips and fill your hands with promises and hope!

For my part, my beloved, on my knees in front of your portrait, and under the calm and steady gaze of my poor dear angel,[a] I'll listen tenderly to the twenty-five anniversaries of our love singing in the depths of my heart, and then I'll try to go to sleep, praying for you.

Good night, my beloved, be happy as much as I love you, and may everything that you desire in this world and the next be given to you!

Letter 124

Guernsey, 21 May 1859
Saturday morning, 8 o'clock

Good morning, my dear beloved; good morning, after, I hope, a good restorative night without headache or boo-boo of any kind! Good morning, I love you!

It should soon be time for the sun to warm up a bit and permit us to go to Sark,[1] for if it continues to rain as it has done for the last two or three months, I can't see our vacation being possible. Besides, I dread the moment as much as I desire it, and I feel very apprehensive about my imminent meeting with your good Charlot.[2]

If I were not the poor woman that I am, I would have sought out the opportunity to share the company of this brilliant young man,[3] but, as it is, I fear coming into contact with him. Alas! Whatever the kindness of his heart and indulgence of his mind might be, I feel I have everything to lose and nothing to gain from the involuntary comparison he cannot fail to make. However, my beloved, I don't want my misgivings to deprive you of the pleasure of being with your son in the happy circumstances that present themselves to the two of you. I will go, cost what it might to my self-esteem, and no matter what might come of this meeting that I did not solicit. I'll love you forever and wherever with all my soul.

Letter 125

Guernsey, 25 May 1859
Wednesday morning, half past 7:00

Good morning, my dear beloved, good morning, my all-beloved, good morning! How are you this morning, my good little man? Your head is better? Are you gayer and happier than you seemed to be last night? *That is this question [sic]* to which you'll reply if you find it appropriate, since for three or four days now you've been full of frowns, without my knowing why.

In the meantime I'm still very worried about my meeting with your son, which is daily losing its spontaneity and simplicity[1] thanks to the officious, tactless, and indiscreet gossip of fat and pompous Guesnard. This event, which in itself is so natural, is becoming as embarrassing and troubling in the midst of the promiscuity and publicity it's receiving from more or less malicious gossip, as it could be charming and sweet in the shade of intimacy and anonymity.

Certainly, none of this adds to the pleasure we've been promising ourselves from this little vacation together, and I feel it could intimidate and embarrass me greatly. However, since the cork has been drawn on the trip to Sark, I'll drink it to your health and to that of your good Charlot, who, like you, like me, like us, cannot do anything about it. And I'll love you with all my soul, there, here, elsewhere, and everywhere!

Letter 126

Guernsey, 23 June 1859
Thursday morning, half past 7:00

Good morning, my dear beloved, good morning, my adorable little man, I love you! I don't always have the time to scribble it to you every day, but I have loved you without pause from one end of my life to the other.

I'm thinking about our little evening together, and I wish that it was already over because I find meeting new people so upsetting, not to mention the emotion I'll feel at being in the company of your son Victor,[a] whom I only glimpsed on the quay that day at Sark. All that troubles me a little in the midst of my happiness at being with you, but I know one cannot always choose one's time, one's society, and one's pleasure. So I'll try to be as happy as possible tonight, despite all the intimidation caused by my stupidity.

I hope, my dear beloved, soon to need to give *back* to you the famous cross I have already had the pleasure of giving you for your dear daughter Mlle

Dédé, for no doubt one of these days she will want to choose a husband.[b] So I consider myself only a very provisional depository for it until it should please this beauty to make someone happy. I hope it will be soon, for her own happiness and for that of her whole family.

My beloved, I kiss you with all my soul.

Letter 127

Guernsey, 17 August 1859
Wednesday morning, half past 6:00

Good morning, my dear beloved, good morning, and may all my life be devoted to blessing you and loving you as I have loved you and blessed you until now!

I thank you for your little table,[1] which nearly caused me much sorrow. I'm certainly not one to disdain the least thing coming from you, and I give you the proof of this every day by religiously collecting and treasuring even the smallest piece of paper on which you've left a word, most often illegible.

It's just that when I saw your table, I said that it didn't seem sufficiently smart for my room, which was quite aside from the feeling that makes it a thousand times more precious to me than the most splendid table in the world. This *misteck [sic]*[a] being now explained, I'm keeping *my* table, not only with love because of its inscription, but also with the *pious respect* due to a pretty ornament. Thank-you, my dear beloved, but another time don't be so quick to get angry, because you run the risk of being unjust toward me and of hurting me a lot!

On another topic, I regret the sudden disappearance of your Charles from our little circle. I had counted on keeping him until the arrival of these ladies, but God and his aunt[b] had decided otherwise. Let their will be done, although not without resentment on my part. If you have the opportunity to convey this to him and to tell him how much I love him, I'd be much obliged.

As for you, my beloved, I adore you!

Letter 128

Guernsey, 19 August 1859
Friday morning, quarter past 7:00

Good morning, my dear beloved, good morning! With the fullness of my heart and with all the admiration and adoration of my soul, I wish you good morning! I don't know whether you had a good night, but personally

I found it impossible to sleep. I don't credit the amnesty[1] with being the cause of this insomnia, although it was certainly something to do with it because of the possible sad changes it could bring to your family circle. And yet when I reflect well on it, it seems to me that there is little to fear, so complete and unalterable are the attachment and devotion of your family. As far as you are concerned anyway, M. Bonaparte will have wasted his time and money on *clemency,* and we'll have the pleasure of spitting on it in passing. As for the exiles who consent to return to France by this back door under the pretext of *ease and convenience,* great good may it do them, but I don't envy them.

Aside from the fact that my love prevents me from living anywhere except where you are, I feel I have a basis of honesty, pride, and virtue in my soul that wouldn't permit me to remain in the same atmosphere as this vile scoundrel. In any case, my dear beloved, I can't even claim the virtue of resignation by staying in exile with you, since *you* are *all* for me.

Juliette

Letter 129

Guernsey, 5 September 1859
Monday morning, half past 7:00

Good morning, my poor beloved, good morning, my blessed love, good morning, and may God be with you in your sorrows and joys!

Poor beloved, you regained a little serenity[1] yesterday only amid the gaiety of your two excellent sons. It's true that it's impossible for you not to feel happy and proud when you look at your two adorable children. If you had seen with what eyes of envy and love they looked at your first grammar,[2] you would have been touched and moved. As for myself, I felt compelled to give it *back* to them immediately, despite my ardent desire not to relinquish voluntarily and before my death all these precious and glorious relics. They refused to profit from an act of generosity that would have cost me eternal regret, and they left it with me with a grace and deference that I'll never forget. I hope that one day I'll be able to prove to them that their trust in me was not misplaced.

On another topic, my sweet, my dear, my revered beloved, the matter of Mlle Allix[3] is settled. It remains for me to find an excuse to explain to my Bretons[a] this change of program, as the *music* especially seemed to entice them greatly. Thus far I don't pity them, since before their departure arranged for this coming Thursday, they can expect to dine with you once or twice more, an honor and a happiness I would envy if I did not share it.

I have not yet thanked you for your beautiful present. That will be for another restitus. Until then, I love you.

Letter 130

Guernsey, 4 October 1859
Tuesday morning, 8 o'clock

Good morning, my dear beloved, good morning, my ray of light, good morning, my joy, good morning, my happiness! I hope you slept well and were not tormented by thirst. It's once again summerlike weather this morning, which tempts one to go rambling through the countryside even when one doesn't have the legs for it, like me. I wonder why I am always so achy? In any case it isn't worth worrying about, since apart from being slower, I'm very well, the proof of which is that I'm already very hungry and that I'd like to devour you forthwith. And as one has an appetite even when one doesn't eat,[a] I'd like to have just a mouthful of your *Légende des siècles* that I have the humiliation of not knowing entirely before its publication.[1] It's the first time since I've been working for you that I must regret the loss of my privileged role as *unique* copyist of your masterpieces. That will teach me to persist in living so long, since I'm no longer good for anything except loving you! However, given that I'm still alive and that I can still draw some scrawl from my pen, I beg you to hurry to give me some copying work—as much and as soon as possible—because you have some and you promised it to me. Dear beloved, I jest to make you see that I love you, that I'm happy, and that I adore you!

Notes

Letter 78

1. On 5 April 1850 Hugo had given a speech at the Assemblée législative **(which succeeded the Assemblée constituante—see above, L. 70, n. 1 [T])** on deportation, a penalty that was described as "the dry guillotine." The reaction on the right of the Assembly was extremely violent (see *OC*, 7:267–80).

Letter 79

1. A revival of *Ruy Blas*. **See above, L. 28, n. 1; 31 and n. 1; 34 and n. 1.**

a. See above, L. 43 and n. a [T].

b. **Don César de Bazan, one of the characters in *Ruy Blas*, is a courtier at the royal Spanish court [T].**

2. An old theater in the boulevard du Temple. **Nigaudème might be a misspelling of the character Nicodème in the fairy play *Nicodème dans la lune*, described by Marian Hannah Winter, *The Theatre of Marvels*, trans. Charles Meldon (New York: Benjamin Blom, 1962), 78, as a "goodhearted simpleton" and as a stock character along the same lines as "characters**

such as Harlequin, Pierrot, Columbine and Pantaloon inherited from Italian Comedy." The Théâtre des Funambules and the Petit-Lazary are described by McCormick, *Popular Theatres*, 34, as two of the three theaters in early nineteenth-century Paris that "remained closest to their fairground origins, and were the lowest in the social hierarchy of the boulevard theatres" [T].

c. Frédérick Lemaître had played the title role in *Ruy Blas* at its opening in 1838—see above, L. 31, n. 1; 34, n. 1 [T].

Letter 80

1. The anniversary of the Mardi Gras of 1833 and not of the precise date.

2. The sculptor Victor Vilain (cf. above, L. 66 and n.1).

a. See above, L. 43 and n. a [T].

b. This expression, "je reste sur le chemin à voir tourner les ombres sur mes pieds," is an evocation of a poem by Hugo (*Les Chants du crépuscule*, XXVII), "La pauvre fleur disait au papillon céleste..." ("The poor flower said to the heavenly butterfly..."), in which a flower laments that the butterfly it loves flies away while the flower must remain rooted to the ground: "Et moi je reste seule à voir tourner mon ombre / A mes pieds" ("And I remain alone, watching my shadow turn at my feet"). This "quote" from Hugo's poem was a favorite one with Drouet to express her sense of isolation and abandonment—cf. also her letters of 10 February 1841 and 22 January 1843, cited by Souchon, *Servitude amoureuse*, 86, 304, respectively [T]. Hugo had given the manuscript of the poem to her (see Pierre Albouy, ed., *Oeuvres poétiques de Victor Hugo*, 2 vols. [Paris: Editions Gallimard, 1964], 1:1450).

Letter 81

a. Blewer (*LVH*, 140, n. 1) notes that "a military review had taken place at the Champ de Mars on 27 June: an opportunity for Bonaparte and his partisans to associate themselves with the army, and an opportunity for the republicans to denounce the political display of 'Caesar'" [T].

b. For the private joke involved in "the rest" see below, L. 103 and n. b [T].

1. Some strawberries sent by Juliette's sister had arrived the previous afternoon (cf. Maison de Victor Hugo α 8572).

Letter 82

a. It was on this day (see also, below, L. 83 n. 1) that Drouet would receive from Léonie Biard a bundle of love letters written by Hugo to Biard, his mistress of the last seven years (see above, Introduction, pp. 18–19), and Drouet's view of her relationship with Hugo would be changed forever. By the end of the day she would be writing a letter very different in tone and with far more serious matters than strawberries in mind (*MUL*, 391) [T].

Letter 83

1. On 28 June Juliette had received a package of love letters from Léonie Biard sent to the latter by Victor Hugo. Juliette, who knew nothing about this seven-year relationship, was devastated. She yielded, however, to Hugo's pleas not to leave him (cf. *MUL*, 391 and 392—two letters that have been lost). It was then that the period of "trials" started, where each tried to convince the other of the sincerity of his and her respective love.

Letter 86

1. Cf. above, L. 83, n.1.

a. The word for "today," "aujourd'hui," is left unfinished as "aujo" [T].

Letter 88

1. Juliette, as we know, had religious faith. This letter in the form of a prayer is a reminder of her education with the Benedictines.

Letter 89

1. That is to say, her rival, Mme Biard.

Letter 90

1. The announced "trials" seemed to Juliette to be turning to her advantage. Hugo had convinced her of it. But an illness of Mme Biard's seems once again to throw everything into question.

Letter 93

a. Blewer (*LVH*, 153 and n. 1) reads "Cabarus," and notes that a certain Cabarrus [sic] was a specialist in disorders of the larynx [T].

1. The wish, expressed by Juliette in the preceding letter, to give her life for Victor Hugo, and the sensed imminence of the coup of 2 December, allow us to see Juliette's future heroism emerging and Hugo's debt to her that, for the rest of his life, he will acknowledge having contracted at this time.

Letter 94

1. After some vain attempts to organize the republican resistance to the coup of 2 December, Victor Hugo had left Paris on the evening of the eleventh for Brussels. Juliette Drouet followed him there with his manuscripts two days later (*LJD*, 194), and Mme Hugo arrived the following week. **The coup d'état of 2 December 1851 was Charles-Louis-Napoléon Bonaparte's seizure of absolute power, by which he abolished the Assemblée legislative and had himself proclaimed emperor**

(Napoleon III) on 2 December of the following year. His Second Empire lasted until his defeat in the Franco-Prussian war (1870) [T].

Letter 95

1. There is an error in the date. It was Sunday, 21 December 1851.

2. A letter from Hugo to his wife, dated 24 January, gives some measure of the limits of the relationship:

> The person of whom [you speak] is indeed here; she has saved my life, you will understand that in due course. Without her I would have been taken and lost at the height of the unrest. Her devotion is absolute, complete, of twenty years duration, and has never failed. Furthermore, profound abnegation and resignation toward everything. Without this person, I tell you as I would to God, I would be dead or deported by now.—She is here in complete solitude. *Never goes out.* Under an assumed name. I see her only after nightfall. All the rest of my life is public. (*OC*, 8:970)

Letter 96

1. These lines are written on the same sheet of paper as the letter of the twenty-eighth. See the letter of the thirty-first from Hugo, *LJD*, 197. **In this letter Hugo expresses his gratitude to Drouet for what she has done for him in the past year: "Be happy remembering that you have been a good, brave, and generous woman, that if I live it is because of you, that if I am happy, even here, it is because of you, that you have devoted yourself to me, and that I kiss your feet and love you!" [T].**

Letter 97

a. Hugo compared Napoleon III to "a sleeping parrot" (*VH*, 280) [T].

1. Esther Guimont, a self-styled "courtesan," had known Hugo at least since September 1848. She had been the mistress of Emile de Girardin **(1806–1881, journalist and husband of Delphine, see below, Letter 106, n. 1 [T])**. She died, according to a note of Hugo's, in December 1861. (See Escholier, *Amant de génie*, and the note by Journet and Robert, *Journal*, 142.) **On Mme Wilmen, a former actress, see *VS*, 4:40ff. [T].**

Letter 99

1. A dating error. It was Sunday, 29 February 1852.

2. Juliette would not make the acquaintance of Charles until 1859 on the occasion of a visit to Sark (see below, L. 124, 125).

Letter 100

1. The representative for the Basses-Alpes at the Assemblée législative. He had protested against the coup and had taken refuge in Brussels. **Blewer (*LVH*, 164, n. 1) adds that Melchior Yvan (1806–1873) was a doctor [T].**

Letter 101

   a. Hugo made himself an embarrassment to the Belgian government with his publication of *Napoléon le petit* (see Glossary), criticizing Napoleon III and comparing him unfavorably with his uncle, Napoleon I, and he was obliged to find himself another place of exile. He chose to go next to the isle of Jersey, one of the Channel Islands and a British possession. He and Drouet would arrive in Jersey on 5 August 1852 [T].

   b. Drouet refers here to Léonie Biard, Hugo's former lover—see above, L. 82, n. a [T].

Letter 102

   a. For an account of the events of December 1851, in general, and of 3 December, in particular, and of Hugo's part in them, see *VH*, 296–306 [T].

Letter 103

   a. This is Drouet's joking reference to the excuse she heard so often when she reached the island of Jersey—see *VHJD*, 1:183 [T].

   1. Doubtless the reference here is to Sandor-Alexandre Teleki (1821–1892), the Hungarian politician exiled in Jersey. Blewer (*LVH*, 168, n. 1) adds that, according to the journal of Adèle Hugo, he was a guest at Hugo's house every Tuesday night (*Le Journal d'Adèle Hugo*, ed. Frances Vernor Guille, 3 vols. [Paris: Minard, 1968–1984], 3:111, entry for 8 February 1854). Lucullus was a first-century B.C. Roman renowned not only for his military prowess but also for his lavish lifestyle, including extravagant meals. Drouet also comments in her letter of 7 March 1853 (*LVH*, 177) on Teleki's "gastronomical inventions" [T].

   b. Blewer (*LVH*, 168, n. 3) notes that this remark relates to the fact that Hugo had persuaded his son François-Victor to send away his mistress, the actress Anaïs Liévenne, who had accompanied him to Jersey a week before. Blewer remarks further that "le reste" ("the rest") is a favorite expression of Drouet's and is an allusion to a fable (*Fables* IX, 2) by La Fontaine: "Mon frère a-t-il tout ce qu'il veut, / Bon soupé, bon gîte, et le reste?" ("Does my brother have everything he wants: good food, good quarters, and the rest?") [T].

   c. Hugo had complimented Drouet on her beautiful hands—see *MUL*, 67. There is a photograph of the cast of Drouet's right hand in *VHJD*, 367. Of course the joke here is probably also that Drouet "has her hands on Hugo" and that she will use them to fight off any competition [T].

Letter 104

   a. Cf. Drouet's letter of 15 July 1853 (*LVH*, 186) in which she comments on Hugo's hats as being "like something out of comic opera." "Norman," that is, from Normandy, since Normans were proverbially renowned for their craftiness—Littré, s.v. "Norman" (2) [T].

Letter 106

    1. The séances of table turning, brought to Jersey by Mme de Girardin, had started on 11 September. Hugo would be much absorbed by them. **Delphine de Girardin (1804–1855), daughter of Sophie Gay (1776–1852), a novelist, was a poet, journalist, novelist, and playwright. In table turning the participants, who sat around a table, received (as they believed) the communications of spirits of the dead through (in the method used in Hugo's séances) the tapping of the table legs on the floor, the taps signifying different letters, which were transcribed and interpreted [T].**

    a. The French word, "tablatures," may be intended to be a pun on the word "tables" [T].

Letter 107

    a. The French word, "farce-*ie*," meaning "stuffed to the point of satiety," has been written in such a way that it draws attention to the word "farce" (as "farce" in English) that it contains within it. There is no way to translate the word and preserve the play on words [T].

    b. Drouet alludes to the fact that Hugo believed great figures of the past spoke to him through the table and dictated poetry and prose to him. On Shakespeare as a visitor to the turning table, see *VH*, 337 [T].

Letter 108

    1. Juliette knew perhaps that on 1 January the table had let it be known that their friend Meurice was in danger of being ambushed in Paris (see *OC*, 9:1273). **On Paul Meurice, see Glossary [T].**

Letter 109

    a. Sark is a tiny (two square miles), precipitous island with beautiful walks, approximately eight miles east of Guernsey [T].

    b. On Auguste Vacquerie, see Vacquerie family, Glossary [T].

Letter 110

    a. "Criminal conversation" was also a technical legal term used to signify adultery and had been used (unknown to Drouet) in the charge against Hugo and Biard in 1845, of which Drouet seems never to have been apprised (*VH*, 253). Blewer (*LVH*, 229, n. 1) notes that "the beautiful lady in the other world" must be the "White Lady" who spoke via the turning table on 1 March as recorded in *OC*, 9:1456–8 [T].

Letter 111

    1. "The representative Charrassin, economist, agronomist, scholar, was at the same time an intrepid man" (*Histoire d'un crime*, III, 2 in *OC*, 8:154).

Letter 112

a. Drouet, Hugo, and his son François-Victor left Jersey for Guernsey, another of the Channel Islands, on the same boat on 31 October 1855. Drouet stayed for the first month at the Crown Hotel, on the quay at Saint Peter Port, and then moved later to lodge at a house at 8 rue de Havelet, around the corner from Hugo, who rented a large house for his family at 20 Hauteville Street (after spending the first few days at the Hôtel de l'Europe, also on the quay). Hugo had been expelled from Jersey after his presence there had become embarrassing to the authorities. Hugo had expressed his support for the *Lettre à la Reine d'Angleterre* (*Letter to the Queen of England*), published originally by French exiles in London and then reprinted in the exiles' newspaper in Jersey, *L'Homme*, in which it was alleged that Queen Victoria was in cahoots with Napoleon III—*VH*, 345ff. [T].

b. See above, Letter 35 and n. a [T].

c. Presumably a pun on "roots," as in vegetables, and "roots" as used with reference to the Latin language [T].

1. Oh shame! . . . all naked . . . the head . . . with a foot that doesn't limp. The expression *"pede non claudo"* is a favorite one of Drouet's that she uses also in letters to her sister and brother-in-law (*LF*, 97, 365). Hugo himself also uses it—see Journet and Robert, *Journal*, 41, 124 and *Claude Gueux, OC*, 5:249 (*"pede claudo"*). It is an allusion to one of Horace's *Odes:* "Raro antecedentem scelestum / Deseruit pede Poena claudo" (3, 2. 31–2), "Rarely does Vengeance, albeit of halting gait, fail to o'ertake the guilty, though he gain the start" (as translated by C. E. Bennett, *Horace: The Odes and Epodes* [London: William Heinemann, 1918]). Here the expression seems to be used mainly as playful evidence of some knowledge of Latin [T].

Letter 113

1. *Les Contemplations* (a collection of poetry by Hugo, on which see Glossary [T]) was published on this day by Hetzel and Michel Lévy.

2. Probably Wheadon, whom Hugo calls in his notebooks "my first barber at Guernsey" (5 March 1857, in *OC*, 10:1401). But there is no expense recorded in Hugo's accounts for this date.

Letter 114

1. What is now called the "lookout" is a glass extension that was not constructed until 1861. When Hugo moved to Hauteville House he gave this name to his bedroom, also on the third floor. The house had been bought on 16 May 1856, but Hugo did not move there until November. **However, in this letter Drouet seems to be talking about two "lookouts"—the one in Hugo's house and the one that she proposes to create for herself, either in the house in question into which she is reluctant to move, or in the one next door, from either of which she would be able to see Hugo in his own lookout. Evidence that the couple used the word**

"lookout" for Drouet's attic window at La Fallue (see below, n. 2) is provided by a letter from Drouet to Hugo dated 2 July 1856 (*LF*, 51, n. 1) in which she anticipates moving into the house at La Fallue and being able to see him in his lookout from her "lookout:" "I have my lucoot [sic] because of you, my ineffably good little man. I'll be able to see you at almost every moment of the day. Oh! How I'll watch you day and night, and how I'll throw my soul across the roofs and my kisses from lucoot to lucoot [sic]" [T].

2. Perhaps La Fallue, where Juliette lived between November 1856 and June 1864.

Letter 115

1. It is Saint Victor's day.

2. It is not known at what date Juliette began to use this word to refer to her letters. Blewer (*LVH*, 169, n. 1) speculates that the word was invented to describe her letters because in them Drouet pays back (French, "restituer") Hugo the affection she owes him [T].

3. This is the dress that Juliette wore in *Lucrèce Borgia*. It is now part of the collection of the Maison de Victor Hugo in Paris. It was as a result of her part in *Lucrèce Borgia*, a play by Hugo (on which, see Glossary), that Drouet met Hugo in 1833—see above, Introduction, pp. 9–10 [T].

4. The arrangement and decoration of Hauteville House was a lengthy process. Hugo devoted much time and energy to it. The "Gallery" (which would come to be called the "Oak Gallery") is on the second floor.

Letter 116

a. "Manche" and "mouffetard" evidently refer to some type of bric-a-brac that Hugo has acquired for his house, but I have not been able to identify them. "Coromandel" is incised and painted black lacquer, sometimes embellished with semiprecious stone and often made into folding screens (which were often later cut up and used as decorative panels for other furniture). They originated in China in the seventeenth century, but received the name "Coromandel" from India's coast, being shipped to Europe by merchants of the English and French East India companies [T].

b. As Blewer (*LVH*, 253, n. 1) notes, this is a parody of the line delivered to Don Salluste by Ruy Blas in Hugo's play *Ruy Blas* (V, 3) where Ruy Blas says, "Pour un homme d'esprit, vraiment, vous m'étonnez" ("For an intelligent man, really you surprise me"). It was a line to which Drouet jokingly alluded more than once in her correspondence with Hugo [T].

c. In the French ("j'en tombe de mon haut, et même de mon niveau d'eau") there is a play on the similar sounds of "astounded" ("j'en tombe de mon haut"—"mon haut" sounds like "mon eau," "my water") and the word "water level" ("niveau d'eau"). The pun cannot be rendered into English and does not affect the meaning of the letter [T].

d. See above, L. 43, n. a [T].

1. A large drawing takes up this page of the letter: a man is showing a fan to a woman who is laughing with her hands on her hips. Hugo greatly relished "chinoiserie," of which there is an abundance at Hauteville House.

Letter 117

1. Probably some drawings.

Letter 120

1. Does this refer to *La Bohême dorée*, to *La Chaise de paille*, to *Crapouillet* (all published in 1859), or to yet something else? The exact order in which Charles Hugo wrote these works is, according to Bernard Leuilliot, impossible to determine with certainty.

a. It is noted at *CL*, 33 that the "mountain," as Drouet called it, was to be found in the west of the parish of Saint-Martin in Guernsey [T].

2. Victor Hugo's dog, whose last illness and death would so sadden her master. Cf. *MUL*, 567, and Hugo's diary, *OC*, 12:1374.

b. On Hetzel, Hugo's publisher, see below, L. 138 and n. 2 [T].

3. Original title of *La Légende des siècles* **(a collection of poetry by Hugo, on which, see Glossary [T])**. When Hugo decided in favor of the definitive title of the collection in April 1859, he would retain *Les Petites Epopées* as a subtitle to the "first series" of the collection.

d. Blewer (*LVH*, 257) reads "attrapée" rather than "attrape." I adopt that reading here [T].

Letter 121

1. Hugo is sick with anthrax in the back and with swollen legs. His last lines, before this serious illness immobilizes him for several weeks, are to Juliette—see *LJD*, 219.

Letter 122

1. The solitary life that Victor Hugo had chosen was less appealing to his wife and children, who, beginning this year, had sought breaks in their exile: the mother and daughter by a stay in Paris, François-Victor by a trip to London. It is the eldest, Charles, who seems to have been most strongly opposed to paternal authority, but François-Victor also would soon speak of a "gentle tyrant." Cf. the entries made by Hugo on the dates of 3 October and 22 December 1858 in *OC*, 10:1456, 1462.

Letter 123

1. See the note from Hugo on the same evening, *LJD*, 220. **In his letter Hugo says in part: "[My letter] will arrive tomorrow . . . and it will tell you that I**

have never loved you more, that you are the necessity of my life, that you are for me a being who is still young, still charming, still adored, my woman and my angel; that life on earth with you forms the foundation of my heart; that life in Heaven with you forms the foundation of my soul" [T].

a. A reference to Drouet's daughter, Claire, who had died in 1846 [T].

Letter 124

1. They will leave in five days for a two-week stay, accompanied by Charles Hugo.

2. See Victor Hugo's reply—*LJD*, 222.

3. This first meeting will have been preceded by reading. On 12 April 1859 Juliette wrote to Hugo: "I continue to have a passion for the novels of *Monsieur Charles*, which isn't as unremarkable as one might imagine given that you have made my taste very difficult to satisfy. So far this *little* novel is a dazzling piece of literary craftsmanship and a masterpiece of grace, gaiety, and tenderness" (Bibliothèque nationale de France, Cabinet des manuscrits, nouvelles acquisitions françaises, 16.380, f°96). The reference is to *Le Cochon de Saint Antoine*.

Letter 125

1. Juliette will not see Charles until the next day, the twenty-sixth. Obviously the letter that Victor Hugo had written to her on 22 May (*LJD*, 222) had not reassured Juliette. The trip to Sark was a complete success.

Letter 126

a. This will be the first time Drouet will have met François-Victor since the beginning of her relationship with Hugo in 1833 [T].

b. Dédé is the nickname of Adèle, Hugo's daughter, who would in fact never marry but would run away from home in 1863 in pursuit of a British officer and end her days in a mental institution—see above, Introduction, p. 22, and below, L. 148 and n. 1 [T].

Letter 127

1. The day before Hugo had noted in his diary: "I gave to J.J. the oak table with spiral legs from my lookout with this inscription: 'I give to Mme J.D. this table on which I wrote *La Légende des siècles*. V.H., Guernsey, 16 August 1859.' J.J. sent me by way of thanks her little table on wheels with the lacquer top and one of the two leather chairs from Brussels. I have put them in the lookout" (*OC*, 10:1488). **The table Hugo gave is now in the Maison de Victor Hugo in Paris. A photograph of it may be seen in Prévost, *L'Homme océan*, 240, # 202, "Table de *La Légende des siècles*"** [T].

a. This is Drouet's spelling of the English word "mistake" [T].

b. On Charles' aunt, Julie Chenay (sister of Mme Hugo), see Glossary. Blewer (*LVH*, 264, n. 3) notes that she had arrived in Guernsey on the previous day [T].

Letter 128

    1. On 16 August *Le Moniteur* published the announcement of an amnesty to political exiles. Hugo learned about it on the eighteenth and in his *Déclaration* of this day he rejected it categorically: "When liberty returns, I will return."

Letter 129

    1. The appearance of fragments of *La Légende des siècles* in the *Revue des deux mondes* of 1 September had surprised and displeased the poet, who was still in the process of correcting the proofs of the work. **On *La Légende des siècles*, see above, L. 120 and n. 3 [T].**

    2. On 22 June 1835 Victor Hugo dedicated the Latin grammar from his school days to Juliette: "Here is one of the first books I read: the last book I shall read will be your heart."

    3. Augustine Allix, daughter of a family of French exiles, often participated in the little festivities of the exiles in Guernsey, which she enlivened with her musical contributions. In a letter of 1855 Juliette describes her as "a pleasant guest with a good appetite and good humor who does honor to the food and the merriment without fuss and in the most agreeable way in the world" (*LVH*, 223).

    a. For the "Bretons," see Koch family, Glossary. According to Hugo's diary, Renée and Louis Koch, Drouet's sister and brother-in-law, arrived on 20 August and left on 9 September, apparently one day later than the "Thursday" projected as the day of departure in this letter. See *LF*, 63 and n. 1 [T].

Letter 130

    a. The French, "l'appétit vient même en ne mangeant pas," is a playful reversal of the usual saying, "l'appétit vient en mangeant"—"the appetite comes with eating," or "the more one eats the more one wants" [T].

    1. *La Légende des siècles* was published on 26 September 1859 by Michel Lévy and Hetzel. Once before Juliette had shared the copying—with Léopoldine, at the time of the publication of *Le Rhin*.

1860s

Letter 131

Guernsey, 25 April 1860
Friday morning, 8 o'clock

Good morning, my all-beloved, good morning! My soul greets you in the name of God and of our love.

Did you sleep well, my dear little man? Your little *Cosette* didn't make too much noise in your head during the night?[1] I didn't actually dream about her, but I think about her all the time with thrills of tenderness and joy, as though waiting for a real little girl from whom we've been unwillingly separated for twelve years. I'm eager to see the little girl again and to learn the fate of her *beautiful doll*. I'm impatient to know whether this monster *Javert* has lost trace of the poor sublime rascal *Monsieur le Maire* and to know whether the poor dwelling on the boulevard Mont-Parnasse has been illuminated by a ray of well-being and happiness since I left it.[a] In short, my poor beloved, I long to renew my acquaintance with all these creations of your genius, whose sadnesses make me suffer and cry more than my own and whose joys are my celebrations and my rays of light. I'm going to do all my chores quickly in order to leave the room free for you. In the meantime I'm delivering you a ton of kisses and caresses, carriage paid. And I also adore you.

Juliette

Letter 132

Jersey, 13 June 1860
Wednesday morning, half past 6:00

Good morning, my dear beloved! Let me wish you from afar[1] a "good morning" even more tender and sweet than if I were close, so as to trick distance of its sadness and gloominess for two beings who love each other as we love.

In two hours you'll be in the packet boat and will be swaying on the same waves as I was yesterday evening. If your eyes gaze upon them and if your thoughts plunge into them as you think of me, you'll find there all the tenderness and kisses my heart and soul dropped there during the crossing yesterday. I hope that nothing will prevent you from arriving in good health, for the weather which was bad last night appears to be very good this morning. I hope the influence of the thirteenth will not be felt by any one of you and that you will all arrive with a voracious appetite. As for me I'm waiting for your arrival to regain my appetite, which until now has completely failed me, although I was served a very substantial dinner yesterday. I could have decided to go and dine with Ch. Asplet[2] this morning. But it would be impossible for me to enjoy anything without you, no matter what the pretext and with whomever it might be.

The only way for me to bear your absence courageously is to remain all alone with your memory, and to love you with a magnetic fixity which brings my soul closer to yours.

Take care on the boat, my dear beloved, and may God bless your crossing!

Juliette

Letter 133

Jersey, 14 June 1860
Thursday afternoon, 2 o'clock

Finally! Finally! Finally![a] You have arrived, my great, my ineffable, my divine beloved! I have got back your sweet glance and your victorious smile, and I have heard your dear voice, the enchantment of my soul—what happiness—although I barely saw you! But I know that you're close to me; I'm sure that you're well and I hope that you love me. I'm happy, happy, happy!

I hope you weren't vexed that Mme Duverdier and I took this little boat with the intention of meeting you sooner and arrived on the wrong quay, to which we had been directed by mistake?[b] I was extremely astonished when I saw you in a boat with your Victor heading toward me, while everybody else was waiting for you on the other quay. I felt you had something constrained and displeased about you when you met me, which I don't deserve either by intention or deed, since for the last two days I've done nothing except walk the path from my house to the jetty and from the jetty to my house, without even going into town to buy myself a toothbrush, which I greatly need, having left mine in Guernsey. I assure you that if I took a false step in following these ladies it was not my fault, and that their solicitude, while very gracious and kind, has more than once been burdensome and embarrassing to me.

If ever necessity should force me to be separated from you again, which please God won't be the case, I would ask God for the supreme compensation of leaving me entirely alone with just your memory for company. I hope this necessity will never present itself. And on this subject I think it won't be long till your Charles arrives, perhaps with his mother and sister if these ladies found themselves well enough to face the crossing.

In the meantime, I adore you.

Juliette

I owed a visit to Mmes Ch. Asplet and Nicolle for all the concern they've shown me these last two days. Now here I am liberated, because I have just paid the visit!

Letter 134

Jersey, 15 June 1860
Friday morning, half past 7:00

Good morning, my dear beloved! I wish you good morning with all the enthusiasms and passions of last night added to my own. How much I regretted that your dear and worthy wife and your noble and courageous daughter could not be at this meeting. What happiness for them and what a glory to be present at this radiant and supreme triumph![1] I assure you I believe I would have sacrificed half my happiness yesterday to procure them the pleasure of seeing and hearing these hurrahs, these bravos, these cries of love, admiration, and veneration from this moved, respectful, and exhilarated crowd. I know the echo of it will reach them in their hearts, but it isn't the same thing.

As long as you are not too tired, my dear beloved, and that you had a good night? I would have liked to stay at the Asplets to serve you, take care of you, adore you, instead of returning foolishly to my hotel. What a stupid prejudice that separates two beings who have but one soul in two parts and one life between the two of them! Anyway, I must accept it, and I'm more than happy if the emotion and fatigue of this memorable night yesterday did not prevent you from sleeping. I'm very happy that you were able to reconcile the Asplet brothers, and happy for my part in acting as a link between the charming Mme Ch. Asplet and her brother-in-law, Philippe.[2] I hope this bond will be solid, although Philippe seemed to me to be cold and constrained yesterday. Perhaps it was emotion? Time will tell. In any case, you have done all you could do to bring together these two hostile brothers. Dear beloved, I am still all dazed with the cheers of yesterday, and my whole being still thrills with admiration and adoration. I can tell you nothing else except that since yesterday I have been drowning in supreme ecstasy.

Juliette

Letter 135

Guernsey, 17 February 1861
Sunday morning, half past 8:00

Good morning, my poor invalid![1] Good morning, my much-much-beloved, good morning!

I was very sorry yesterday to have made you speak more than you could, my poor beloved, and I reproached myself for it every time I woke up. I hope this little excitement didn't prevent you from sleeping? This thought torments me more than the seriousness of the illness in itself, which isn't great and can't be more than that of a bother and preoccupation to you—which is already too much, but not in any way life threatening. However, the idea that you feel ill is so unbearable to me that I long for the time when you can have a change of air. To that end there is nothing that I won't do, being only too happy to be able to contribute to the restoration of your dear health, which is my life itself. So, my adored beloved, I beg you not to trouble yourself over me in the different arrangements that will still perhaps materialize between you and your family, sure as you can be in advance that I will do whatever you want, when you want, as you want. As long as your health strengthens and your gaiety and happiness return, I am the happiest of women and I thank God.

I haven't yet mentioned the wonderful page you wrote yesterday inspired by our sweet anniversary,[2] my dear beloved, so much preoccupied am I with the thought of curing you, which is to say, so much do I love you, for it's the same thing. And yet God knows with what tender and religious emotion I read and reread this page—this page that I would have believed dictated by my soul, so much does it resemble the love, faith, and hope that I have in my heart. Thank-you, my beloved, for having spoken so well for you and for me. Thank-you! I love you, I smile upon you, I bless you in the eyes of our two loved ones.[a]

At the very moment that I invoke these two angels as witnesses to my love and implore their protection of you, a delightful ray of sunshine reaches my pen and seems to caress it, saying: *trust, love, happiness.* I believe in this omen and I want to make you share it, my dear beloved. Yes, trust, love, happiness, all of that is contained in this ray of sunshine from Heaven, in this ray of health promised by God, in this ray of love from my soul to yours. I kiss your dear little feet and I adore you!

Juliette

Letter 136

Guernsey, 20 March 1861
Wednesday morning, 8 o'clock

Good morning, my dear beloved, good morning, you,[a] good morning if you're smiling at me and if you've had a good night and are continuing with yesterday's revival! If not, *"Goodnight!"* I'll put on my gloomy nightcap[b] and never laugh again.

Dear beloved, it's very true that it's only your nerves that are affected.[1] If it were otherwise, then you would not have at one moment this state of complete health and at another moment this state of complete illness that cheers us or afflicts us as the wind blows. So, my dear little man, I'm convinced that travel will cure you *as if by hand* and in very little time. So we must hurry to make preparations to seize the first fine day that comes. For that reason you and M. Charles must hurry to send me your things, so that I can pack them as soon as possible. You must also buy the bag for your manuscript this very day.[2] We'll go together, and I'll make my little purchases at the same time. My blessed Victor, I love you, I love you, I love you!

Letter 137

Mont-Saint-Jean, 17 June 1861
Monday evening, 8 o'clock

Dear beloved, while you relax amid the sweet joys of your family,[1] I rally all my physical and moral strength so as not to sink into too great a sadness during your absence.

As long as my eyes could pick out the omnibus, I followed the road to Gronandael, that is to say as far as the Betterave Renaissante. At that point I had to give up the sweet illusion of my dear little black dot on the horizon and confess to myself I could no longer see anything except the immense void of your twenty-four-hour absence. So not knowing what to do nor how to *kill the time*, I went to the church at Waterloo by a path across the fields that was not too tiring, and I came back via the village without having visited the church, despite the insistent offers of an old woman who called me her "dear friend." I got back to the hotel at exactly six o'clock. I took advantage of the half hour until dinner to freshen up and wash from head to toe, then I put on my *robe de chambre* and went down to our little dining room, where I ate without hunger and drank without thirst, so much is my poor heart already disoriented and discouraged as soon as you're not there. I had to be very convinced I couldn't accompany you to Brussels without bringing upon ourselves more or less malicious curiosity to impose on myself the sad duty of staying here. This conviction doesn't console me, however, and I'm just as unhappy as if it had been only up to me whether or not to take the opportunity of making this little trip with you. Decidedly, human respectability is a wretched pest more malevolent and annoying than any midge's most venomous bite, and no ointment in the world can treat it.

The bites I don't overly notice, moreover, for my arm is already better, while my heart suffers more and more. Dear beloved, try at least on your side to put to profit this time, which costs me so dear! Be happy! I love you, I bless you, and I adore you!

Juliette

Letter 138

Guernsey, 5 October 1861
Saturday morning, 8 o'clock

Good morning, my dear beloved, good morning, my dear little man! I send you my whole heart in a kiss. I hope you slept well despite the inevitable agitation of yesterday's big event.[1] It would be annoying if this inevitable outcome—an outcome that could perhaps have been better still, especially if the possible competition had been better known—it would be annoying, I say, if this outcome should have given you a night of insomnia. I hope it didn't. I hope also that if you *guide* me well I'll finish your copying, perhaps even without any help. To that end I'm going to leave the running of my house completely in the hands of Suzanne throughout the time that this dear copying lasts. On your part, my dear little man, you mustn't leave me without *labor*. This morning I could have copied two or three pages at least if you had given me a little provision of your manuscript, because I had already finished yesterday what you had brought me the day before. Now I'm waiting. Toto, my little Toto, don't let me languish! It's your new publisher who's shouting this to you via my pen, and all the members of the public who say it to you via my heart. Quick, quick, some *copying!*

Anyway it seems that M. Lacroix must have had a good, if not a *fine* crossing, for the sea is as smooth as oil. Poor *Hetzel!* What is he going to say! Despite it being his fault or that of his partners, he won't be any less furious about the way things have turned out—*on the contrary*. I pity him, because I understand on the basis of my own feelings how much he must care about publishing this book of books, quite aside from the question of profit.[2] Anyway one cannot please everybody and Hetzel, and you were right to settle this matter in a way that is satisfactory to you. And I'd do better to hold my tongue and mind my own business and love you like the dog that I am!

Letter 139

Guernsey, 12 November 1861
Tuesday morning, half past 7:00

Good morning, my dear beloved! Good morning and a smile if you slept well last night; and, if your boo-boos of the head and the insides have gone ... Oh, well then happiness! happiness! happiness! As for me I slept quite well, and I think I'll be fine as soon as I've properly woken up and started work on my dear little task that I prefer more than anything except you. This is the feeling that will subdue my natural savagery and make me receive your sister-in-law without too much sullenness, I hope.[1] The pleasure of hearing your wonderful book read aloud will prevail over all my tetchiness as an old bear.

As we wait for the arrival of this good little person, I see that her husband will have a good crossing.² I'm glad for him and for me, one of whose most beautiful and dearest pictures he is taking with him. I hope he'll not keep it too long and that he'll be very careful with it. Anyway, it's no less of a great sacrifice for me to be separated even for a very short time from something that you have given me, especially when this something is a masterpiece created by you. I console myself and find patience in the thought that brave M. Chenay will make good use of it and that we will have nothing to regret, you for your independence and I for my trust. My Toto, I adore you.

Letter 140

Guernsey, 6 December 1861
Friday morning, half past 8:00

Good morning, my dear beloved, good morning! I love you and I'm happy if you had as good a night as mine, as I desire and hope that you did. So now the first part of *Les Misérables* has been delivered.¹ No more changes can be made, it's finished, and happy Lacroix will carry it in a few hours over the ocean, the one carrying the other... Ocean, *Les Misérables*! What an effect it's going to have on everybody! Just thinking of it makes my heart swell and my hand tremble. I'd like to be all eyes, all ears, and all soul to witness all the light, all the admiration, all the adoration that this book is going to elicit from every heart and soul when it is published.

As always, excessive emotion makes me ramble when I speak to you. But that doesn't prevent me from feeling sublime things that are worthy of being laid at your feet.

Another good piece of news is the arrival of your daughter,² which means your wife also will soon be returning and probably your son Charles too. And although this good news must extinguish a part of my own joy in my poor little house, I'm nonetheless glad for you, for your son Victor, and for Mme Chenay to know you're all happy and that everything is back to normal. It is too bad for me if I'm a little too bewitched with the happiness of having you all day and every day. That will teach me not to taste unwittingly the forbidden fruit of the legitimate and legal happiness of the family!

Letter 141

Guernsey, 1 January 1862
Wednesday morning, quarter to 8:00

Good morning, my ineffable beloved, good morning! A fine day, happiness, smiles, tenderness, love, I send you all that in a single kiss. I waited a long time for the day when I would have my dear little letter.¹ Finally, I hold it! I read it! I kiss it! I adore it! But I hear you opening your window, I'm putting it down to run to you . . .

I did it! I saw you! My eyes were filled with your gaze! My heart with your kisses! My soul with ecstasy! Thank-you, my sweet beloved! Thank-you! May all the blessings of God be on you and on all those that you *[paper torn]*[a] and may He grant you all that you ask of Him, as I make my ardent and incessant prayer that He never separate us one minute in this life or in the next. I hope that He will harken to us, my adored beloved, and that He will spare us such pain—I was going to say *shame*, since I feel I would be dishonored if I had the unhappiness of surviving you by a single day. So I hope God will give us the happiness and will do us the honor of calling us to Him at the same time and that He will weld our two souls together for eternity.

Dear beloved, I'm all shaken, as always happens whenever I receive a letter from you. Your love in this form is a divine elixir that inebriates my whole soul. However, even in the midst of my bedazzlement I feel I don't deserve all that you think of me, for my worth lies only in loving you. Aside from my love, I am a very ordinary poor woman, very uncultured and imperfect, I know it, I know it, I know it! And I could almost say that I don't mind about it as long as you don't suffer for it. My virtue is to love you. My body, my blood, my heart, my life, my soul are employed in loving you. Beyond my love, I am nothing, I understand nothing, I want nothing. Loving you, loving you, loving you, that is my one and only perfection. I couldn't, and wouldn't, know how to have other virtues even if I desired to, because all my strength and all my will are absorbed in loving you.

Be blessed, my generous beloved, for all the rays of light with which you surround my love, and may my gratitude and my blessings be so much more happiness and felicity in your life! I say all these things in a sort of fever of the soul so that I don't know what I'm writing to you, but the foundation of the first word to the last is that I love you, that I'm very happy, that I bless you, and that I embrace your angel and mine with my love and benedictions.

My Victor, I adore you. I smile at you, I bless you, in the past, the present, and the future!

Letter 142

Guernsey, 4 March 1862
Mardi Gras, 8 o'clock in the morning

Good morning, my dear beloved, good morning! I hope your dear wife didn't leave in this weather?[1] *What a surprise!* It's almost as though God wanted to create some local color in honor of this special day to better remind me that this day was, is, and always will be, the finest of my life. However this decoration—which in moderation looks very good with the landscape—is anything but pleasant for traveling; so I suppose it's unlikely that Mme Hugo set off in this Siberian snow. As for myself, no matter what the temperature that comes with the name *"Mardi Gras,"* on this date all the flowers of love that you have sown in my heart come back into bloom again, and my soul blossoms as in a ray of sunshine.[a] So it is with all joys, all tendernesses, all smiles, and all happinesses that I send you my morning greetings.

Dear, dear beloved, for today let us be young, let us be in love, let us be happy as at the time of our first kiss!

Juliette

Letter 143

Guernsey, 4 April 1862
Friday morning, half past 7:00

Good-day, my great beloved, a *fine* day in honor of the triumph of *Les Misérables*,[1] my heart full of love, and admiration from all sides—this is what I offer you this morning in my own name and in the name of all those who will by now have read your miraculous book!

I hope the distant rumbling of this glorious fanfare didn't prevent you from sleeping last night and that your headache has completely gone this morning? In the meantime until I know for sure, I'll give you my bulletin, which is as good as can be, because I slept very well all night and I feel very well despite yesterday's rather disagreeable incident. If you are not happy, it is because you're unjust, but in any case I pardon you, such is my *weakness*. Besides it has been glorious weather since yesterday. It would be good, it would be just, if the spring—that is to say, the *rebirth* of this year—should date from the date of the publication of your book, which is a moral creation as great as the earth itself. Dear beloved, my heart is too moved to express my emotions well. I feel that I love you and admire you with all my being all at the same time, that's all!

Juliette

Letter 144

Guernsey, Tuesday noon, 20 May 1862

Thank-you, my great beloved, thank-you for making me the flesh of your flesh and the soul of your soul! Thank-you for linking the humble memory of me with the most glorious date in your life, with *Les Misérables*! My heart is swollen with love and gratitude fit to burst. My eyes are filled with tears of tenderness. My whole being thrills with emotion as if something divine had just penetrated me and fixed itself there forever.

This *thing*, this ray, this perfume, this music, this joy, this happiness, it is your dear little letter[1] that I see, that I touch, that I read, that I kiss, that I adore. I'm so happy to feel you delivered, at least relatively speaking, from this titanic work that your genius has carried, with mind braced, for so long, that I would like to be able to shout with joy from the four corners of Heaven and earth: "What happiness! What happiness!! What happiness!!! What happiness!!!!"

I kiss your dear little feet still dusty from your voyage across humanity, and I shade my eyes with my hand so as not to see your divine halo from too close. I kiss you on my knees!

Letter 145

Guernsey, 30 September 1862
Tuesday morning, 8 o'clock

Good morning, my dear beloved, good morning—joy and smiles if you have had a good night, as I hope!

It's now two weeks since there swarmed around you at Brussels[1] all the bees of intelligence who had come expressly to bring you their tribute of admiration, the sweet honey of glory. What fine fluttering of wings! What a fine celebration! What rays of light! What emotion! What love and what bedazzlement! No, not since the time of Christ has anyone witnessed anything as grand, as august, as saintly, and as splendid as this sublime *Lord's Supper* where the bread of the soul and of the body abounded as at the banquet of the man-God.

And to think that I have seen all these things! That I have heard all these harmonies! That I have been penetrated by all these perfumes of intelligence and genius and that I have not been struck by blindness or dumbness for the rest of my days like the lowly mortal that I am—there is the miracle of miracles! From all this enchantment, all these ecstasies, all these marvels of the mind, my love emerges yet greater, yet more beautiful, yet more eternal, and I place it at your divine feet.

Letter 146

Guernsey, 2 o'clock in the afternoon, 2 December 1862

Dear beloved, I would like this anniversary, which in itself is so sad for the hideous crime that it recalls, to be greeted by a smile of recognition and love by you as well as me; far from bearing it ill will on my own account, I bless

The view from Juliette Drouet's window at 20 Hauteville Street afforded a glimpse of Hugo's balcony. In this photo his house is the most distant building, a small section of the side of which is outlined against the sky. The railing of the balcony, to which Hugo would attach a towel indicating that he had got up, is dimly visible. (Photo taken by translator with kind permission of Richard and Elizabeth Soar).

it for allowing me to love you without trouble and without fear for the last eleven years.ᵃ

Perhaps I show bad taste in vaunting a happiness derived from something that has cost so dear to many poor victims and to France itself. But as my egoism has no bearing on events, I can be very happy in my little corner, especially if you regret nothing and desire nothing in place of my love. Chance has it that my "festival" today will occur almost at the same time and on the *same day* as the dinner we had together on the same date in the place de la Bastille eleven years ago.ᵇ Do you remember, my beloved? At that moment, as now, my happiness would have been to die for you. Blessings on you in your sacrifice and your glory!

Letter 147

Guernsey, 19 May 1863
Monday afternoon, half past 1:00

There is no going back on it now, my poor beloved, the act separating our two homes has been signed and countersigned[1] for a quarter of an hour, and I still don't know whether to rejoice or mourn over it.

If I am to believe your solemn promise, this distance in space, instead of separating us *in body*, will bring us closer together. If that is so, as I hope, the resolution we have taken is not to be regretted too much, since my health will benefit from it as much as my happiness. Everything depends on you, my sweet beloved, and that is what makes me confident about the future. In the meantime I would much have liked to spend the rest of the day with you, so much have I need to reassure myself about the consequences of the act we have just *committed* by signing this lease, you and I. Your immediate departure leaves me even more alone at this moment than usual, and it seems to me that my house has already receded away from yours as far as La Fallue is from Domaille's house.ᵃ This impression brings on a sadness that I cannot overcome whatever I do. I need to see you and to assure myself that you love me as much as before. Then I can get back my smile and my joy, with which my tenderness would like to inundate you as by a ray of sunshine.

J.

Letter 148

Guernsey, Friday morning, half past 7:00, 19 June *[1863]*

I sense that you must have had a bad night, my poor beloved, and I fear that you are suffering more than you want anyone to see.[1] I love you, my sublime, resigned martyr. I don't dare to touch your pain, and yet I would like to make it stop at any price God might set. The thought that you are suffering in your dear soul is hateful and unbearable to me. But what can I do, what can I do, my God, to prevent it? Yesterday I saw you struggling against your painful preoccupation and a terrible headache, and my heart was overwhelmed with anguish and pity. I would like to have absorbed you entirely into my love to force you to see nothing, feel nothing, and understand nothing except it.

Last night I got up several times, trying in my soul to sense through your dark and silent window whether you were sleeping, and every time I went back to bed more tormented. Since early this morning I've been looking out for when you would get up, while wanting you to stay in bed as long as you need for the rest of your body and mind. Until now you haven't yet appeared. O my poor beloved, rest, don't let yourself go with grief! Everything will turn out better than we dare to hope, I sense it with my love, which desires your happiness. I hope you'll receive news that will calm your anxiety and explain many things to you in a satisfactory way, as far as that is possible for your poor ruffled heart.

As for myself, my adored beloved, happy or sad I can only love you. I laugh when you laugh, I suffer when you suffer, and always, always, I love you. I wish I could do more, but God doesn't permit anyone to encroach upon His power, which means that all that I can do is love you.

Letter 149

Guernsey, 3 July 1863
Friday afternoon, half past 3:00

I'm ready, my dear beloved, I've received my visitors who will be yours also this evening. They are fine people; the wife, whom we already know, is very pleasant and expansive; the husband, completely English, but very enthusiastic about *Les Misérables*. He says that the man who created this prodigious book is a great saint, whatever the religion to which he subscribes. This was said to me by his wife, who translated into French as he was talking. They also offer us a place to stay should we ever go to the part of England in which they live.

It is impossible to be more likably English that this old-fashioned young couple. They want to see the children's dinner next Thursday,[1] so as to be able to speak about it knowledgeably on their return. I told them the doors are always open and they don't need permission to attend. They stayed only about ten minutes, but long enough for this woman to have time to call me *"Mme la Comtesse"*[a] a dozen times without my being able to hit on a way to disabuse her of this notion of *nobility [sic]* with which she glamorizes me—I don't know why, as I've often protested to her sister that I'm not entitled to this form of address. The only title that I claim is that of your faithful dog, all others are worthless. And then I adore you. Take that!

Letter 150

Guernsey, 21 November 1863
Saturday morning, quarter to 8:00

You abuse my love and make me suffer without any other reason than to test how far I'm willing to submit to your caprice. I will forgive you until the time when my humiliated love will eventually raise its head and bow no longer, nor even look anymore in your direction.

I hope you had a better night than mine, and I look forward to the explanation of the coldness you showed me last night with equal malice and persistence. I know it's the order of the day in your *group* to make fun of *cooing*, fidelity, and exaggerated sensitivity and that you are all victimized by feminine delirium. But I, being the age I am and in my right mind, do not wish to be mocked, nor to have my heart played with as though it were a twenty-five-sou accordion. This demand I make absolutely and resolutely. It is not the first time I have told you this, but perhaps it will be the last, for I am wounded deep in my soul and in what I have most immaculate in me—my love. This is not a threat, about which you would care little in fact, but the honest and sincere warning of a woman who refuses to have her most sacred possession slighted.

J.

Letter 151

Guernsey, 21 December 1863
Monday morning, quarter to 10:00

I hope you're still sleeping, my dear little man, and I'm happy about it for you must be very tired, not only because of going to bed unusually late, but also because of Lacroix's[1] reiterated attempts to wrest as many things as possible from your splendid reserve of masterpieces. How far he has succeeded I don't know, but he seemed very joyful and triumphant when he left us last night. I hope his joy didn't cost you too dear and that you slept all the better for it the rest of the night. This morning I saw M. Ulbach[2] making himself a bouquet in your garden before leaving. Just now I saw the boat that's taking them away depart at full steam. So "bon voyage" to our two fine visitors, including one *publisher*. So here we are once again back to just ourselves; if I were to think only of myself, who am never more happy than when it is just the two of us, I would almost say, "So much the better." But it can't be the same for you and still less for your dear little Toto,[a] so I repress my egotistical satisfaction and wish you this kind of visitor as often as possible.

Anyway I profited from the few hours that remained of the night to sleep like a log. I feel completely restored this morning from the fatigues and annoyances of the day before yesterday, and ready for the next derailment.[3] I'm sorry now that I spoke to you about it. I must have been crazy to bother you with my servant troubles. Another time I'll try to keep it to myself. Until then I take courage and love you by trial of fire, water, and servants! What beautiful weather today, my dear little man, and how I would like to be sure to be able to take advantage of it, arm in arm with you! But I have so very, very, many things to do between now and then, even without counting the collation with Mme Chenay. I adore you!

Letter 152

Guernsey, 23 April 1864
Saturday afternoon, quarter to 1:00

What news from Paris today, my dear beloved? Has the veto on the banquet been confirmed?[1] They may show their claws and snouts and have their policemen seize the empty chair of Victor Hugo, but they will never prevent your splendid book on Shaskespeare [sic] from shining at the zenith of the literary and humanitarian heavens of this time, and of all time past and to come. As for myself, I jubilate over their impotent rage, and I congratulate you from the depths of my heart on your new *poetic* and *political* success. You are more than crowned, you are haloed, and you are the saint of saints of art and progress in all its forms. I say this to you unwittingly and in a state of bewilderment, because admiration overwhelms me without giving me the wherewithal to convey it. But, fortunately, you're not short of that kind of praise and it's just a question of who will lay it at your feet first. Personally, I'm on this earth to love you, and I acquit this task conscientiously. I hope that your bust[2] will finish as it has started, going from good to better to perfect to ideal. I hope, also, that if it is to be given to someone outside the immediate family, I will be able to make my rights felt with the artist. In the meantime I once again wish good luck to this bust, and I kiss the original from the ends of his hair to his little toe.

J.

Letter 153

Guernsey, 20 December 1864
Tuesday morning, 8 o'clock

Good morning, my dear little early bird, *good* morning if not *fine* morning! How are you in this gloomy[a] weather? Did you sleep well? Are you pleased with the night you had, my dear little man? If everything with you is as my heart desires, then I smile on you, bless you, and adore you. Now it's your turn to speak. I have forgotten to tell you I slept admirably well all night and that I have the health today to match—*admirable.*

Thank-you, my sweet beloved, thank-you for your beautiful little portrait, which I'll always wear, thanks to your gracious generosity. I'm impatient to have this dear little portrait so as to be able to enjoy it more quickly—that is, for longer. Thank-you again and everlasting love!

Dear beloved, it's not because I doubt the charming and kind welcome that your noble and worthy wife would give me that I'm not going to your touching little children's party,[1] but out of a feeling of reserve which is fundamental to my nature. This reserve must be invincible if it makes me resist, as it does, all the seductive opportunities that I'm offered to associate with your family outside my home.

But what discretion commands me to do in flesh and blood has no control over my thought and heart, and I'll be present all the same, invisibly, at your dear charity *Christmas [sic].* And that's without counting the fact that I'll be represented there by my two servants, eager to serve you and help you in your care of the dear little poor children. May God reward you in happiness for all your good deeds, and may He allow me the right to admire you and love you all until my last breath!

J.

Letter 154

Guernsey, 17 January 1865
Tuesday morning, quarter to 8:00

Good morning, my great, my ineffable beloved, good morning! Be blessed on the earth and in Heaven and in people's hearts and souls! I adore you. Your balcony is still empty, but I hope the absence of your dear little signal[1] is no indictment of your night, and that you slept well despite all the sad reasons for agitation that you have at the moment.[2] The weather, although still very overcast, seems quite mild, and the sea is very calm, which promises your two dear fugitives a good crossing for tomorrow. If it was only a question of desiring something ardently to make it come true, I could predict it for them with certainty. Unfortunately, that's not sufficient, which means I won't be tranquil on their behalf until they've arrived in Brussels without too much fatigue.

As for me, I slept very badly, but I don't complain about it for I seem to have been let off easily by my fiendish gout, which wants only to play the devil with me. And what are a few hours of sleep more or less compared with the frightful pain of this hideous ailment? Besides it's enough, according to our convention, that one of the two of us sleeps and is well to restore the balance of sleep and health in the other. This is why I'm counting on making up with your good night what was lacking in mine.

I'm glad to have done a little bit of good for your dear little Victor by opening my door, and more than that—my arms and heart—to this poor stricken family that he loves and esteems. It will be through no fault of mine if they don't find all the consolation in me and at my house that they need. When I say consolation, it's *diversion* I mean, for the supreme consolation, the one that can overcome any sorrow, is *you*, who will give that to them in the wreath of light you will lay on the grave of their child on Thursday. I'm sorry that my moral scruples prevent me from being present at the funeral. But from afar as near my thoughts will not leave you, and my soul will hear everything your soul says to this poor little dead one, so loved and mourned on this earth.

I kiss your beloved feet.

J.

Letter 155

Guernsey, 4 February 1865
Saturday evening, quarter to 6:00

Don't be surprised at the unseemly hour of my restitus, my dear beloved, which has as its excuse a bath taken this morning, three days' shopping if not to do, then at least to *have* done, which is worse, a *thorough* combing, a *thorough* walk—you'll see I haven't wasted my time, since there's enough left for me to scribble to you: *I love you*. This declaration, which I make with my eyes, my mouth, my heart, and my soul to everything I see and to everything that hears me, to God and to men, I make again to you with as much emotion as if I were revealing an unexpected secret. You cannot know, my sweet beloved, with what kind of young and serious love I love you. I could spend my whole life enumerating to you all its many tendernesses before exhausting them. I'm obliged to sum them all up with: I adore you!

Don't forget to tell your dear little Victor when you write to him how happy his nice little letter[1] made me. I feel I deserve it, but it is very generous and charming of him to have written to me. Tell him that I love him through you with the affection he deserves. And when I say *him*, I mean his brother, his admirable mother, in fact all those who have rights to your love. I have so much love for you that I can give some of it to your whole family without depriving you of an iota.

I don't know if you'll be able to read my scribble, because I can't see to write any longer. I kiss you with a blind stroke of my pen until I can write you something better.

J.

Letter 156

Guernsey, 30 April 1865
Sunday morning, 7 o'clock

Good morning, my adorable beloved, good morning, may God protect you! I bless you! I didn't dare announce yesterday the great event of your having finished your book that very morning,[1] not knowing if you wanted it to be known immediately. My heart was so full of joy that I almost committed an indiscretion despite myself, but in the end I was able to contain myself and wait until it should please you to reveal the great news yourself! What pleasure it's going to give your family over in Brussels! What envy it's going to arouse among the publishers! What excited impatience and curiosity in the public and what admiration and happiness in the whole world when it can be read! I wish that moment were already here so that I could take my part in it. The hope of being the first to see this dear new book as I collate it with Mme Chenay gives me a feeling of delight and agitation that I cannot express, but which is the anticipatory ferment of my admiration mixed with my love for you.

I hope you spent a good night, my divine swot, and that you are as well as you could wish this morning. I wish we were already at midday, so I could know for sure. In the meantime, I love you with all my soul.

Letter 157

Guernsey, 6 May 1865
Saturday morning, 7 o'clock

Good morning, my dear adorable beloved, good morning and happiness if you had a good night, as I hope you did! I don't know how long your signal has been gleaming on the railing of your balcony,[a] because I no longer get up early, as you will have noticed some time ago. There used to be a rivalry between our two houses about getting up, by which I mean I eagerly waited for the moment when I would see you appear at your dear little window. Now that I can't see anything any longer except your inert signal, laziness takes me over, and I have no heart for anything until I see you again. This regret for your sweet proximity I have every morning and all the day, for I used to have the feeling that my soul entered you along with my gaze and that I penetrated you with it.

Nowadays it's no longer like that, alas, and our silent chatter is restricted to my noticing the presence or absence of your ... towel. But I'm only too happy to have this little bit of a rallying sign; it has an interesting meaning for my heart, since I know more or less, according to the time when you hoist it, whether you've had a good or a bad night.

In consequence of all this, one would think I would be eager to seize every opportunity of being with you, and one would be right, for it's the preoccupation and ambition of every moment of my life, with one situation excepted—that being the one that presents itself next Tuesday. Permit me to decline the happiness and honor of it in the name of the thirty years of reserve, discretion, and respect that I have maintained toward your house as also toward my own. If ever I am to be your guest there, which I do not foresee, it must not be by *chance* but with the *premeditated* consent of everybody that I should be invited to your house. Permit me not to depart from this lifelong line of conduct and to keep intact the dignity and sanctity of our love!

Letter 158

Guernsey, 25 June 1865
Sunday morning, 6 o'clock

Sleep, my sweet beloved, I love you! I hope you've had a really good night this time, but until I know for certain, I send you everything that is best and most tender in my heart as a prayer and a blessing upon your awakening.

I'm thinking of all the things you still have to do, and I doubt that we can leave on Wednesday.[1] I remind you that there isn't a single sheet of paper left at my house, in case you should need some. Unfortunately, I can't help you, which humiliates and saddens me. If you want to trust the copying of your comedy to me, I can do it during our stay in Brussels.[2] I'll try hard to hide my poor handwriting. Anyway, my dear beloved, I'd be very happy and proud if I could be good to you for something, whatever it might be. In the meantime I adore you, but that's not enough.

Letter 159

Guernsey, 16 January 1866
Tuesday morning, quarter to 8:00

Good morning, my dear beloved! Permit me to deduce from your august nose and Olympian beard that the day is still wearing its nightcap over its eyes as though in the depths of 21 December. You will say that there's no need for me to see any more clearly than that to scribble my daily sublimities, and I grant you that's true; but fact is fact and I take note of it! I'd also like to be able to take note of the fact that you slept well the whole night. Not having that certainty, I abstain from complimenting you on it, which deprives me of a great happiness.

Is it today that you may have the verdict on the lawsuit against Lacroix?[1] I suspect that you won't, in fact. But what *is* certain is the fact of your corrected proofs that you'll return *ready for press*.[2] What happiness for you and what a service to the poor publishers submerged in the ocean of their stupidity! You're Gilliat[a] in flesh and blood and genius, and you will get them out of it. But like the hero of your book, you'll not be rewarded for it except by the most calm and arrogant ingratitude. Fortunately, universal recognition and the eternal admiration of all great hearts will not fail you, nor even those of protozoa[b] like myself; the proof being that I bless you as though I were *authorized*, winged, and haloed by God. Such is the audacity of my love for you.

Letter 160

Guernsey, 24 January 1866
Wednesday morning, quarter past 8:00

Good morning, my dear beloved, good morning! I don't know how long you have been up as I have only just opened my shutters,[a] having tried to make up a little for the horrible night I had. I wouldn't mention this melancholy incident to you if it weren't for the fact that you demand to be kept informed of the reasons for all my random *sighs*. That done, I come back to *you*, my dear *Master*, who are the sole preoccupation of my heart and life, and ask you if you slept well, if the buzzing in your ear has stopped, and if your outrageous *flirtaiehioune [sic]* of yesterday doesn't weigh a bit on your conscience today? Consult it a little, I beg you, and ask it, in private conference with your heart and soul, what it thinks about it. As for myself, I abstain from passing judgment. I observe and that is all.

The weather is fine this morning, but I doubt that I can profit from it, my indisposition not being of the kind that seeks the light. I won't even take my bath this morning. This is a very gloomy scribble in form and content—it would have been better not to indulge in it; but *in sum, dear Master*, it proves that, ill or well, gay or sad, happy or unhappy, my scribble is at its post like my love. Take it as it is and give, in exchange, faith and the future!

Letter 161

Guernsey, 17 June 1866
Sunday afternoon, half past 4:00

In haste[1] *[sic]*—now is the time if ever to let this idiom fly, seeing as I haven't the time to speak any language or to think about anything except the action of battle, for which read *trip*. Since four o'clock in the morning when I got up, I haven't yet taken the time to wash my heart and soul in a good bath of tenderness and love. It's stupid, and I'm handing in my resignation from *everything*. Note that I still have the traveling bag to do, isn't that ridiculous?

I would like us to leave, no matter what the weather, on Wednesday.[2] In the meantime I looked for your *vade mecum* by the tourist Alfred Busquet,[a] and I found it with a signature in Monsieur Charles' handwriting. I've also chosen two pictures that I take the liberty of thrusting at your feet *in place* of the "original." I seem to be abusing *capital letters* and *italics*, forgive me, and I remain, in lowercase, your very humble servant, Juju, *born*[b] in the department of Ille et Vilaine.

Letter 162

Guernsey, 2 December 1866.
Sunday morning, half past 7:00

Good morning, my much-beloved, good morning, bless you! I smile this morning on this date execrated by all good people—*2 December*—because for me, alone, it's a happy date.[a] If my recognition is an offence against humanity and civilization, I humbly ask God and man forgiveness.

I'm tormented by the thought that you didn't perhaps sleep well and by the fear that your *ache* has become an actual *pain*. If I could be reassured on these two points of anxiety, I'd be very happy this morning. Unfortunately, I'm not going to know until quite late, when you come to bathe your dear eyes. Your eyes make me think of those of your dear wife. It seems to me that if it wasn't certain they would be cured she wouldn't be detained so long in Paris, far from her family, in winter. My desire that she should entirely recover the sight of which she made such noble and admirable use in her fine book, *Victor Hugo raconté*,[1] makes me regard the postponement of her return here a good omen for her imminent recovery.

I pray God for it with love!

Letter 163

Guernsey, 23 January 1867
Wednesday morning, 8 o'clock

No signal yet,[a] but so much the better, I hope, as a sign of a *very good* *[sic]*[b] night. I also slept very well and I love you, I love you, I love you!

Oh, how right you were to decide in your dear wife's favor last night by giving her the key to all her beautiful drawing rooms.[1] It's so just that she should enjoy them by doing the honors of them, as she alone can do, that I rejoice over it as over a personal victory.

I stand security for the tail of Sénat and the rest, and I'm sure this honest Sénat won't offend me by betraying my good opinion of his manners. As soon as you think the moment opportune for returning to Mme Hugo the visit with which she honored me yesterday, I'll do so immediately. In the meantime I'm glad to know that she's happy and you also, and I love you all from the depths of my heart.

Letter 164

Guernsey, 24 March 1868
Tuesday morning, quarter past 7:00

My good night throws its arms around your good morning, and asks it how you slept, how you are, and how you love me? I expect, I desire, I hope for, a good response to these three questions. I wasn't fool enough to be sick today, you understand. Even had I wished to be, I would have been unable, for only to have touched the edge of a page in your manuscript would have miraculously cured me like the robe of Jesus. Now you know the power of this panacea on me, and I lay on you henceforth the responsibility for my boo-boos and my carcass! What happiness!!!!!! After a year of deprivation, to find oneself again in the midst of genius in your beautiful, terrible, and sublime book***![1] Just thinking of it fills me with joy, sunshine, and admiration. I have springtime in my heart, and my soul is blossoming in adoration.

Letter 165

Guernsey, 29 April 1868
Wednesday morning, half past 7:00

How was your night, how is your heart, my dear beloved? Without waiting for your reply, I say, "Very good, I adore you." It's up to you now to try to catch me in this *stepple chease [sic]* of sleep and love.

You see I was right not to take any notice of the rain yesterday! I have the stubbornness and hooves of a mule. As far as my more or less perilous infirmities are concerned, you must just let me follow my whim. My animal instinct is worth more in that respect than all the science of Corbin.[1]

What wonderful portraits those of Lady Josiane and Lord David are![2] You couldn't have painted them better *at the time when you were called Rembrand [sic]*.[a] What a beauty this woman is, and this man, and what monsters also! It's dazzling and scary.

Letter 166

Brussels,[a] 28 August 1868
Friday morning, 8 o'clock

I put your sleep last night under the protection of your wife's dear soul, my poor dear beloved, praying that it would dismiss from your dreams all the painful memories of the gloomy day yesterday.[1] I hope she heard me and that you slept well. Henceforth it is this sweet and glorious witness of your life in this world, and now your radiant protector in the presence of God, whom I will petition for the peace and happiness you need to complete the great humanitarian work to which you are devoted. May God bless her and you as I bless her and you!

The more I think about this evening's sad journey, the more I feel that I must abstain from taking part in it. My heart's pious homage to this great and generous woman must not be exposed to the misinterpretation of the indifferent and malicious. Still this last sacrifice to human malice before we can have the right to love each other openly henceforth—isn't that so, my dear beloved? And then that nothing should separate us here below nor there above, this is my ardent wish!

Letter 167

Thursday evening, quarter past 5:00, 16 December 1869

You're plunged in the news, my dear beloved, and it isn't because I'm discrete that I don't read it over your shoulder, so eager am I to know all that interests you. But I don't have the gift of second sight, and first sight hardly serves me even with the aid of glasses. So I hasten on with all my heart the moment when you'll be able to tell me, yourself, what is happening. Here you are right now! What happiness! . . . Enough for today.

Notes

Letter 131

1. According to the Guernsey diaries, it was on 25 April that Victor Hugo took out from the "manuscript trunk" the manuscript of *Les Misérables*. The work had been interrupted on 21 February 1848. See *OC*, 10:1514 **and above, L. 68 and n. 1. Cosette is the young female heroine of *Les Misérables*. She has been abandoned as a baby to the care of the evil Thénardier family by her mother,**

Fantine, who is compelled by her poverty to seek work elsewhere. Cosette is treated cruelly by the Thénardiers, innkeepers, and is forced to act as an unpaid servant. Cosette is rescued from the Thénardiers by Jean Valjean (see above, L. 68, n. 1), who arrives at their inn one night and singles out Cosette with the gift of a splendid doll [T].

a. Javert is a police officer who pursues Jean Valjean, a former convict, throughout much of *Les Misérables*, and who is responsible, in particular, for penetrating Valjean's assumed identity as Monsieur Madeleine, mayor of a town in northern France. In the final version of the novel the boulevard Montparnasse is mentioned briefly (*Les Misérables*, ed. René Journet, 3 vols. [Paris: Garnier-Flammarion, 1979], 2:218) as one of the places of residence of the churchwarden, M. Mabeuf, as he slowly descends into poverty [T].

Letter 132

1. Hugo had been invited to Jersey to speak on behalf of Garibaldi; Juliette made the trip the day before him. See Hugo's reply, *LJD*, 226. Drouet stayed with her servant, Suzanne, at the Hotel Southampton in Jersey (*MUL*, 541), and Hugo with the Asplets (see below, n. 2). The visit would last from 12 June (14 June for Hugo) until 20 June. The purpose of Hugo's speech was to help raise money for Giuseppe Garibaldi (1807–1882) in his struggle for Italian unity. Hugo agreed to return to Jersey, from which he had been expelled, only on condition that a petition, with a large number of signatures from the people of Jersey supporting his visit, be collected first (*VH*, 372). Hugo and Garibaldi exchanged correspondence during the 1860s but never actually met—Gaudon et al., *Exilium*, 134 [T].

2. Charles Asplet was a close friend of the Hugos, and it was to Mme Charles Asplet that Mme Victor Hugo made a gift of the album known under the name of the Album Asplet, preserved at Chantilly in the Bibliothèque Spoelberch de Louvenjoul. On Charles and his brother, Philippe, see below, L. 134, n. 2 and Asplet family, Glossary [T].

Letter 133

a. Hugo had been scheduled to arrive on 13 June, the day after Drouet arrived, but his boat was delayed by bad weather (see *LJD*, 226), and he was not able to leave Guernsey until the fourteenth. In a state of increasing anxiety Drouet had waited seven and a half hours on the quay for his arrival on the thirteenth until friends had compelled her to give up (*MUL*, 542). In the meantime Hugo had sent her a telegram to reassure her (*LJD*, ibid.) [T].

b. It is not completely clear what intention Drouet had or what the mistake was. Robb (*VH*, 372–3) interprets it thus: "He [Hugo] was deposited by the boatman on the wrong side of the harbour, glowered at Juliette, who had landed there so as not to embarrass her heroic Toto in public, walked across the quay and was greeted there by a cheering crowd." Souchon (*MUL*, 544) sees Hugo's irritation as arising from the fact that Drouet did not wait at the hotel to meet him there. Concerning Mme Duverdier, see *LF*, 318, n. 4: Prosper Duverdier (1798–1881) was an exile, living first in Jersey and then in Guernsey [T].

Letter 134

1. The return of Victor Hugo to Jersey was seen as a sort of compensation for his expulsion in 1855. The speech that Hugo delivered on 14 June was a passionate plea for the liberty and right of peoples to self-determination (see the text in *OC*, 12:839–44). On 18 June Hugo will reply to the toast in his honor by a very fine speech evoking and erasing what he calls "the misunderstanding of 1855" (ibid., 844–6).

2. Philippe Asplet, a chandler, was a *centenier* and a friend of the exiles. See in *Les Hommes de l'exil* by Charles Hugo the account of his interview with the governor of Jersey, Sir Love (*OC*, 9:1509–11).

Letter 135

1. "Chronic laryngitis," according to a notebook of Hugo's (24 January 1861 in *OC*, 12:1532).

2. See *Le Livre de l'anniversaire*, *LJD*, 347.

a. I adopt the reading of Blewer (*LVH*, 272), "bien-aimées." This is a reference to Drouet and Hugo's two dead daughters, Claire and Léopoldine [T].

Letter 136

a. In French there is a play on the familiar and polite words for "you"—"bonjour, toi, bonjour, vous"—which cannot be rendered in English. Cf. above, Letter 66 and n. a [T].

b. This is a reference to the expression "triste comme un bonnet de nuit" ("sad like a nightcap") [T].

1. For three months Hugo has been suffering from sore throats and insomnia. On 17 March his doctor advised him to go on a trip.

2. On the following day Hugo will note in his account book: "Bought a *waterprooff* [sic] bag for the manuscript of *Les Misérables*." He will leave Guernsey on the twenty-fifth, accompanied by Juliette and his son Charles, to make a trip to Belgium and the Netherlands.

Letter 137

1. On 7 May they had taken rooms at the Hotel des Colonnes at Mont-Saint-Jean, near the battlefield of Waterloo. Hugo had made a scrupulous tour of the site, before leaving Juliette on 17 June to go to spend three days in Brussels with his wife and daughter. As soon as he returns on the nineteenth he will set to work again on *Les Misérables*. On the thirtieth he will write: "I have finished *Les Misérables* on the battlefield

of Waterloo and in the month of Waterloo" (*OC*, 12:1535). **Mont-Saint-Jean is a village in Belgium, south of the village of Waterloo and north of the battlefield. It is some fifteen miles from Brussels. Drouet and Hugo's stay at the Hotel des Colonnes in May lasted for about two months [T]**.

Letter 138

1. The publisher Lacroix arrived at Hauteville House on 3 October to negotiate the purchase of *Les Misérables*. Next morning Juliette wrote: "So your aspiring publisher is come, my dear beloved. "He's short of charm on the surface, perhaps he's all the more solid for it. Let's hope so, especially if you have to deal with him" (Bibliothèque nationale de France, Cabinet des manuscrits, nouvelles acquisitions françaises, 16.382, f° 115). They signed the contract on the same day: three hundred thousand francs for the rights to twelve years, including the translation rights.

2. This was in fact, since the beginning of his exile, the first time that Hugo had not dealt with Hetzel, and the latter was deeply offended by it. He obviously did not have the means to lay hands quickly enough on a sum comparable to the one offered by Lacroix. The relations of Hugo with Hetzel were profoundly affected by this episode. Juliette shows herself to be particularly perceptive here. **Pierre-Jules Hetzel (1814–1886) a publisher of some of Hugo's major works, was exiled from France following the coup d'état of 1851—cf. Joseph-Marc Bailbé and Christian Robin, *Un Editeur et son siècle: Pierre-Jules Hetzel* (Saint-Sébastien: ACL, 1988) [T]**.

Letter 139

1. Julie Foucher, sister of Mme Victor Hugo, had married the engraver Paul Chenay in 1859. She was due to arrive in Guernsey the following day to help with the copying.

2. Paul Chenay had already engraved one of the "hanged men" by Hugo and had published it with great success. He took advantage of this to seek permission to engrave an album of twelve drawings by Victor Hugo. The enterprise will turn out disastrously. **Hugo had made three drawings of a hanged man, arising from his interest in abolishing the death penalty—see Gaudon, *Exilium*, 128. On Hugo's dislike of the "disastrous" engravings, see *MUL*, 535 and *VH*, 390–1 [T]**.

Letter 140

1. After a four-day visit, the publisher Lacroix was leaving Guernsey with the manuscript of *Fantine*. **"Fantine" is both the name of a character in *Les Misérables* (see above, L. 68, n. 1 and 131, n. 1) and the title of the first of the novel's five parts [T]**.

2. Adèle Hugo and her mother will return to Guernsey on 16 December.

Letter 141

1. See *LJD*, 228. **In his letter Hugo expresses the desire that he and**

Drouet should die at the same time. "We will die loving each other to be reborn adoring one another, and the paternity of God will be over us." He promises to watch over her if he should happen to die before her and invokes the spirits of their two dead daughters, Claire and Léopoldine—the two "angels" to whom Drouet refers here in her reply [T].

 a. Blewer (*LVH*, 281) reads "love" [T].

Letter 142

 1. Mme Hugo left on this morning for Paris, after a two-and-a-half-month stay on the island.

 a. **Mardi Gras was the anniversary of Drouet and Hugo's first night together as lovers in 1833—see above, L. 80, 135, and Introduction, pp. 10–11 [T].**

Letter 143

 1. The first part of *Les Misérables*, *Fantine*, appeared in Brussels on 30 March and in Paris on 3 April. Already on the third, Hugo had noted in his diary: "The newspapers arrive full of quotations" (*OC*, 12:1391).

Letter 144

 1. See *LJD*, 262. On this day **(according to Blewer [*LVH*, 285, n. 1])** Hugo sent Lacroix the end of the manuscript of *Les Misérables*. **In this letter Hugo associates his joy at finishing *Les Misérables* with the joy of celebrating at the same time Drouet's feast day, the day of Saint Julie [T].**

Letter 145

 1. On 13 September there took place at Brussels the "Banquet of *Les Misérables*," organized by the publishers of the novel; eighty guests, including numerous writers and journalists, honored the author of *Les Misérables*.

Letter 146

 a. **This is a reference to the coup d'état of 2 December 1851, by which Louis-Napoléon Bonaparte overthrew the government, a fact that led to Hugo's current exile [T].**

 b. **For an account of what Hugo did on 2 December 1851, see *VH* 296–300 [T].**

Letter 147

 1. On this day Hugo signed a lease for a house at 20 Hauteville Street, farther away from his but considered to be less damp than the one in which Juliette had been

living since 1856: he will call it "Hauteville-Féerie." Juliette will not move there until 16 June 1864. **20 Hauteville Street is really only a few more steps away from Hauteville House than La Fallue, where Drouet is currently living. Psychologically the house seems a long way away to her because it does not directly overlook Hauteville House in the way that La Fallue does. Nevertheless, Drouet was still able to see Hauteville House and glimpse part of the balcony of Hugo's lookout from a front-bedroom window (cf. *MUL*, 618) and also from her garden at the back of the house [T].**

    a. Thomas Domaille is the owner of 20 Hauteville Street, from whom the house was rented and then bought—see *JDD*, 301, 309f. [T].

Letter 148

    1. On 18 June Adèle Hugo left her father's house "with violence and mystery," as Hugo will say (*OC*, 12:1221). In this escapade in pursuit of the man she loved, a British officer named Pinson, she will lose her remaining sanity. It is in this way that Hugo will lose his second daughter. **See above, Introduction, p. 22 [T].**

Letter 149

    1. Since March 1862 Victor Hugo had been offering a weekly meal to twelve poor children on the island. The majority were the children of French parents. The number grew rapidly; for Christmas 1863 there were thirty-seven.

    a. "Madam Countess" [T].

Letter 151

    1. Albert Lacroix, publisher of *Les Misérables* (see above, L. 138, n. 1) had arrived in Guernsey on the nineteenth to negotiate the purchase of *William Shakespeare*. On the twentieth he accepted Hugo's draft contract.

    2. Louis Ulbach (1822–1899), writer and journalist, drama critic at the time for *Le Temps*. He had arrived with Lacroix to spend two days on the island.

    a. François-Victor, Hugo's son [T].

    3. Suzanne, her longtime servant, had been drinking for several months.

Letter 152

    1. For the third centenary of the birth of Shakespeare, a Shakespeare committee formed by the friends of Victor Hugo had planned a banquet. The celebration was to take place in Paris on 23 April 1864, and the chairman of the committee, Victor Hugo, was to be represented there by an empty chair. The imperial veto occurred on the sixteenth.

    2. The sculptor Lebeuf started a bust of Victor Hugo on 22 April 1864. The work will take a little more than three weeks. It is preserved now at the Maison de Victor Hugo.

Letter 153

a. I follow the reading of *LVH*, 295—"grimaud" rather than "primaud" [T].

1. The invitation would have permitted Juliette to enter officially into the intimacy of the family **(on the meals for poor children given by Hugo, see above, L. 149 and n. 1 [T])**. It was not until 22 December that Adèle invited her in writing to the meal for the poor children (*OC*, 12:1321):

> We are celebrating Christmas today, Madame. Christmas is a celebration in honor of children and, consequently, of ours. It would be very gracious of you to attend this little ceremony, a celebration also in honor of your heart. Kind and sincere regards,
>
> Adèle Victor Hugo

Juliette replied immediately:

> Madame, your invitation is my celebration. Your letter is sweet and generous and I am touched by it. You know my solitary habits and will bear me no ill will if today I content myself with the happiness of your letter. This happiness is great enough. Please permit me to remain in the shade to bless you all while you do good. Tender and profound devotion,
>
> Juliette Drouet

Letter 154

1. The signal that indicated to Juliette that Hugo had got up: a cloth that Hugo tied to the balcony. **From a window of her house at 20 Hauteville, Drouet could see the balcony and lookout of Hugo's house higher up the street (see above, L. 147, n. 1) [T].**

2. Emily de Putron, François-Victor's fiancée, died on the fourteenth. Mme Hugo will leave for Brussels with her distraught son on 18 January, the day before the burial. Victor Hugo's speech on this occasion will be collected in *Actes et Paroles* (*OC*, 12: 895–6). **Emily de Putron (1834–1865) was the daughter of a Guernsey shipowner, who helped François-Victor with his translations of Shakespeare and died from tuberculosis before they could marry [T].**

Letter 155

1. On 2 February François-Victor had written: "You have always been so indulgent toward me, so kind about everything that is dear to me, so hospitable, so gracious, so nobly considerate toward all of us, that you make gratitude toward you the sweetest of my duties" (*OC*, 12:1695–6).

Letter 156

1. On 29 April Hugo noted in his diary: "I finished the book *L'Abîme* at eleven o'clock this morning" (*L'Abîme* was the first title of *Les Travailleurs de la mer*) (*OC*, 12:1492). **On *Les Travailleurs de la mer*, a novel by Hugo, see Glossary [T].**

Letter 157

    a. See above, L. 154 and n. 1 [T].

Letter 158

    1. The departure for Brussels, via London, will indeed take place on Wednesday, 28 June. They will return at the end of October, having traveled in Belgium and Germany.

    2. The reference is to *La Grand' Mère*, written in six days and finished on 24 June. It was Julie Chenay who had made the copy of *L'Abîme* (see above, L. 156, n. 1). **On *La Grand' Mère*, see Glossary [T].**

Letter 159

    1. The posthumous publication of *Les Evangiles annotés* by Proudhon cost Lacroix a lawsuit. It is not until 30 January that Hugo, having learned the verdict, will write to Lacroix: "How empty and null are these notes of Proudhon's! What shameful scoundrels your judges are!" (*OC*, 13:756). Lacroix was sentenced to a year in prison and a fine of Fr 1,800. **Pierre-Joseph Proudhon (1809–1865) was a journalist, politician, and radical thinker on social questions whose opinions had led to his imprisonment [T].**

    2. The final proofs of *Les Travailleurs de la mer*. The novel will appear on 12 March.

    a. Gilliat is the hero of *Les Travailleurs de la mer*, who salvages the boat engine belonging to the father of the girl he loves and in so doing battles with a giant octopus [T].

    b. Hugo frequently notices the similarity between great things and small and stresses the importance of both. In *Les Misérables* he equates "l'évolution de la comète dans le firmament" ("the orbit of the comet in the firmament") to the "tournoiement de l'infusoire dans la goutte d'eau" ("twisting of the protozoon in a drop of water"), *Les Misérables*, ed. Journet, 2:416 [T].

Letter 160

    a. Drouet means that because her shutters were closed she did not see at what time Hugo tied the cloth to the balcony, signaling that he had got up—see above, L. 154 and n.1 [T].

Letter 161

    1. One of the English phrases that Victor Hugo most liked to use in his letters.

    2. The annual trip will last from Wednesday, 20 June until 10 October. Hugo will spend most of his time working on *L'Homme qui rit*. **On this novel by Hugo, see Glossary [T].**

    a. Blewer notes that Busquet was a "journalist and poet (1820–1883), suitor of Adèle after a stay at Hauteville House (1860), publisher

of François-Victor with Pagnerre, and traveling companion of Hugo and Charles in Germany in 1863 and 1864" (*LVH*, 305, n. 3) [T].

b. "Born" ("née," is written as the same-sounding "nez," meaning "nose") [T].

Letter 162

a. Anniversary of the 2 December coup d'état of 1851, which brought Hugo into exile—see above, L. 146 and n. a [T].

1. *Victor Hugo raconté par un témoin de sa vie* (1863), a biography written by Mme Hugo with the collaboration of Auguste Vacquerie. Mme Hugo had given a copy of it to Juliette Drouet at the time of her first return to Guernsey after the publication of the book.

Letter 163

a. The cloth tied to the balcony that indicated to Drouet, who could see it from her house, that Hugo had got up—see above, L. 154 and n.1 [T].

b. "Very good" is written in English. [T].

1. Mme Hugo returned to Guernsey from 18 January to 6 March 1867. She paid a visit to Juliette on 22 January, which must have required lengthy negotiations. Juliette will return the visit on the twenty-fourth without great enthusiasm, speaking of "formal courtesy." **This was the first time that Mme Hugo and Juliette Drouet had officially visited one another in the thirty-four years of Drouet's liaison with Hugo, although, as Sabourin (*JDD*, 319) points out, Drouet had dined with Hugo and his wife several times in Brussels the previous year. Hauteville House had been finely decorated with Hugo's very active involvement over a number of years. It contains several extremely ornamental drawing rooms as well as several other highly ornamented rooms not officially designated as "salons." Evidently, Hugo was accustomed to keeping them locked up, fearing, among other things, that the dog, Sénat, would spoil them** [T].

Letter 164

1. Juliette will begin on this very day to collate the copy of *L'Homme qui rit* with Julie Chenay. The three asterisks are explained by the fact that the title has not yet been chosen. The copying had been finished up to the end of the fourth book of part II.

Letter 165

1. The doctor who was taking care of Juliette.

2. These portraits are in Book I of part II of *L'Homme qui rit*. **Duchess Josiane of Clancharlie and Lord David Dirrymoir are two of Hugo's satirized English aristocrats in this novel** [T]. The phrase about Rembrandt is a comic illustration of the theory of metempsychosis.

a. The words "stepple chease," that is, the English "steeplechase," and "Rembrand" appear as given [T].

Letter 166

a. Drouet and Hugo have been in Brussels (where Mme Hugo, and Hugo's son Charles, and Charles' wife, Alice, are living) from 27 July and will stay until 9 October. During this time a second son, Georges (see Glossary), is born to Charles and Alice. The first Georges had died of meningitis in April of this year [T].

1. Mme Victor Hugo had died on the previous day in Brussels. She will be buried at Villequier. Hugo will accompany the funeral procession, the evening of the twenty-eighth, as far as the French border, **but Drouet has decided, as this letter shows, that it would be best for her not to attend. Mme Hugo will be buried next to her daughter Léopoldine, who had drowned twenty-five years before [T].**

1870s

Letter 168

Guernsey, 7 August 1870
Sunday afternoon, half past 3:00

Whatever you decide and whatever you do, my dear beloved, I'm with you, heart, body, and soul. So don't hesitate to make and unmake plans until you find one you like and can put into action.[1] But above all, no separation, not even for a second, whatever happens! Happiness or unhappiness or death must find us inseparable. This is our contract that neither one of us any more than the other has the right to break. It must be accepted once and for all and never breached, no matter what the circumstances and events that present themselves. I harp on it so that you won't make me any more nasty propositions for the future. For this once, I forgive Papapa.[2]

I see that the Rimmel fellow and the Austrian fellow have the capital luck of dropping into Hauteville House precisely on the day when you're doing your Charles the favor of reading him some poetry! Happily, I'll benefit from it also along with him, along with them, and along with all the company present at that moment. What happiness! What happiness!! What happiness!!!

Letter 169

Bordeaux, 27 February 1871
Monday evening, 5 o'clock

Dear beloved, far from filling me with joy, this beautiful day gives me, on the contrary, an immense desire to cry. It's because I'm thinking of our dear little paradise lost, in Guernsey, of our sweet walks around the island that we will perhaps never take again, of our life that was so peaceful and so happy, of your undisputed glory, of your genius shining over everybody, of your sublime word heeded religiously at all four points of the compass—compared with what happens here[1] and what threatens you in the future—and I'm sad right to the depths of my soul.

I don't dare to wish for an egotistical happiness by asking God to return to me what I miss so bitterly, because I'm not sure that your heart feels the same need as mine. But I ardently beg Him to keep at a distance all the chalices that are extended toward you all at the same time and to preserve you from all perils.

Letter 170

Brussels, 28 May 1871
Sunday afternoon, 4 o'clock

Is it possible, my great beloved, that it's because of your letter that was so sublime, so magnanimous, and so generous for the vanquished and the victorious, that the attempt was made, almost successfully, to assassinate you last night at your house, perhaps risking the life of your two little grandchildren and of their mother, the poor widow of your son Charles?![1] It is hard to believe, and it puts this country to shame and reveals the black ingratitude of those you defend, which is as great as that of your opponents. I am devastated and overwhelmed by it more than I have ever been by anything in my life, long and full of trials as it has been.

Here is Suzanne back from your place. The superintendent of police was just at your house. He came to ask you not to sleep there tonight. Not that he doesn't answer for[2]

Letter 171

Paris,[a] 27 January 1872
Friday evening, 4 o'clock

I hope, my great swot, that you haven't decided to take the key to the fields or the key to the woods or to the wildflowers in this season of frogs and Gribouilles?[b] On this topic, I remind you that your umbrella is here.

You must have received the letter containing the three hundred francs for Charroin that Suzanne was to deliver to you personally this morning. I give you this little reminder so you won't forget it in the midst of all the things you have to do, not to mention all the fish you have to fry. Tell me now, *Mister Poet*, to what astonishing nurse are these gallant verses dedicated that you thought inappropriate to have me copy?[1] This little scruple of conscience probably hides a big infamy for which my poor old heart will have to suffer, alas! The proof is that the strained smile I tried to put on as I began this question ends with my eyes filling with tears. I'm wrong still to have these painful curiosities, but I'm yet more wrong to love you in 1872 with the same ardent and jealous passion as I had in 1833. This anachronism is more than a fault, it's an absurdity for which I ought to atone. Too bad if I love you too much!

Letter 172

Paris, Thursday morning, 7 o'clock, 11 April *[1872]*

Permit me, my great beloved, to send you my sixty-six years all newly burst forth from their buds for you this morning! Give them a good welcome,[1] these good old things all blazing with love for you as if they were born only yesterday! I ask little Jeanne to kiss you for me sixty-six million times today; not a kiss less and a few more. I hope little Georges has not had any more nosebleeds since yesterday and that he had, along with you all, a very good night. As for myself I slept like a log last night, and I'm in perfect health this morning. I feel a youthful verve that is probably due to the sixty-six springtimes I've resolutely absorbed without a fuss. The sky itself is playing its part by pouring over them the cream of its sunshine. So long live *our* love first of all—for a bit of egotism doesn't spoil happiness, especially that one—and then long live love for all those whom we love! Be blessed, my great beloved, in all those whom you love! I adore you.

Letter 173

Thursday, half past 3:00, 13 June 1872

My dear beloved, if there is *someone or something* between you and me, it's not of my doing and I know nothing about it.[1] All that I know is that I love you alone, sincerely, faithfully, and sacredly, that *I want never to see either my daughter or you again in the hereafter if there is someone on this earth that I love more than you,* and I sign

J.

Now, my beloved, smile at me as I smile at you, and trust in me as I trust in you!

Letter 174

Guernsey,[1] 1 July 1873
Tuesday morning, half past 6:00

Dear great and ineffable beloved, my eyes, my heart, my soul are in quest of you, your night, and your health. So far I have received no visible sign,[a] but I'll be very happy if you have had a good night. In the meantime I help with the preparations for the departure of poor Blanche—not without emotion, although I have, or believe that I have (which is the same thing), many reasons not to be sad about her leaving.[2] Besides, she herself wanted to go, and at this moment her face is beaming with joy. I hope sincerely and with all my heart that she finds in Paris the happiness she is hoping for and to which she has a right; and if it were possible for me to contribute to it, I would do even that with speed and pleasure, provided that it wasn't to the detriment of my own happiness. That being said, I pray to God to protect and bless her, as I pray to Him to protect you and bless you and to let me live and die by your side.

Letter 175

Paris,[a] 8 September, 1873
Sunday afternoon,[1] quarter to 2:00

Whatever you say, my dear great beloved, you allow yourself to be a little too encumbered by the *Fair Sex*. By dint of aspiring to the fine title of "Little Blue Cloak of Tarts in a Bind,"[2] you'll end up not knowing where to give chase or where to blow your horn, even if you had Hernani's.[b] If I were in your place, I wouldn't lend myself so benevolently to this systematic exploitation of your time, your purse, and your influence without knowing who has a right to it and who profits from it. Your latest client appears to me to be an Agnès[c] very experienced in the art of exciting curiosity by means of mysteriousness and poste restante addresses. It's true that what succeeds with you would be far from interesting to me, and would indeed have the opposite effect. That's why I hasten to recognize the futility of my observations, which are of no use to you. In short, what I find tiresome naturally appears to you very agreeable, which is why you do right to lend yourself to it and to persist with it. "A sultan must have sultanas, a dagger its pearls!"[3] I thank you nonetheless for having offered to go out with me just now, but my very real cold forces me to keep my room for a few days more. You've given me something to give me patience until you return. I'm going to profit from it immediately, so that you can give me other marvels to copy tomorrow. I adore you.

Letter 176

Paris, 16 October 1873
Thursday afternoon, 4 o'clock

There are some things that are not revealed by witnesses and inquests, my dear beloved, but which make themselves felt. One of these is true love, without limit and incorruptible, another is pitiless betrayal, permanent and cowardly, by the woman of the man or, vice versa, by the man of the woman. Which of the two of us has the right to take God as witness of his or her love, which of us must avow to being guilty in his heart of hearts? God knows it, and it is to Him I turn in this infernal contest between your love and my love, which is always being called into question. My soul is so distracted I can no longer distinguish between you and me. All I know is that I'll not last long in this constantly renewed battle between my old love and the young temptations that are offered to you, even though they may be unsolicited by you—which is anything but proven, alas! All I know, and God knows I don't lie, is that in this new and painful trial there are some things that only you and I know and no one could have guessed.

Now I forgive you because I want God to forgive you also, He Who alone has the right to punish and the power to deliver me as quickly as possible from this terrestrial Hell where my poor heart has been tortured since the first minute that I gave myself to you. I ask Him to spare you all the sufferings I endure and to absolve you from the imprudent oaths sworn, and sacrileges committed, on the life of your sick son.[a]

Letter 177

Paris, 28 December 1873
Sunday morning, half past 10:00

My dear beloved, you will not be alone today as you climb the road to Calvary.[1] All those who feel with you (and the number is great), all those who suffer your pain, all those who find hope in God as you do, all those who, like I, venerate you, admire you, adore you, and bless you will be there to prevent you from falling on your knees and to uphold your courage until you reach the end of your painful journey.

Dear beloved, bless me as I bless you!

Letter 178

Paris, 28 July 1874
Tuesday morning, 8 o'clock

I thought I noticed, my dear beloved, that you were sad and vexed last night when you left me,[a] and I have been trying to find the reason for it. I think I have found it in your excessive kindness for everybody, which makes you simultaneously the object of the black ingratitude of some and of annoying importunities from others. Hence the disappointments and vexations of your life.

But what is to be done about it? The remedy, if there were one, would be worse than the malady for your generous and gallant nature. You have a need to oblige all those who address themselves to you, and you love persiflage of any kind, even that of chance encounters. Hence the distaste and vexations of your life and heart. It's no use my trying to become indifferent to them or ignore them, I cannot do it. And even if I were to reach this unhappy point, you would be no more tranquil or happy or free because of it, for the temptations follow one another and resemble one another to the point of irritating your desire rather than satisfying it. In vain do you throw your happiness and mine into this Danaids' cask, you will never succeed in filling it sufficiently to find there even a drop of the pleasure you desire to drink so thirstily.

You are not happy, my poor beloved, and no more am I. You are suffering from an open sore caused by the female sex that continually grows bigger because you don't have the courage to cauterize it once and for all. *I* suffer from loving you too much. We each have our own incurable disease. Alas! Who knows if we won't in fact carry it with us to the hereafter? This *that is the question [sic]* is horrible!

Letter 179

Guernsey, 27 April 1875
Tuesday morning, 5 o'clock

Good morning, my beloved, good morning, my fine sun of Guernsey,[a] my blessings on both of you, I adore you both! The weather this morning seems filled with promise, not only for our departure today but also for our imminent return to all our dear little loved ones in Paris. In the meantime, some ill-wishers found it funny yesterday evening to break a pane of the staircase window, and last night a windowpane in the kitchen. This attack against my house, strangely reminiscent of the sinister events in Brussels,[1] is completely inexplicable to me, a poor woman without initiative of any sort except to love you more and better than any other living being on this earth or than any soul in Heaven. I think it's just to say that I don't deserve either this excessive honor or this indignity, and that it's an insult to both my modesty and my pride. I hope these rascally tricks will end with our departure, otherwise the upkeep of the house will be ruinous and impossible. Perhaps it's only a stupid prank, but it doesn't make it any less expensive or worrying. Perhaps, too, you would be wise to take steps to make sure it doesn't happen again in our absence. I kiss your blessed forehead.

Letter 180

Paris, 7 September 1875
Tuesday morning, 9 o'clock

Good morning, my great little man, good morning! I adore you, and how about you—do *you* adore *me?* While awaiting your response, there's a charming little letter here from Georges with a picture of his hotel, which is really very beautiful and makes one want to go and surprise your beaming brats in this nest of verdure and waterfall.[a] Unfortunately, your grandeur detains you on another shore, which means your girl is mum and that I keep quiet about all my desires for travel and sojourn in the country. On another topic,[b] Lemonnier has finally made up his mind to ask you for your representation at his Peace

Congress, which will take place next Sunday, that's to say, in four days;[1] this gives you very short notice, but that's not something that worries you, fortunately. I'm not worried, either, when it's a question of telling you about my heart from the beginning to the end, from "I love you" to "I adore you."

I almost forgot to tell you—little Jeanne has written a nice little letter full of big, big butterflies.

Letter 181

Paris, 1 November 1876
Wednesday evening, half past 6:00

Dear beloved, I agitate myself greatly for very little result. Though I put all my courage and all my heart into it, at the end of my day there's nothing to show for it except proof of my useless love.[a] This sad daily demonstration must annoy you as much as it does me, and in particular inspire you to alter this state of things as soon as possible, since it's impeding your great life, which is so gloriously necessary for humanity. The solution would be to put in my place someone more capable, if not more devoted—for I have the proud conviction that you'll find no one anywhere, no matter of what sex or of what age, more ardently devoted to your person, to your interests, and to your glory than my poor old heart, which venerates you and adores you. I feel this harsh necessity for a change in the management of your household, and I'm ready to resign myself to it . . . from a distance, as I'm afraid I won't be able to tolerate at close quarters the person whom you'll necessarily invest with your trust and authority.

I beg you to let me go and finish my days in Guernsey[b] or elsewhere where I'll have the right to adore you without encumbering and saddening your house, which ought to be a luminous and serene Mecca for everybody.

Letter 182

Paris, Thursday, noon, 6 June 1878

Dear great and sublime man of justice, your letter to Dupanloup[1] has a formidable and crushing effect. Nothing could be more powerfully contemptuous, more serenely honest, more sovereignly terrible, and more astrally sublime than this lofty and laconic letter.

Dear beloved, I don't have the art of speaking and writing as grammar dictates, but my heart, as my soul, knows how to admire you and adore you in your work and in your person with a perfection that no one on earth or in Heaven can surpass. This syntax is worth just as much as the other kind, isn't it?

Good old Boulet, who did my hair this morning, is delirious with enthusiasm, and all those who read *Le Rappel* while waiting for their turn in the barber's chair are even more so, according to what he says. Which I don't find hard to believe, judging by my own feelings—I have never admired or adored you more than at this moment. Bless you!

Notes

Letter 168

1. France had declared war on Prussia on 19 July. Since then Hugo had been wondering what course of action to take. He will leave Guernsey for Brussels on 15 August.

2. The name given to Victor Hugo by his grandchildren, Georges and Jeanne, who were then in Guernsey with their parents.

Letter 169

1. Having been elected deputy on 8 February, Victor Hugo, accompanied by his family, has reached Bordeaux where the Assemblée nationale has been sitting. **Drouet and Hugo, accompanied by his son Charles and his family, as well as Drouet's nephew, Louis Koch (who had been visiting Guernsey for a few days), had left Guernsey for Brussels on 15 August 1870. From there, on 5 September, Hugo, Drouet, and Charles and his family had returned to Paris shortly before the beginning of the siege of Paris by the Prussians, to stay with Paul Meurice—the first time Hugo and Drouet had set foot in France in nineteen years. The siege finished on 28 January 1871 with France's capitulation to Prussia. On 8 February 1871 Hugo was elected to the Assemblée nationale and went to Bordeaux, but will resign a month later as a protest over the reactionary tendencies of the assembly and their annulment of the election of Garibaldi. This "beautiful day" may refer in part to the fact that it is Hugo's birthday (he was born on the twenty-sixth but often celebrated it on the twenty-seventh) [T].**

Letter 170

1. Concerning the serious incident of 27 May 1871 which led to the expulsion of Victor Hugo from Belgium, see the text of *Actes et Paroles* in *OC*, 15:1292ff. Charles had died on 13 March 1871. **Hugo and Drouet had come to Brussels on 21 March so that Hugo could settle the estate of Charles, who had been living in that city before dying suddenly, at the age of forty-four, in Bordeaux. Hugo had published a letter protesting against Belgium's agreement to extradite back to France any Communards who sought refuge there. An angry mob had attacked Hugo's house, and he was expelled from Belgium by the government for breaching the peace—*VH*, 467–8. Hugo and Drouet would seek refuge in Luxembourg from 1 June to 23 September 1871, returning to France and ultimately Paris on 24 September [T].**

2. The letter is interrupted here.

Letter 171

a. In Paris Hugo lived at 66 rue de la Rochefoucauld and Drouet across the road at 55 rue Pigalle—*cf. JDD*, 352 [T].

b. This sentence is full of puns that cannot be translated into English. The expression "to take the key to the fields," meaning "to take to one's heels" or "to bolt," is followed by a joke about taking the key also to the woods and to "amourettes" ("cowslips," "wildflowers"), meaning also "casual love affairs." "Grenouilles" ("frogs") are not just amphibians but also whores, and the close-sounding word "Gribouilles" appears in the expression "fin comme Gribouille qui se jette dans l'eau crainte de pluie," meaning "cunning like Gribouille, who throws himself into the water out of fear of the rain" (*Littré*, s.v. Gribouille), to refer to someone who, in order to avoid one danger, courts another. Here "gribouilles" seems to occur just because it sounds similar to "grenouilles" and is associated, like frogs, with the rain—hence the reference to the umbrella [T].

1. This poem ("Si dans ce grand Paris, ô charmante infirmière ...") ["If in this great Paris, O charming nurse ... "]) is in the collection entitled *Le Moi* in *Toute la lyre* (*OC*, 15-16.2:140).

Letter 172

1. See Hugo's response, *LJD*, 265. It reads: "My sweet angel, there is no old age for light. You are my ray. You are young here, as you will be in Heaven. Already I see you as an angel. I love you." Drouet's letter is a celebration of her sixty-sixth birthday on 10 April [T].

Letter 173

1. This letter is a response to a parallel declaration made by Victor Hugo to Juliette in his letter of Thursday morning (*LJD*, 267). The flirtation with Judith Mendès, daughter of Théophile Gautier, is not yet in full swing. **For the relationship with Judith Mendès, see *VS*, fascicule 6. In his letter, to which Drouet replies here, Hugo says:**

> Listen, my beloved, I haven't slept all night, I am deeply sad. It seems to me that there is *someone or something* between us. However, I am sure that it is not on my side. Last night you asked me a question that leads me to say to you, and to write to you, this: I want never to see either my daughter or you again in the hereafter if there is someone on this earth that I love more than you.—And I sign
>
> V.
>
> Write to me and sign with *J.* for me the same declaration, and I will sleep tonight. I adore you.
>
> V. [T].

Letter 174

1. Since August 1872 Victor Hugo and Juliette have been staying in Guernsey. **They will return to Paris on 30 July 1873 [T].**

a. **Meaning that Drouet has not yet seen through her window Hugo's towel tied to his balcony signaling that he has got up—see above, L. 154 and n. 1 [T].**

2. Juliette had only suspicions about this girl in her service, and no doubt it was Hugo who decided to send her away. But we know that it was only a ruse. Blanche Lanvin, who according to Louis Barthou (*Les Amours d'un poète* [Paris: Louis Conard, 1919]), had been the lover of Victor Hugo since 1 April, returns clandestinely by 12 July. This love affair will last, through various crises, until 1878. **See above, Introduction, p. 24 [T].**

Letter 175

a. **Drouet and Hugo are staying in a furnished house in Auteuil to be close to Hugo's son François-Victor, who is ill with renal tuberculosis, *JDD*, 365 [T].**

1. An error in the date: it is Sunday, 7 September 1873.

2. Edme Champion (1764–1852), an orphan who had grown up to make a fortune in the jewelry business, distributed alms on the streets dressed in a little blue cloak, whence his nickname "the man in the little blue cloak." His ostentatious generosity impeded his political ambitions.

At this time Hugo is completely preoccupied with his love for Blanche Lanvin. His more or less concealed acts of liberality are known from his notebooks. On this particular day no new "client" is mentioned there. Juliette will discover the liaison with Blanche on 19 September and will flee to Belgium without leaving an address. **Hugo kept records of his payments to women for sexual favors by noting them as "secours" ("assistance")—*HS*, 76. According to Sabourin (*JDD*, 366), Drouet's departure was precipitated by the discovery of a letter written to Hugo by a mentally disturbed woman with whom Hugo was not, in fact, having an affair, and that it was not, in fact, the discovery of the true extent of Hugo's relationship with Lanvin at this point that brought about this particular crisis (375). In any case, Hugo will be tremendously upset about Drouet's disappearance. The extent of his anguish can be seen in Letters 241–5 in *LJD* in which the phrase "to lose you is to die" recurs. In Letter 244 (*LJD*, 292) he makes the statement: "You are my joy, my life, my thought, my supreme necessity, my happiness in this world, my hope in the next, my prayer day and night, my sweet Juliette, my eternal love." During this time Hugo did not know of Drouet's whereabouts and dispatched letters to friends and relatives with whom she may have taken refuge in Guernsey, Belgium, and Germany. She will finally return on 26 September [T].**

b. There is an untranslatable pun here on the word "corps" ("body") and "cor" ("horn"). The reference to "Hernani" is to the hero of Hugo's play *Hernani* (see Glossary), who carries a horn with which he can summon his comrades and which is used by the aged Don Ruy Gomez de Silva to reclaim the young Doña Sol from her young lover, Hernani. There may also then be a sly dig here at Hugo's pursuit of women much younger than himself [T].

c. This is a reference to the young romantic heroine in the 1662 comedy *L'Ecole des femmes* by Molière. Agnès is a young woman who has been brought up in a state of total sexual innocence but nevertheless becomes embroiled in a triangular love affair [T].

3. "La Sultane favorite," *Les Orientales*, XII (a collection of poetry by Hugo, see Glossary [T]).

Letter 176

a. It seems that Hugo must have sworn on the life of his sick son, François-Victor (see above, L. 175 n. a), in promising fidelity to Drouet. Cf. *HS*, 114 [T].

Letter 177

1. François-Victor Hugo died on the twenty-sixth. He was buried on the twenty-eighth in the Père-Lachaise cemetery. Hugo followed the procession on foot. He wrote in his notebook: "The people followed you, as I did" (*OC*, 15–16.2:842).

Letter 178

a. Since April 1874 Hugo, Drouet, Hugo's grandchildren, Georges and Jeanne, and their mother, Alice, have been living at 21 rue de Clichy. Hugo, the grandchildren, and their mother occupy the fourth floor, while Drouet lives on the third floor (*JDD*, 377) [T].

Letter 179

a. Blewer (*LVH*, 333, n. 1) notes that "this brief stay in Guernsey (from 20 to 27 April) allowed Victor Hugo to retrieve from the bank the trunk of manuscripts that he had deposited there in 1870 before returning to France." Drouet feared this would be the last time she would ever see her house and Guernsey where she had been so happy, and she writes in a letter of 21 April (*MUL*, 730): "The thought that we will not come back again to these houses that are ours, where we have suffered, where we have been happy together, breaks my heart as though I were already attending our funerals." In fact they would return once more to Guernsey from 5 July to 9 November 1878 [T].

1. See above, L. 170.

Letter 180

a. Hugo's grandchildren, Georges and Jeanne, and their mother, Alice, had gone on a trip to Italy [T].

b. The French says "autre guitare" ("another guitar"), which is a reference (see n. 1 below) to the title of one of Hugo's poems [T].

1. Hugo will content himself with sending to the Peace Congress an address dated 10 September, which will be reproduced in *Actes et paroles* (*OC*, 15–16.1:1365–6). "Autre Guitare" is the title of a poem in *Les Rayons et les ombres* (XXIII). **The poem called "Autre Guitare" ("Another Guitar") follows the poem called "Guitare." ("Guitar"). Both are poetic evocations of guitar music. Drouet's reference to the poem "Autre Guitare" seems to be no more than a joking way of moving on to another topic but without any specific reference to the content of the poem. According to Guimbaud (*VHJD*, 2:502), these poems were inspired by Drouet** [T].

Letter 181

a. After the return to Paris from exile, Drouet acted as Hugo's secretary-cum-housekeeper. Her age and failing health made the task increasingly difficult for her. Several letters (for example, that dated 22 August 1874 [*CL*, 80–1]) among the collection in *CL* testify to the same situation [T].

b. A letter dated 18 December 1878 (*CL*, 95) shows that Hugo did offer to send Drouet to live in Guernsey at his expense, but she rejects the idea outright in this letter [T].

Letter 182

1. On 30 May 1878 Hugo had delivered an important speech to commemorate the centenary of the death of Voltaire (*OC*, 15–16.1:1428–34). François Dupanloup, Bishop of Orléans, had replied to Victor Hugo in an open letter. It was to this letter that Hugo replied on 3 June in *Le Rappel* (*OC*, 15–16.1:1435–6). **Voltaire (1694–1778), historian, poet, philosopher, while reviled by Hugo at an early stage in his career, was admired greatly by him in the latter stages of it. Hugo's 1878 speech on Voltaire was eulogistic. Dupanloup (1802–1878), who had built his reputation on his reactionary views, disliked Hugo's admiration for this liberal philosopher.**

1880s

Letter 183

Paris, 20 May 1880
Thursday morning, 8 o'clock

"Double restitus," is all I have to say to you! Tremble! My pitiless love won't spare you a single scribble or a single tenderness! Too bad! That'll teach you to make yourself too much loved! You were too sleepy just now for me to dare to ask you how you slept; but if your experience was anything like mine, you slept like a log.

Dear beloved, tomorrow is the *twenty-first*, the eve of the *twenty-second*, as good old Jocrisse would say; *I* say the eve of Saint Julie's day, that is, of a nice little letter from you, awaited, desired, and blessed in advance.[1]

Nothing has changed in the order of the day today at the Senate.[a] Open session at two and no office. The stock of letters very few and not at all interesting. The weather, overcast, gloomy, and cold like an old maid wearing the bonnet of Saint Catherine.[b] Talking about Saint Catherine, we're having to dinner tonight the one who bears this name but not the bonnet—Mme Catherine Glaize—with her husband and her valiant uncle, Auguste Vacquerie;[c] plus the three Houssayes[d] and Saint-Hérem; in all fourteen people to dine. That reminds me that apart from the housekeeping money that you must give me today, you also have to pay the locksmith's bill for Fr 18.45. You see that the items of expense are never ending—on the contrary. All of that can hardly excite your imagination on my behalf, as I harp on the subject every day. It's one of the biggest nuisances among my responsibilities, but one that I carry out without fear or disgrace and with all the courage of which I'm capable.

You have received from the Société des gens de lettres[e] a form invitation to attend the funeral of Paul de Musset, which will take place today at noon precisely, at the Eglise de la Madeleine. "Signed Emmanuel Gonzalès." I inform you of it, not so you'll go there, but so you can give the dead man a thought of sympathetic regret at the appropriate time.

Dear beloved, my scribbling is feeling the absence of sun, but under this tiresome grayness there is a sublime and radiant love that I put at your feet.

[Addressed] Monsieur Victor Hugo.

Letter 184

Paris, 15 October 1881
Saturday morning, half past 7:00

"Morning showers gladden the pilgrim" ... in the autumn, they say. So by this reckoning you will probably have very fine weather this afternoon for the ceremony of laying the foundation stone of the school in your *arrondissement*.[a]

And on this subject I renew my advice that you put on your new overcoat to attend it, as your dear little Georges, who will be going with you, will be turned out very smartly as usual. I give you notice in the meantime that today the rents are due to the *Princess* and for the rue de Clichy[b] as well as the gardener's bill, which amounts to *Fr 95.95*, of which *Fr 90* is for the quarter.

The flow of letters rises, rises, rises to the point of submersion. Soon I alone won't be able to open them all without a steam engine of several donkeys' power. There is hardly enough time to botch together my restitus for you at a scribbling gallop. I adore you en masse, heart, body, and soul, without pausing for breath.

[Addressed] Monsieur Victor Hugo.

Letter 185

Paris, 5 March 1882
Sunday morning, half past 11:00

Dear beloved, like the doublet of Don César, I'm struggling rather badly,[1] especially this morning, I must confess. The night passed well enough, but hardly had my feet touched the floor than sporadic vomiting took hold of me, which has lasted until now. Every time I move, it comes back, which tires me horribly. Hence it's impossible to busy myself with anything whatever, and this puts me behind with everything, even my poor little restitus. But I'm talking to you about nothing except myself, which nauseates me yet further. To revive my soul a little, I come to you whom I adore. How was your night? According to my *estima [sic]*, as they say in Guernsey, your night was so-so, which isn't enough. Fortunately, it's nice weather, so we can have a little walk, but we'll make sure there's no interruption to your work with the good fellow Lesclide.[2] In the meantime he's reading and filing the letters from this morning and the past week, as well as the books and the pamphlets, while I am adoring you.

[Addressed] Monsieur Victor Hugo.

Letter 186

Paris, 11 July 1882
Tuesday morning, half past 7:00

Dear beloved, I have just left you in a deep sleep, but that tells me nothing one way or another about your night's rest. May it have been as good as mine was bad, that's all I ask!

I don't know when or how it will end, but I suffer every day more and more and get weaker from hour to hour. At the moment I have hardly the strength to hold my pen and I have great difficulty concentrating on what I'm writing to you. However, I cling to life with all the strength of my love, so as not to leave you on earth too long without me. But alas, nature resists and is unwilling!

I beg your pardon for this lamentable scribble. But the weather itself is in no better humor than I. Dear beloved, I'd like to find something cheerful to say to you before writing the last word of this pitiful restitus, and I can find nothing except this: I love you, I admire you, I venerate you, and I adore you.

[Addressed] Monsieur Victor Hugo.

Notes

Letter 183

1. See *LJD*, 322. In this letter celebrating Drouet's feast day, Saint Julie's day, Hugo expresses the hope that he and Drouet will die at the same time and looks forward to their eternal life together in Heaven. It includes the statement: "I love you. I need you. You are the necessity of my life" [T].

a. Hugo had been elected to the Senate as a senator for Paris on 30 January 1876. The sessions were held in Versailles, and Drouet would accompany him there, waiting in a carriage outside (*JDD*, 379) [T].

b. The French, "comme une vieille fille coiffée par Sainte Catherine" ("like an old maid wearing the bonnet of Saint Catherine"), is a reference to the expression "coiffer sainte Catherine," meaning to have reached the age of twenty-five without marrying [T].

c. Léon Glaize (1842–1931) was the great-nephew of Auguste Vacquerie (see Glossary, Vacquerie family). Glaize was an artist and he illustrated Hugo's work *Les Châtiments* [T].

d. Houssaye (1815–1896) was a man of letters and former director of the Comédie-Française (see above, Introduction, passim). He refers in his memoirs (*Confessions*, 5:310) to his habit of dining at Hugo's house with his son, Henry (1848–1911), and Henry's wife [T].

e. A society founded in 1838 to promote the rights of authors pertaining to copyright issues, and so on, as well as to help writers in need. Paul de Musset (1804–1880), a writer, was the brother of the more famous Alfred de Musset (1810–1857), poet, novelist, and dramatist [T].

Letter 184

a. Blewer (*LVH*, 346, n. 1) notes that this school was the lycée Janson-de-Sailly, on the rue de la Pompe in Passy [T].

b. Hugo resided on the rue de Clichy before moving to his present address on the avenue d'Eylau (later renamed Avenue Victor Hugo). Arsène Houssaye tells us (*Confessions*, 5:304–5) that Hugo's house on this avenue was owned by the princesse de Lusignan, hence no doubt the reference to paying rent to the "princess" [T].

Letter 185

1. "My doublet has followed me into my misfortunes. It is struggling!" (*Ruy Blas*, IV, 2). In this play by Hugo the missing grandee, Don César, arrives unexpectedly back at court, entering by the chimney and thereby ripping his clothes [T].

2. Victor Hugo's secretary. **Richard Lesclide (1825–1892), author of a volume of reminiscences on Hugo,** *Propos de table de Victor Hugo,* **was a doctor by training and served Hugo for a time as secretary** [T].

Glossary

ADELE
See Hugo, Adèle (I), (II).

ALICE
See Hugo, Charles.

ANGELO
A prose drama by Hugo (1835) set in sixteenth-century Padua, involving the consequences of a courtesan's conflict between sexual and maternal passion and the revelation of hitherto concealed identities and pasts.

ASPLET family
Philippe Asplet was a *centenier*, or elected magistrate, in Saint-Helier, Jersey, and a friend of the exile community. His brother, Charles, and Charles' wife, were also friends of the Hugo family and of Juliette Drouet.

BERTIN family
Hugo was friendly with the Bertin family: the father, Louis-François (1766–1841), editor of the *Journal des débats*, a paper famous for its political and cultural articles; his sons, Armand and François-Edouard; and his daughter, Louise (1805–1877), a poet and musician, and composer of the music for the opera *La Esmeralda* (q.v.). The Bertin family had a country house, the château des Roches, in the vallée de la Bièvre, where Hugo and his family used to stay.

BIARD, Léonie
Léonie Biard, née d'Aunet (1820–1879), was the wife of an artist, François Biard (1799–1882), a genre painter and portraitist, who was very popular in his time and favored by Louis-Philippe. Léonie, pregnant with his child, married Biard after making a voyage with him to Spitsbergen in the Arctic Circle. Hugo met Léonie in 1844 (probably through Pradier) and their liaison lasted until

1851, although he continued to provide her with financial aid thereafter. Subsequently she published several ephemeral novels, such as, *Un mariage à province* (1856), *Une vengeance* (1858), *Etiennette, le secret* (1859), and the play *Jane Osborn*, performed in 1855 at the Porte-Saint-Martin. She had two children: Henriette (1840–1897) and Georges (1844–1934).

BIARD, Mme
See Biard, Léonie.

BLANCHARD, Suzanne
From 1839 onward she was Drouet's faithful servant and accompanied her into exile in the Channel Islands.

BLANCHE
See Lanvin family.

BURGRAVES, LES
Hugo's drama in verse (1843) is a story about the epic "Titanomachy" between the medieval warlords, the "burgraves," who inhabited castles along the banks of the Rhine, and the emperor of Germany. Hugo acknowledges in the preface to the play that it was inspired by his visit to the Rhineland in 1840.

CHANSONS DES RUES ET DES BOIS, LES
A collection of poems by Hugo (1865), written almost entirely in 1859 and 1865. They are lighthearted "songs" ("chansons") or lyric poems concerning less the city ("les rues," ["the streets"]) than the countryside ("les bois," ["the woods"]).

CHANTS DU CREPUSCULE, LES
A collection of poetry by Hugo (1835), expressing, in Hugo's words in the preface, "this strange twilight ['crépusculaire'] state of the soul and of society in the century in which we live."

CHARLES
See Hugo, Charles.

CHARLOT
See Hugo, Charles.

CHATIMENTS, LES
A collection of poems by Hugo, written shortly after going into exile and published in Brussels in 1853, denouncing the regime of Napoleon III. It was banned in France and did not appear there in unexpurgated form until 1870.

CHENAY family
Julie Chenay, née Foucher (1822–1905), was the much younger sister of Mme Hugo. She moved to Guernsey in 1860 and acted as housekeeper of Hauteville House from 1861. She also helped with the copying of Hugo's manu-

scripts. She was unhappily married to an engraver, Paul Chenay (1818–1906), who became estranged from his brother-in-law and published the defamatory reminiscence *Victor Hugo intime*.

CHENAY, M.
See Chenay family, Paul Chenay.

CHENAY, Mme
See Chenay family, Julie Chenay.

CLAIRE
See Pradier, Claire.

CLAUDE GUEUX
A tale by Hugo that appeared first in *La Revue de Paris* in 1834. The story concerns Claude Gueux, who like Jean Valjean in *Les Misérables*, is jailed for having stolen a loaf of bread to feed his family, and is about the brutality of the social system that destroys him.

CONTEMPLATIONS, LES
A two-volume collection of poetry by Victor Hugo published in 1856, the proceeds from the best-selling sales of which enabled Hugo to purchase Hauteville House in Guernsey.

DEDE
See Hugo, Adèle (II).

DIDINE
See Hugo, Léopoldine.

DORVAL, Marie
Marie Dorval (1798–1849) was a celebrated actress in her time. She took the part of Marion in Hugo's *Marion de Lorme* (q.v.) (1831, 1838), Catarina in *Angelo* (q.v.) (1835) as well as Tisbe (1836), Doña Sol in *Hernani* (q.v.) (1838), and Jane in *Marie Tudor* (q.v.) (1844). Her most celebrated role was Kitty Bell in the play *Chatterton* (1835) by Alfred de Vigny (1797–1863), who was her lover at the time. Although so feted at its peak, Dorval's career ended in obscurity, and she died from grief, some said, at the death of a beloved grandson.

DROUET, Eugénie
Eugénie Drouet (1816–1850) was the daughter of Françoise Drouet (q.v.), Juliette Drouet's aunt, and most likely the illegitimate child of an adulterous relationship. She attended the same pension as Claire Pradier (q.v.) and later became the lover and probably wife of Victor Vilain (q.v.), the sculptor. She had an illegitimate son, Jules-Charles (born 1836), with the painter Jules Ziegler.

DROUET, Françoise
Née Marchandet, Françoise Drouet (1779–1858) was the sister of Juliette Drouet's mother. She and her husband, René-Henry (q.v.), assumed the care of

Juliette after her parents' early death. After the couple moved to Paris with Juliette in 1815, Françoise lived separately from her husband and became involved to some degree in artistic circles. She had an illegitimate daughter, Eugénie (q.v.), in 1816. Françoise seems to have been manipulative, exploitative, and interfering. In 1833 she wrote a letter to Hugo in which she attempted to besmirch Drouet by revealing details of her past life.

DROUET, René-Henry

René-Henry Drouet (1774–1842) was a native of Brittany, uncle of Juliette Drouet, and her adoptive father, whose surname she took. He was married to Françoise Marchandet (see Françoise Drouet), sister of Drouet's mother. He served in the army and retired in 1814. He and his wife came to Paris to live in 1815 (although they would live separately), bringing Juliette, whom they installed in a convent. Drouet was very fond of her uncle.

ESMERALDA, LA

An opera adapted from the novel *Notre-Dame de Paris* (q.v.), with libretto by Hugo and music by Louise Bertin (see Bertin family). It was first performed at the Opéra in 1836 and was not a great success with the public.

FEUILLES D'AUTOMNE, LES

Les Feuilles d'automne is a collection of poems, published in 1831, in which Hugo evokes the charms of children, childhood, and domesticity and also expresses sadness at the passing of time.

FRANÇOIS-VICTOR

See Hugo, François-Victor.

GAUTIER, Théophile

Théophile Gautier (1811–1872) was a Parnassian poet, novelist, and journalist, and friend of Hugo. He was at the forefront of the Romantic movement, and led the Romantics in the "Battle of *Hernani*" (see *Hernani*), at which he wore a famous cherry-colored waistcoat. He was the father of Judith (1845–1918), with whom Hugo pursued a flirtation late in life.

GEORGES

See Hugo, Georges.

GRAND' MERE, LA

La Grand' Mère is a play by Hugo (1865) about the development of a woman from a harsh mother to a compassionate grandmother.

HERNANI

A drama by Hugo (1830) that revolves around the chivalry of the sixteenth-century Spanish nobleman-turned-bandit Hernani, and his love for the noble lady Doña Sol. On their wedding night they hear the sound of the horn that Hernani had given to Don Ruy de Gomez, Doña Sol's old guardian and former fiancé, promising to kill himself whenever he heard it. Both Hernani and

Doña Sol take poison and die in each other's arms. The famous "Battle of *Hernani*" between traditionalists and Romantics took place during the play's first two performances.

HOMME QUI RIT, L'

A novel by Hugo (1869) set in seventeenth-century England that contains some of the elements of *Notre-Dame de Paris:* the central character, Gwynplaine, is a young man whose face was mutilated after he had been stolen as a child by vagrants, so that it appears to be set in a perpetual grin. He is loved by a blind girl, Dea, whom he rescued as a child and who believes him to be beautiful. Their love story turns out tragically, and Gwynplaine dies for his love.

HUGO, Abel

Abel Hugo (1798–1855), the eldest brother of Victor Hugo, was involved in financial affairs, which were for the most part unsuccessful. He was also a writer, and published lengthy multivolume works such as *La France pittoresque* (1833–1835), and *La France historique et monumentale* (1835–1843).

HUGO, Adèle (I)

Née Foucher, Adèle Hugo (1803–1868) was the daughter of a civil servant at the ministère de la Guerre. She knew Hugo as a child and married him in 1822. Early in the marriage she engaged in an affair with a literary critic and friend of Hugo, Charles-Augustin Sainte-Beuve (1804–1869). After Hugo went into exile in the Channel Islands, his wife spent long periods of time abroad, particularly in Brussels, where she died. In 1867 after Hugo's relationship with Juliette Drouet had been going on for thirty-four years, she finally formally met Drouet, and a symbolic reconciliation was effected.

HUGO, Adèle (II)

Adèle Hugo (1830–1915), also known as "Dédé," was Hugo's youngest child. She ran away from home in 1863 in pursuit of a British officer named Pinson with whom she had become obsessed. She followed him to Canada and then to Barbados. She returned to France finally in 1872 and was confined by her father in a psychiatric institution. She remained incarcerated for the last forty-three years of her life.

HUGO, Charles

Charles Hugo (1826–1871), "Charlot," was Hugo's elder son and the father of Georges and Jeanne (q.v.). He was a novelist and journalist. After leaving the Channel Islands, where he went into exile with his father, he married Alice Lehaene in 1865 and lived in Brussels. He died suddenly in 1871 in Bordeaux, where his father was sitting in the Assemblée nationale.

HUGO, Eugène

Eugène Hugo (1800–1837), elder brother of Victor Hugo, was incarcerated in a mental institution from 1823 until the end of his life.

HUGO, François-Victor

François-Victor Hugo (1828–1873) was also known, like his father, Victor Hugo, as "Toto." While in exile with his father, François-Victor spent much time on translating Shakespeare's plays (1859–1865) with which he was assisted by his fiancée, Emily de Putron (1834-1865), daughter of a Guernsey shipowner. She died from consumption before they could marry. He himself died at an early age from renal tuberculosis.

HUGO, Georges

Georges Hugo (1868–1925) was the son of Hugo's son Charles and his wife, Alice. He was the brother of Jeanne (q.v.) and Hugo's beloved grandson.

HUGO, Jeanne

Jeanne Hugo (1869–1941) was the daughter of Hugo's son Charles and his wife, Alice. She was the sister of Georges (q.v.) and Hugo's beloved granddaughter.

HUGO, Léopold

Léopold Hugo (1773–1828) was father of Victor Hugo and his two brothers, Abel (q.v) and Eugène (q.v). Although of humble origins, being the son of a joiner, Léopold enjoyed a brilliant military career in Napoleon's army, and with the patronage of Joseph Bonaparte (1768–1844; created King of Naples and King of Spain [1808–1813]), was named Count of Sigüenza and governor of several Spanish provinces. Like all of his sons he had literary interests and published several works, including his memoirs (1823). He married Sophie Trébuchet (1772–1821), Victor Hugo's mother, in 1797, but early in the marriage both acquired lovers and were eventually legally separated. Sophie's lover was Fanneau de Lahorie (1766–1812), a friend of her husband's, who was eventually executed for suspected Royalist sympathies. After the death of Sophie, Léopold married his mistress, Catherine Thomas (1775–1858).

HUGO, Léopoldine

Léopoldine Hugo (1824–1843), also known as "Didine," was Hugo's favorite child. She drowned with her husband, Charles Vacquerie (see Vacquerie family), in the river Seine at Villequier in 1843.

HUGO, Mme

See Hugo, Adèle (I).

HUGO, Victor

Victor Hugo (1802–1885), son of Léopold Hugo (q.v.) and his wife, Sophie Trébuchet (1772–1821), and brother of Abel (q.v.) and Eugène (q.v.). Renowned and prolific poet, novelist, and dramatist, and leader of the French Romantic movement. He married Adèle Foucher (see Adèle Hugo I), whose father had been a professional associate of Hugo's father, in 1822, but became involved with Juliette Drouet in 1833 in a relationship that lasted the rest of his life. He was active in politics and evolved from a youthful Royalist position toward much more Republican sympathies later. He spent the years (1851–1870) of Napoleon III's regime (Second Empire) in exile, first in Brussels and then in the Channel Islands.

JEANNE
See Hugo, Jeanne.

KOCH family
Née Gauvain, Renée Françoise Koch (1800–1885) was Juliette Drouet's sister and married to Louis Koch (1801–1881), who was born in Germany. They lived in Brittany for most of their lives. Their son, Louis (1835–1912), carried on an affectionate correspondence and relationship with his aunt, Juliette Drouet, and became in 1903 the first curator of the Maison de Victor Hugo in Paris.

K., Mme
See Krafft, Laure.

KRAFFT, Laure
Laure Krafft (ca. 1801–1874), daughter of an architect, was a friend of Drouet's. She had two sons born in 1818 and 1820, at which time her profession was given as "musician." In 1844 Laure married Jean Luthereau, artist, writer, and lithographer, and they went to live in Brussels. It was for Luthereau's establishment that Hugo claimed to be heading, when he left France in the guise of a typographer after the coup d'état of 1851. The Luthereaus helped Hugo and Drouet in Brussels. They later returned to Paris.

KRAFFT, Mme
See Krafft, Laure.

LANVIN family
Antoinette Lanvin (1804–1880), whose husband was Jacques-Firmin Lanvin (1803–ca. 1880), was a servant of James Pradier (q.v.) when Juliette Drouet met them through their relationship with Pradier. She and her husband would later perform numerous duties for Drouet, especially chaperoning Claire Pradier (q.v.) to and from school. After Claire's death the couple maintained her grave while Drouet was in exile. It was Lanvin's identity and passport that Hugo used to escape to Belgium after the coup d'état of 1851. Blanche (1849–1909) was the Lanvins' adopted daughter and illegitimate grandchild. She was the daughter of Augustine Lanvin (1825–1849), who committed suicide shortly after Blanche's birth (*VS*, 6:33-4). Blanche Lanvin entered into Drouet and Hugo's service as a lady's maid on 7 April 1872, and she became the object of Hugo's last great passion. Blanche married Emile Rochereuil in December 1879.

LANVIN, M.
See Lanvin family, Jacques-Firmin Lanvin.

LANVIN, Mme
  See Lanvin family, Antoinette Lanvin.

LEGENDE DES SIECLES, LA
Epic poems by Hugo, published in three series (1859, 1877, 1883), comprising a kind of spiritual history of mankind.

LEMAITRE, Frédérick
Frédérick Lemaître (1800–1876), whose stage name was "Frédérick," was one of the most celebrated actors on the nineteenth-century French stage. He was a versatile actor, who first achieved celebrity performing in popular theater and who later took some of the leading roles in Hugo's plays, such as Gennaro in *Lucrèce Borgia* (q.v.) and Ruy Blas in *Ruy Blas* (q.v.).

LEOPOLDINE
See Hugo, Léopoldine.

LUCRECE BORGIA
A drama in prose by Hugo (1833) about the notorious Lucrezia Borgia, involving murder, incest, and adultery. It was through her part in this play as the Princesse Negroni that Drouet met Hugo.

MARIE TUDOR
A historical prose drama by Hugo (1833) about Mary of England, set in sixteenth-century England. She is in love with an Italian adventurer, Fabiani. The latter has seduced Jane, daughter of Earl Talbot, who has been adopted by the righteous craftsman, Gilbert, to whom she is affianced. When Mary Tudor finds out about Fabiani's betrayal, she engineers his execution but is then overcome by remorse.

MARION DE LORME
A historical drama in verse (written in 1829 but not performed, owing to censorship, until 1831) about the famous seventeenth-century courtesan Marion Delorme whose love for the good man Didier has "remade her virginity" and prevented him from discovering her true identity. To save Didier from the scaffold, to which he has been condemned for having fought a duel for her honor, Marion promises herself to the magistrate de Laffemas. Didier rejects Marion and his salvation in disgust when he discovers the truth. The two are reunited in love as he goes to his death.

MEURICE, Paul
Paul Meurice (1818–1905), journalist, dramatist, novelist, was a lifelong friend and admirer of Hugo and his literary executor after his death. He was introduced to Hugo by Auguste Vacquerie (q.v.), his schoolfellow, while just an adolescent.

MISERABLES, LES
A massive epic novel, published by Hugo in 1862. It is a story about social inequality and injustice centered on the hero, Jean Valjean, and the

female character, Fantine. A subplot concerns the love affair between the young aristocratic hero, Marius, and his sweetheart, Cosette, daughter of Fantine.

NAPOLEON III

Napoleon III (1808–1873) was the son of Louis Bonaparte, Napoleon I's brother. His mother, Hortense, was the daughter of the Empress Joséphine, Napoleon I's wife, by her marriage to her first husband. Napoleon III gained a foothold on power by means of the 1848 Revolution when he was elected to the Assemblée constituante, later becoming Prince-President of the Republic, and with his coup of 2 December 1851 finally becoming (in 1852) Emperor Napoleon III. His downfall was the Franco-Prussian war and the disastrous battle of Sédan, in which he personally took part. He ended his life in exile in England.

NAPOLEON LE PETIT

Hugo's historical account (1852) of the events from December 1848 to April 1852, the point of which is to satirize Napoleon III as the unworthy successor of his uncle, Napoleon I, "le Grand." It was written in Brussels after Hugo fled France and it made him an embarrassment to the Belgian government.

NOTRE-DAME DE PARIS

A novel by Hugo (1831), set in fifteenth-century Paris, about the love for Esmeralda, a gypsy girl, on the part of the evil archdeacon, Claude Frollo, and his ugly, but noble-hearted, adopted son, Quasimodo, the hunchbacked bell ringer.

ORIENTALES, LES

An 1829 collection of poems by Hugo, many on Oriental themes.

OZY, Alice

Alice Ozy (1820–1893), whose real name was Julie-Justine Pilloy, made her debut at the Variétés in 1840. She was the mistress of the duc d'Aumale and of a series of other wealthy men. She left the stage in 1855. She was pursued in the 1840s by both Hugo's son Charles (q.v.) and Hugo himself.

PIERCEAU, Mathilde

Mathilde Pierceau (ca. 1804–1844) was a dressmaker and friend of Drouet's. Her lover, with whom she had five children, was Félicité Desmousseaux, an actor at the Comédie-Française.

PIERCEAU, Mme

See Pierceau, Mathilde.

PRADIER, Claire

Claire Pradier (1826–1846) was the illegitimate daughter of Juliette Drouet by James Pradier (q.v.). As a baby she was sent to a nurse near Mantes and then in 1828 to a pension, where Drouet's cousin, Eugénie Drouet (q.v.), was already boarding. In 1834 the pension was moved to Saumur, and Claire went too. Juliette brought her back to Paris in 1836 to a pension at Saint-Mandé, where she spent the remaining ten years of her life, first as a pupil and then as an instructor. Although she had already shown signs of a decline in health, she fell seriously ill in early 1846 after failing her teacher's examinations. She died in June 1846 from tuberculosis. She is buried at Saint-Mandé along with Drouet.

PRADIER, James

James Pradier (1790–1852) was a sculptor of Huguenot descent, born in Geneva. He was highly successful among French academic artists, maintaining a studio in Paris and achieving many honors. He was the father of Juliette Drouet's daughter, Claire (q.v.), born 1826. He married the wealthy nineteen-year-old Louise d'Arcet (see Louise Pradier) in 1833 and legally separated from her in 1845, following numerous infidelities on her part (as on his), and the accumulation of enormous debt.

PRADIER, Louise

Née d'Arcet, Louise (1814–1885) married the architect Antoine-Florent Dupont in 1832. He died a few months later of cholera. She then married James Pradier (q.v.) in 1833. They had three children: Charlotte (1834–1855), John (1836–1912), Thérèse (1839–1915). Charlotte spent the years 1845–1846 (after the separation of her parents) at a pension in Saint-Mandé, along with her half sister, Claire Pradier (q.v.). According to the *Mémoires de Madame Ludovica* written about 1848 by Louise's confidante, Louise-Françoise Boyé, John was the son of an official in the ministère de la Marine, and Thérèse was the daughter of the painter Louis Jadin. Numerous other men are said to have been Louise's lovers. Pradier obtained a legal separation from her in 1845. She provided the inspiration for Emma in Flaubert's *Madame Bovary*.

QUATREVINGT-TREIZE

A historical novel by Hugo (1874) concerning the Royalist insurrection in Brittany during the revolution in 1793 ("Quatre-vingt-treize"), which divides two members of one family. The young leader on the Republican side ("les bleus") is named "Gauvain"—an allusion to Juliette Drouet's true surname and her Breton origins.

RAYONS ET LES OMBRES, LES

A collection of Hugo's poems, published in 1840, including the famous "Tristesse d'Olympio."

RHIN, LE

A descriptive travelogue of the Rhineland (1842, revised 1845) with a political subtext, based on letters Hugo wrote to his wife during several trips with Juliette Drouet. The work is heavily dependent on the works of others, including *La France pittoresque* (1835) by his brother Abel (q.v.).

ROI S'AMUSE, LE

A drama in verse by Hugo (1832), set in sixteenth-century France. François I seduces the beloved daughter of Triboulet, the court jester. Triboulet has the king murdered, but just as he is about to throw into the Seine the sack containing, as he believes, the king's body, he discovers that it contains, in fact, the body of his daughter. She tells him before she dies that she loved the king and had chosen to sacrifice herself in his place.

RUY BLAS

Ruy Blas is a drama in verse by Hugo (1838) set in seventeenth-century Spain, involving the tragic consequences of the love between a noble-hearted valet, Ruy Blas, and the queen, Doña Maria de Neubourg, who is unaware of his true identity and social status.

SUZANNE

See Blanchard, Suzanne.

TORQUEMADA

A drama in verse, composed in Guernsey in 1869 but not published until 1882 and not performed during the life of the author. The play revolves around the consequences of fanaticism, incarnated in the medieval Spanish inquisitor, Torquemada.

TOTO

See Hugo, Victor and Hugo, François-Victor.

TOUTE LA LYRE

A posthumous collection of Hugo's poetry, published in two series in 1888 and 1893.

TRAVAILLEURS DE LA MER, LES

A novel by Hugo (1866, originally entitled *L'Abîme*), written in Guernsey where its action takes place. Déruchette, the adopted daughter of Mess Lethierry, offers, on finding that her father's steamboat has been wrecked, to marry the man who can salvage the boat's engine. Gilliat, a fisherman who has loved her from afar for some time, retrieves the engine but then discovers that Déruchette is in love with another man. He nobly facilitates Déruchette's marriage to the man of her choice but allows himself to die as the tide rises to engulf him.

VACQUERIE family

While still an adolescent, Auguste Vacquerie (1819–1895) made the acquaintance of Victor Hugo in 1835, becoming his lifelong friend and admirer and introducing to Hugo his schoolfriend, Paul Meurice (q.v.). Auguste Vacquerie's brother, Charles (1817–1843), married Léopoldine Hugo (q.v.) and drowned with her at Villequier.

VILAIN, Victor

Victor Vilain (1818–1899) was a successful sculptor, winner of the Prix de Rome in 1838, and student of James Pradier (q.v.). He became acquainted with Eugénie Drouet (q.v.), Juliette Drouet's cousin, through her friendship with

Claire Pradier (q.v.), Julliete Drouet's daughter, who was at school with Eugénie. He was her lover and later, probably, husband.

VICTOR
See Hugo, Victor and Hugo, François-Victor.

WILLIAM SHAKESPEARE
Prose work by Hugo (1864), originally intended as an introduction to his son François-Victor's translation of Shakespeare, but in the event too long to serve that purpose. The subject of it extends beyond Shakespeare to the nature of genius itself. It has been described as "one of the most inaccurate lives of Shakespeare ever published," whose real subject is "the greatest geniuses of all time, who belong to 'the region of Equals' and are therefore above comparison" (*VH*, 399).

Note on the French Edition

The text that we present here has been established directly from the original letters in the handwriting of Juliette Drouet. Certain of these letters have been published partially or completely in the past; almost a hundred are, to our knowledge, completely unpublished. With virtually only one exception, we have in every instance reproduced the handwritten text. Their sources can be found in the list at the end of this volume.

Given that these letters were never intended for publication, a certain number of adjustments have been necessary. Our intervention has been limited to the following: restoration of capital letters at the beginning of sentences, in the titles of books, and in proper nouns; the regularization of excessively light punctuation; the addition between square brackets ([ ]) of some missing words and dates, when these can be determined; the regularization of agreements between subject and verb and between noun and adjective, except when it is a question of a foreign word. In the latter case all errors have been scrupulously respected, since it is important not to invest the author with knowledge that she did not have. For this same reason, although we have corrected rare anomalies in the spelling, we have kept the current spellings of the time period (for example *tems*, *longtems*, *la plus part*, *poëte*, etc.), as well as the sometimes surprising spelling of proper nouns. These are all cultural realities that do not in any way impede

---

Some of the information in this note on the French edition is applicable only to that edition and not to my translation where, obviously, original spellings, punctuation, and so on often cannot be preserved or imitated. For emphasis Drouet very often underlines or writes in bigger letters certain words. These instances have been rendered in italics in the French edition. Wherever possible I have preserved this original emphasis (note, however, that italics within square brackets represent editorial interpolations). On a few occasions I have added italics of my own where the translation called for such emphasis [T].

the reading. Finally, Juliette occasionally invents a word; it would be unforgivable not to *copire* ("copy") these faithfully.

As it is inconceivable that the famous "deposition" (L. 7) should be excluded from our collection merely because of its inaccessibility, we have exempted it from our rule of giving only texts that we have established from the original: as an exception we reproduce here the text published by Paul Souchon.

EVELYN BLEWER

List of Sources

The letters published in this volume are to be found in two public collections in Paris: the Cabinet des manuscrits at the Bibliothèque nationale (collection entitled "nouvelles acquisitions françaises") and the Maison de Victor Hugo. Except where marked MVH, (Maison Victor Hugo), and *MUL* (see Abbreviations), all references are to the Cabinet des manuscrits at the Bibliothèque nationale. The number of the volume in the collection "nouvelles acquisitions françaises" is given first, then the number of the folio, and finally the number of the letter in this book.

16.322, 1–2, Letter 1
16.322, 19–20, Letter 2
16.322, 78–9, Letter 3
16.322, 21–3, Letter 4
16.322, 40–1, Letter 5
16.322, 269–70, Letter 6
MUL, 51, Letter 7
16.322, 204–5, Letter 8
16.322, 165–6, Letter 9
16.322, 175–6, Letter 10
16.322, 196–7, Letter 11
16.322, 200–1, Letter 12
16.322, 202–3, Letter 13
16.322, 211–2, Letter 14
16.322, 141–3, Letter 15
16.323, 5–6, Letter 16
16.323, 229–30, Letter 17
16.324, 170–1, Letter 18
16.324, 358–9, Letter 19
16.326, 47–8, Letter 20

16.326, 143–4, Letter 21
16.326, 189–90, Letter 22
16.326, 280–1, Letter 23
16.327, 53–4, Letter 24
16.328, 132–3, Letter 25
16.331, 83–4, Letter 26
16.331, 309–10, Letter 27
16.335, 145–6, Letter 28
16.335, 149–50, Letter 29
16.335, 169–70, Letter 30
16.335, 173–4, Letter 31
16.335, 181–2, Letter 32
16.335, 191–2, Letter 33
16.335, 199–200, Letter 34
16.335, 275–6, Letter 35
16.340, 11–12, Letter 36
16.340, 63–4, Letter 37
16.340, 65–6, Letter 38
16.340, 151–2, Letter 39
16.340, 173–4, Letter 40

16.343, 34, Letter 41
16.343, 121–2, Letter 42
16.343, 131–2, Letter 43
16.343, 137–8, Letter 44
16.343, 189–90, Letter 45
16.343, 257–8, Letter 46
16.343, 291–2, Letter 47
16.343, 293–4, Letter 48
16.345, 219–20, Letter 49
16.351, 147–8, Letter 50
16.351, 241–2, Letter 51
16.352, 105–6, Letter 52
16.352, 109–10, Letter 53
16.352, 111–2, Letter 54
16.355, 111–2, Letter 55
16.355, 217–8, Letter 56
16.360, 7–8, Letter 57
16.360, 53–54, Letter 58
16.360, 252–3, Letter 59
16.360, 324–5, Letter 60

16.360, 326–7, Letter 61	16.373, 25–6, Letter 103	16.383, 197, Letter 145
16.363, 5–6, Letter 62	16.373, 413–4, Letter 104	16.383, 257, Letter 146
16.363, 53–4, Letter 63	16.373, 437–8, Letter 105	16.384, 129, Letter 147
16.363, 175–6, Letter 64	16.374, 360–1, Letter 106	16.384, 161, Letter 148
16.363, 221–2, Letter 65	16.374, 372–3, Letter 107	16.384, 175, Letter 149
MVH, 7851, Letter 66	16.375, 7–8, Letter 108	16.384, 258, Letter 150
MVH, 7876, Letter 67	16.375, 271–2, Letter 109	16.384, 288, Letter 151
16.366, 39–40, Letter 68	16.376, 94–5, Letter 110	16.385, 110, Letter 152
16.366, 83–4, Letter 69	16.376, 193–4, Letter 111	16.385, 270, Letter 153
16.366, 133–4, Letter 70	16.377, 28–9, Letter 112	16.386, 15, Letter 154
16.366, 153–4, Letter 71	16.377, 126, Letter 113	16.386, 31, Letter 155
16.366, 157–8, Letter 72	16.377, 164, Letter 114	16.386, 111, Letter 156
16.366, 159–60, Letter 73	16.377, 196–7, Letter 115	16.386, 117, Letter 157
16.366, 163–4, Letter 74	16.378, 52, Letter 116	16.386, 160, Letter 158
16.366, 203–4, Letter 75	16.378, 65, Letter 117	16.387, 16, Letter 159
16.366, 207–8, Letter 76	16.378, 84, Letter 118	16.387, 24, Letter 160
16.366, 215–6, Letter 77	16.378, 164, Letter 119	16.387, 164, Letter 161
16.368, 95–6, Letter 78	16.379, 85, Letter 120	16.387, 219, Letter 162
16.368, 215–6, Letter 79	16.379, 136, Letter 121	16.388, 24, Letter 163
16.369, 47–8, Letter 80	16.379, 279, Letter 122	16.389, 85, Letter 164
MVH, 8573, Letter 81	16.379, 364, Letter 123	16.389, 118, Letter 165
MVH, 8574, Letter 82	16.380, 135, Letter 124	16.389, 237, Letter 166
16.369, 97–8, Letter 83	16.380, 141, Letter 125	16.390, 323, Letter 167
MVH, 8591, Letter 84	16.380, 149, Letter 126	16.391, 215, Letter 168
16.369. 115–6, Letter 85	16.380, 187, Letter 127	16.392, 11, Letter 169
16.369, 147–8, Letter 86	16.380, 189, Letter 128	16.393, 88, Letter 170
16.369, 221–2, Letter 87	16.380, 199, Letter 129	16.393, 23, Letter 171
16.369, 230–1, Letter 88	16.380, 223, Letter 130	16.393, 97, Letter 172
16.369, 260–1, Letter 89	16.381, 95, Letter 131	16.393, 166, Letter 173
16.369, 406–7, Letter 90	16.381, 143–4, Letter 132	16.394, 196, Letter 174
16.369, 412–3, Letter 91	16.381, 149–50, Letter 133	16.394, 261, Letter 175
16.369, 426–7, Letter 92	16.381, 151–2, Letter 134	16.394, 292, Letter 176
16.369, 464–5, Letter 93	16.382, 46–7, Letter 135	16.394, 360, Letter 177
16.369, 470–1, Letter 94	16.382, 78, Letter 136	16.395, 148, Letter 178
16.369, 484–5, Letter 95	16.382, 83, Letter 137	16.396, 108, Letter 179
16.369, 500–1, Letter 96	16.382, 116, Letter 138	16.396, 234, Letter 180
16.370, 15–16, Letter 97	16.382, 150, Letter 139	16.397, 291, Letter 181
16.370, 27–8, Letter 98	16.382, 171, Letter 140	16.399, 149, Letter 182
16.370, 157–8, Letter 99	16.383, 1–2, Letter 141	16.401, 133–4, Letter 183
16.370, 197–8, Letter 100	16.383, 56, Letter 142	16.402, 229, Letter 184
16.371, 177–8, Letter 101	16.383, 83, Letter 143	16.403, 16, Letter 185
16.372, 225–6, Letter 102	16.383, 129, Letter 144	16.403, 134, Letter 186

Works Cited

Bailbé, Joseph-Marc, and Christian Robin. *Un Editeur et son siècle: Pierre-Jules Hetzel.* Saint-Sébastien: ACL, 1988.
Barthou, Louis. *Les Amours d'un poète.* Paris: Louis Conard, 1919.
Baudelaire, [Charles]. *Oeuvres complètes.* Ed. Marcel A. Ruff. Paris: Editions du Seuil, 1968.
Bennett, C. E., trans. *Horace: The Odes and Epodes,* by Horace. London: William Heinemann, 1918.
Blewer, Evelyn. "Abel et Victor, les frères amis." *Europe,* March 1985. 104–15
———, ed. *Lettres à Victor Hugo: Correspondance, 1833–1882,* by Juliette Drouet. Paris: Jean-Jacques Pauvert et Silène-Har/Po, 1985.
———, ed. *Lettres à Victor Hugo: Correspondance, 1833–1882,* by Juliette Drouet. Paris: Arthème Fayard, 2001.
Caso de, J., G. Garnier, C. Lapaire, I. Leroy-Jay Lemaistre, and D. Siler. *Statues de chair: Sculptures de James Pradier.* Paris: Editions de la Réunion des musées nationaux, 1985. Published in conjunction with the exhibition at the Musée d'art et d'histoire, Geneva, and at the Musée du Luxembourg, Paris.
Caso de, J. "Comprendre Pradier." In de Caso et al., *Statues de chair: Sculptures de James Pradier.* Paris: Editions de la Réunion des musées nationaux, 1985. Published in conjunction with the exhibition at the Musée d'art et d'histoire, Geneva, and at the Musée du Luxembourg, Paris. 13–47.
Chenay, Paul. *Victor Hugo à Guernsey: Souvenirs inédits de son beau-frère Paul Chenay.* Paris: Félix Juven, n.d.
Cox, Gregory Stevens. *Victor Hugo in the Channel Islands.* Guernsey: The Guernsey Press, 1996.
Cunnington, C. Willett. *English Women's Clothing in the Nineteenth Century.* 1937. Reprint, New York: Dover Publications, 1990.

Dow, Leslie Smith. *Adèle Hugo: La Misérable*. Fredericton, Canada: Goose Lane Editions, 1993.

Drouet, Juliette. *The Love Letters of Juliette Drouet to Victor Hugo*. Ed. Louis Guimbaud. Trans. Lady Theodora Davidson. New York: McBride, Nast, 1914.

———. *"Mon grand petit homme . . . ": Mille et une lettres d'amour à Victor Hugo*. Ed. Paul Souchon. Paris: Gallimard, 1951.

———. *Lettres à Victor Hugo: Correspondance, 1833–1882*. Ed. Evelyn Blewer. Paris: Jean-Jacques Pauvert et Silène-Har/Po, 1985.

———. *"Je ne veux qu'une chose, être aimée": Cinquante lettres de Juliette Drouet à Victor Hugo*. Ed. Simonne Charpentreau and Jacques Charpentreau. Paris: La Maison de Poésie, 1997.

———. *Lettres à Victor Hugo: Correspondance, 1833–1882*. Ed. Evelyn Blewer. Paris: Librairie Arthème Fayard, 2001.

———. *Lettres familiales*. Ed. Gérard Pouchain. Condé-sur-Noireau: Editions Charles Corlet, 2001.

Escholier, Raymond. *Un Amant de génie: Victor Hugo: Lettres d'amour et carnets inédits*. Paris: Librairie Arthème Fayard, 1953.

Fertel, Bernard. "Hugo, Juliette, lettres détruites." *L'Intermédiaire des chercheurs et des curieux*, September 1979. Cols. 894–7.

Frey, John Andrew. *A Victor Hugo Encylopedia*. Westport, CT: Greenwood Press, 1999.

Garnier, G. "La Carrière d'un artiste officiel à Paris." In de Caso et al., *Statues de chair: Sculptures de James Pradier*. Paris: Editions de la Réunion des musées nationaux, 1985. Published in conjunction with the exhibition at the Musée d'art et d'histoire, Geneva, and the Musée du Luxembourg, Paris. 77–96.

Gaudon, Jean, ed. *Lettres à Juliette Drouet, 1833–1883. Le Livre de l'anniversaire*, by Victor Hugo. Paris: Jean-Jacques Pauvert, 1964.

———, ed. *Lettres à Juliette Drouet: Correspondance, 1833–1883, suivi de Le Livre de l'anniversaire*, by Victor Hugo. Paris: Librairie Arthéme Fayard, 2001.

Gaudon, Sheila. "James Pradier, Victor Hugo et l'Arc de Triomphe de l'Etoile," *Revue de l'histoire littéraire de la France*, September–October 1968. 713–25.

Gaudon, Sheila, and Danielle Molinari, eds. *Exilium vita est: Victor Hugo à Guernsey*. Paris: Paris-Musées, 2002. Published in conjunction with the exhibition at Hauteville House, Saint Peter Port, Guernsey.

Gautier, Théophile. *Victor Hugo par Théophile Gautier*. Paris: Charpentier, 1902.

Gray, Francine du Plessix. *Rage and Fire: A Life of Louise Colet: Pioneer Feminist, Literary Star, Flaubert's Muse*. New York: Simon & Schuster, 1994.

Grossiord, Sophie. *Hauteville House: General Guide*. Paris: Paris-Musées, 1994.

Guillemin, Henri. *Hugo et la sexualité*. Paris: Gallimard, 1954.

Guimbaud, Louis. *Victor Hugo et Juliette Drouet: D'après les lettres inédites de Juliette Drouet à Victor Hugo et avec un choix de ces lettres.* 2 vols. Paris: Auguste Blaizot, 1914.

Houssaye, Arsène. *Les Confessions: Souvenirs d'un demi-siècle.* 6 vols. Vols. 1–4, 1830–1880; Vols. 5–6, 1830–1890. Paris: E. Dentu, 1885–1891.

Houssaye, Arsène. *Man About Paris: The Confessions of Arsène Houssaye.* Trans. and ed. Henry Knepler. New York: William Morrow, 1970.

Huas, Jeanine. *Juliette Drouet: Le Bel Amour de Victor Hugo.* Paris: Gaston Lachurié, 1985.

Hugo, Abel. *La France pittoresque, ou description pittoresque, topographique et statistique des départements et colonies de la France.* 3 vols. Paris: Delloye, 1833–1835.

Hugo, Adèle. *Le Journal d'Adèle Hugo.* Ed. Frances Vernor Guille. 3 vols. Paris: Minard, 1968–1984.

Hugo, Victor. *Oeuvres complètes.* Ed. P. Meurice, G. Simon, C. Daubray. 45 vols. Paris: Albin Michel; Imprimerie nationale; Ollendorff, 1904–1952.

———. *Correspondance.* Ed. C. Daubray. 4 vols. Vol. 1, *Lettres à la fiancée*; 1814–1848; Vol. 2, 1849–1866; Vol. 3, 1867–1873; Vol. 4, 1874–1885. Paris: Albin Michel; Imprimerie nationale; Ollendorf, 1947–1952. (Part of *Oeuvres complètes*, 1904–1952).

———. *Lettres à Juliette Drouet, 1833–1883. Le Livre de l'anniversaire.* Ed. Jean Gaudon. Paris: Jean-Jacques Pauvert, 1964.

———. *Oeuvres poétiques de Victor Hugo.* Ed. Pierre Albouy. 2 vols. Paris: Editions Gallimard, 1964.

———. *Journal de ce que j'apprends chaque jour (juillet 1846–février 1848).* Ed. René Journet and Guy Robert. Paris: Flammarion, 1965.

———. *Oeuvres complètes.* Ed. Jean Massin. 18 vols. Paris: Club français du livre, 1967–1971.

———. *Choses vues: Souvenirs, journaux, cahiers.* Ed. Hubert Juin. 3 vols. Paris: Gallimard, 1972.

———. *Les Misérables.* Ed. René Journet. 3 vols. Paris: Garnier-Flammarion, 1979.

———. *Le Rhin: Lettres à un ami.* Ed. Jean Gaudon. 2 vols. Paris: Imprimerie nationale, 1985.

———. *Correspondance familiale et écrits intimes.* Ed. Jean Gaudon, Sheila Gaudon, and Bernard Leuilliot. 2 vols. Vol. 1, 1802–1828; Vol. 2, 1828–1839. Paris: Robert Laffont, 1988–1991.

———. *Lettres de Victor Hugo à Léonie Biard.* Ed. Jean Gaudon. Paris: Claude Blaizot, 1990.

———. *Lettres à Juliette Drouet: Correspondance, 1833–1883, suivi de* Le Livre de l'anniversaire. Ed. Jean Gaudon. Paris: Librairie Arthème Fayard, 2001.

Laster, Arnaud. *Victor Hugo.* Paris: Pierre Belfond, 1984.

Leroy-Jay Lemaistre, I. "Pradier et les musées de France." In de Caso et al., *Statues de chair: Sculptures de James Pradier.* Paris: Editions de la Réunion des musées nationaux, 1985. Published in conjunction with the exhibition at the Musée d'art et d'histoire, Geneva, and the Musée du Luxembourg, Paris. 97–105.

Lesclide, Richard. *Propos de table de Victor Hugo*. Paris: E. Dentu, 1885.

McCormick, John. *Popular Theatres of Nineteenth-Century France*. London and New York: Routledge, 1993.

Mérimée, Prosper. *Correspondance générale*. Ed. Maurice Parturier with Pierre Josserand and Jean Mallion. 17 vols. Paris: Le Divan, 1941–1964.

Pouchain, Gérard, and Robert Sabourin. *Juliette Drouet ou "la dépaysée."* Paris: Librairie Arthème Fayard, 1992.

Pradier, James. *Correspondance*. Ed. Douglas Siler. 3 vols. Vol. 1, 1790–1833; Vol. 2, 1834–1842; Vol. 3, 1843–1846. Geneva: Droz, 1984–1988.

Prévost, Marie-Laure, ed. *Victor Hugo: L'Homme océan*. Paris: Seuil, 2002. Published in conjunction with the exhibition at the Bibliothèque nationale de France.

Robb, Graham. *Victor Hugo*. New York: W. W. Norton, 1997.

Savant, Jean. "Madame Krafft et Madame Luthereau." *L'Intermédiaire des chercheurs et des curieux*, September 1979. Cols. 884–6.

———. "Juliette Drouet." *L'Intermédiaire des chercheurs et des curieux*, October 1979. Cols. 1007–8.

———. *La Vie sentimentale de Victor Hugo*. 6 fascicles. Fasc. 1, *Juliette ou le supplice de la chasteté*; Fasc. 2, *Léonie d'Aunet: Madame Biard avant le scandale*; Fasc. 3, *Léonie d'Aunet: Du Scandale au coup d'état et à l'agonie*; Fasc. 4, *Les Amants de Juliette: L'Histoire de ses dettes et les personnages de sa vie*; Fasc. 5, *Amours et légendes: Le Faune et ses cent nymphes: Hypothèques abusives et lectures fautives*; Fasc. 6, *Adorations ultimes: Marie Mercier et la rue des 40 géants: Blanche Lanvin: Judith Gautier*. Paris: Chez l'auteur, 1982–1985.

Siler, Douglas. *Flaubert et Louise Pradier: Le Texte intégral des* Mémoires de Madame Ludovica. Paris: Minard, 1973.

———, ed. *Correspondance*, by James Pradier. 3 vols. Vol. 1, 1790–1833; Vol. 2, 1834–1842; Vol. 3, 1843–1846. Geneva: Droz, 1984–1988.

Souchon, Paul. *Juliette Drouet: Inspiratrice de Victor Hugo*. Paris: Jules Tallandier, 1942.

———. *La Servitude amoureuse de Juliette Drouet à Victor Hugo*. Paris: Albin Michel, 1943.

———. *Les deux femmes de Victor Hugo*. Paris: Jules Tallandier, 1948.

———, ed. *"Mon grand petit homme . . . " Mille et une lettres d'amour à Victor Hugo*. Paris: Gallimard, 1951.

Ubersfeld, A. *Le Roi et le buffon*. Paris: Corti, 1974.

Viennet, Jean Pons Guillaume. *Fables nouvelles suivies de deux épîtres*. Paris: Amyot, 1851.

Winter, Marian Hannah. *The Theatre of Marvels*. Trans. Charles Meldon. New York: Benjamin Blom, 1962.

Index

JD = Juliette Drouet; VH = Victor Hugo. Italics in endnote references denote letter numbers: Read 72n.*4*.2 as "page 72, second note to letter #4."

Abîme, L' (Hugo), 193n.*156*.1, 194n.*158*.2, 227. See also *Travailleurs de la mer, Les* (Hugo)
Académie française, 60, 76n.*26*.2
    VH's election to, 71, 80n.*39*.1, 80n.*40*.1
    VH's reception speech at, 109n.*49*.1
Actes et paroles (Hugo), 210n.*180*.1
Alaux, Jean, 73n.*9*.1
Allix, Augustine, 151, 162n.*129*.3
Anacreon, 77n.*26*.b
Angelo (Hugo), 57, 75n.*17*.1, 76n.*22*.2, 78n.*28*.2, 217, 219
Arnould, Auguste, 111n.*58*.1
Artiste, L' (magazine), 8
Asplet, Charles, 188n.*132*.2, 217
Asplet, Mme Charles, 166, 167
Asplet, Philippe, 167, 217
Assemblée constituante, 104–6, 114n.*74*.1, 114n.*76*.1, 114n.*77*.1, 152n.*78*.1, 225
Assemblée législative, 152n.*78*.1
    dissolved, 154n.*94*.1
Assemblée nationale, 206n.*169*.1

Aumale, duc d', 100, 112n.*66*.1, 113n.*66*.2
"Autre Guitare" (Hugo), 210n.*180*.1

Baa, Mme (servant), 22
Baudelaire, Charles, 35n.*10*
Beaudoin, Mlle (Louise-Atala Beauchêne), 13, 78n.*31*.1, 79n.*34*.1
Belles Femmes de Paris, Les, Gautier's tribute to JD in, 5
Bertin, Armand, 217
Bertin, François-Edouard, 217
Bertin, Louise, 217, 220
Bertin, Louis-François, 15, 74n.*16*.1, 217
Besancenot, Jonas, 85, 86, 108n.*46*.1
Besancenot, Mme (JD's neighbor), 86, 108n.*46*.1
Besancenot, Résisieux, 69, 80n.*38*.2, 86, 108n.*46*.1
Biard, François-Auguste, 17, 41n.*71*, 217
Biard, Georges, 218
Biard, Henriette, 218
Biard, Léonie d'Aunet, x, xi–xii, 17–19, 111n.*59*.2, 154n.*89*.1, 217–18
    beginning of relationship with VH, 41n.*71*, 110n.*56*.1, 110–11n.*58*.1
    falls ill, 126, 154n.*90*.1
    Hugo abandons, 20

Biard, Léonie d'Aunet *(continued)*
    JD acquiesces in VH's affair with, 22, 126
    JD contrasts own virtue with, 134
    VH arrested in flagrante delicto with, 110n.*57*.1, 110–11n.*58*.1
    VH's letters to, 31
Blanchard, Suzanne, 18, 90, 121, 122, 142, 192n.*151*.3, 200, 218
Blanqui, Louis-Auguste, 103, 114n.*70*.2
Bonaparte, Joseph, 222
Bonaparte, Louis, 225
Bonjour, Casimir, 71, 80n.*40*.1
Boulet (hairdresser), 206
Boyé, Louise-Françoise, 226
Briché, Mme (JD's acquaintance), 87
Burgraves,Les (Hugo), 109n.*51*.1, 218
Busquet, Alfred, 185, 194n.*161*.a

Cabarrus (physician), 154n.*93*.a. *See also* Labarne
Chagrin de l'absence, Le (Pradier), 3
Champion, Edme, 208n.*175*.2
Chansons des rues et des bois, Les (Hugo), 21, 218
Chants du crépuscule, Les (Hugo), 14, 218
Charlot. *See* Hugo, Charles
Charrassin (representative), 141, 157n.*111*.1
Châtiments, Les (Hugo), 215n.*183*.c, 218
Chatterton (de Vigny), 219
Chenay, Julie Foucher, 150, 161n.*127*.b, 171, 179, 190n.*139*.1, 195n.*164*.1, 218–19
Chenay, Paul, 7, 190n.*139*.1, 219
Chez Victor Hugo par un passant (C. Hugo), 21–22
Chomel (physician), 98
Claude Gueux (Hugo), 51, 72n.*8*.1, 219
Clovis (Viennet), 76n.*26*.2
Cochon de Saint Antoine, Le (C. Hugo), 161n.*124*.3
Colet, Louise, 3
Comédie-Française, 12, 53, 73n.*11*.2, 75n.*20*.2, 80n.*40*.1, 109n.*51*.1, 215n.*183*.d. *See also* Théâtre-Français
Contemplations, Les (Hugo), 21, 27, 141–42, 158n.*113*.1, 219

Coquette vengée, La (Lenclos), 114n.*71*.1
Corbin (physician), 186, 195n.*165*.1

d'Angers, David, 35–36n.11, 36n.21
d'Arcet, Louise. *See* Pradier, Louise d'Arcet
d'Aunet, Léonie. *See* Biard, Léonie d'Aunet
Davidson, Lady Theodora, 32
Dédé. *See* Hugo, Adèle
de Girardin, Delphine, 155n.*97*.1, 157n.*106*.1
de Girardin, Emile, 155n.*97*.1
de Lahorie, Fanneau, 222
Delorme, Marion, 224
Demousseaux, Félicité, 88, 225
de Putron, Emily, 22, 193n.*154*.1, 222
de Vigny, Alfred, 219
Didine. *See* Hugo, Léopoldine
Dix ans de la vie d'une femme (Scribe and Terrier), 7
Domaille, Thomas, 192n.*147*.1
Dorval, Marie, 6, 7, 75n.*17*.1, 219
Drouet, Eugénie, 2, 3, 36n.20, 219, 220, 225, 227–28
Drouet, Françoise Marchandet, 1, 2, 36n.20, 219–20
Drouet, Jean-Charles, 219
Drouet, Juliette (Julienne Gauvain)
    affair with Alphonse Karr, 8–9, 10
    affair with James Pradier, 2
    affair with Scipion Pinel, 4, 7
    atonement for sexual and financial sin, 14–15
    at Auteuil, 208n.*175*.a
    becomes VH's lover, 10, 38n.45, 47
    bibliography on, 33
    birth and childhood of, 1–2
    in Brussels, 132–34
    candor of, 29
    and Claire's virginity, 42n.87
    complains of sexual deprivation, 16
    daguerrotyped, 83
    on death, 25
    debts, 37n.31, 49, 68, 72n.*4*.2, 72n.*6*.1, 85
    descriptive precision of, 28
    diction of letters, 28, 32

education, x, 2
engaged by Comédie-Française, 12, 13, 53, 73n.*11*.2, 75n.*20*.2
epistolary style and agenda, 26–31
on Eugénie Drouet, 36n.*20*
in exile on Guernsey, 23, 24, 158n.*112*.a
in exile on Jersey, 135–41
in Florence, 7
goes into exile, 20, 130
on Hugo's infidelities, 24
invited to dinner by VH's wife, 193n.*153*.1
last years in Paris, 23–26
leaves VH for Belgium, 208n.*175*.2
leaves VH for Brittany, 53, 73n.*11*.1
at Les Metz, 74n.*14*.1, 96
lithograph by Noël, x, 8
on *Marion de Lorme*, 43n.*110*
"marriage" to VH, xi, 69
meetings with VH's wife, 185–86, 195n.*163*.1
meets VH, 9
meets VH's children, 148, 149
metaphoric oral sex promise, 40–41n.*67*
as Mlle Juliette, 5
models for Pradier, 36–37n.*23*
monopolized by VH, 14
moves to Hauteville-Féerie, 176
on Napoleon III amnesty offer, 151
need for written word, 15–16
at the Odéon, 6–7
parts played by, 37n.*33*
portrait by Gautier, x, 5
on reading *Torquemada*, 25–26
relations with VH's children, 131
religious faith, 154n.*88*.1
retires from stage, 12–14
retrieves mss. from Guernsey, 209n.*179*.a
returns from exile, 23
and the revolution of 1848, 102–3
roles played by, 10
on séances, 137, 138, 139, 140
sexual dissatisfaction, 41n.*68*

simplistic biographies of, ix
style of letters, x–xi
sued for debt, 7–8, 9, 10, 50
textual notes on the letters, 229–30
at the Théâtre de la Porte-Saint-Martin, 5–6, 7, 12–13
at the Théâtre du Parc, 5
at the Théâtre du Vaudeville, 5
at the Théâtre Molière, 10
theatrical debut, x, 5
translation issues, 32–33
vegetation imagery, 27
and VH's family, xi
on VH's infidelities, 133–34
on VH's relations with his children, 147
on VH's retrieval of letters, 42n.*102*
as VH's secretary/housekeeper, 210n.*181*.a
visits Brussels with VH (1865), 183
visits Belgium from Guernsey, 189n.*136*.2, 189–90n.*136*.1
visits Brussels with VH, 194n.*158*.1
visits Waterloo, 169
whereabouts of her letters, 31–32
Drouet, René-Henry, 1–2, 107n.*44*.2, 219, 220
Dumas, Alexandre, 74n.*15*.1
Dupanloup, Bishop François, 205, 210n.*182*.1
Dupont, Antoine-Florent, 226
Duverdier, Prosper, 189n.*133*.a

Education, L', ou les deux cousines (Bonjour), 80n.*40*.1
"11 July 1846, on coming back from the cemetery" (Hugo), 112n.*65*.1
Esmeralda, La (Hugo and Bertin), 76n.*25*.1, 106n.*41*.1, 217, 220
Etiennette, le secret (Biard), 218
Evangiles annotés, Les (Proudhon), 194n.*159*.1

Fables nouvelles suivies de deux épîtres (Viennet), 76n.*26*.2
Fallue, La, 142, 143, 159nn.*114*.1–2, 192n.*147*.1

Fantine (Hugo), 173, 190n.*140*.1, 191n.*143*.1
Ferrier, Ida ("Mlle Ida"), 33, 74n.*15*.1
Feuilles d'automne, Les (Hugo), 47, 71–72n.*2*.1, 220
Fils de Zambular, Le, 10
Flaubert, Gustave, 3, 35n.10, 36n.16, 41n.71
Foucher, Adèle. *See* Hugo, Adèle Foucher
Foucher, Julie. *See* Chenay, Julie Foucher
France historique et monumentale, La (Abel Hugo), 221
France pittoresque, La (Abel Hugo), 108n.*46*.1, 221, 226
François, Mlle (dressmaker), 67
Franco-Prussian war, 206n.*168*.1, 206n.*169*.1

Garcia, Marie, 19
Garibaldi, Giuseppe, 188n.*132*.1, 206n.*169*.1
Gautier, Judith. *See* Mendès, Judith Gautier
Gautier, Théophile, 30–31, 39n.52, 113n.*67*.1, 207n.*173*.1, 220
    on JD in *Lucrèce Borgia*, 9–10
    on Mlle Juliette, x, 5
    portrait of JD, x
Gauvain, Armand, 1, 35n.3
Gauvain, Julien, 1
Gauvain, Julienne. *See* Drouet, Juliette
Gauvain, Marie, 1
Gauvain, Renée. *See* Koch, Renée Gauvain
Gauvain, Thérèse, 1
Gay, Sophie, 157n.*106*.1
George, Mlle (Marguerite Joséphine Weimer), 9, 13
Glaize, Catherine, 213
Glaize, Léon, 215n.*183*.c
Gonzalès, Emmanuel, 213
Grand' Mère, La (Hugo), 183, 194n.*158*.2, 220
Grangé (military substitute), 113n.*67*.2
Guérard, Mme (JD's acquaintance), 87
Guimont, Esther, 131, 155n.*97*.1
"Guitare" (Hugo), 210n.*180*.1

Harel, Jean-Charles, 9, 13
Hauteville-Féerie, 42n.89, 175, 176, 191–92n.*147*.1
Hauteville House, 21, 42n.89, 142, 158n.*114*.1, 160n.*116*.1, 195n.*163*.1, 219
Hernani (Hugo), 13, 24, 202, 208–9 n.*175*.a, 219, 220–21
    "Battle of," 39n.52, 220, 221
Hetzel, Pierre-Jules, 146, 170, 190n.*138*.2
Homme au masque de fer, L' (play), 10
Homme du monde, L' (Ancelot and Santine), 6
Homme qui rit, L' (Hugo), 21, 186, 194 n.*161*.2, 195n.*164*.1, 195n.*165*.2, 221
Houssaye, Arsène, 3, 18, 19, 40n.63, 113n.*67*.b, 213, 215n.*183*.d, 216n.*185*.2
Houssaye, Henry, 213, 215n.*183*.d
Houssaye, Mme Henry, 213, 215n.*183*.d
Hugo, Abel, 108n.*46*.1, 221
Hugo, Adèle ("Dédé"), xi, 12, 21–22, 109n.*49*.2, 150, 161n.*126*.b, 171, 190n.*140*.1, 221
    courted by Alfred Busquet, 194n.*161*.a
    leaves to pursue Lt. Pinson, 22, 192n.*148*.1
    returns and is incarcerated, 22
Hugo, Adèle Foucher, 160n.*122*.1, 171, 173, 221
    absence from Guernsey, 20, 22
    burial of, 196n.*166*.1
    death of, 23, 187
    early awareness of VH's affair with JD, 42n.94
    on expenditures, 39n.51
    frustrates JD's hope of *Ruy Blas* part, 78n.*31*.1
    given Alaux's Hugo miniature, 73n.*9*.1
    has affair with Sainte-Beuve, 11–12, 23
    invites JD to charity dinner, 193n.*153*.1
    leaves Guernsey for Paris, 191n.*142*.1

on marital relations, 39n.48
meetings with JD, 185–86,
  195n.163.1
rapprochement with JD, xii, 23
returns to Guernsey, 190n.140.1
VH's letters to, x
vision impaired, 185
Hugo, Alice, xii, 209n.178.a,
  210n.180.a, 221
  children born to, 196n.166.a
Hugo, Blanche-Laura, 138
Hugo, Charles ("Charlot"), 109n.49.2,
  132, 148, 149, 155n.99.2, 160n.122.1
  accompanies VH to Guernsey, 21–22
  affair with Alice Ozy, 18, 225
  attends VH's Académie acceptance speech, 88
  children born to, 196n.166.a
  dies, 206n.170.1
  JD acts as copyist for, 134, 146, 160n.120.1
  meets JD, 161n.125.1
  and national guard service, 101, 113n.67.2
  returns to Paris, 206n.169.1
  and VH's letters to Léonie Biard, 41n.77
  as VH's traveling companion, 161n.124.1, 189n.136.2, 189–90n.136.1, 195n.161.a, 221
Hugo, Eugène, 42n.109, 221
Hugo, François-Victor ("Toto"), xi, 109n.49.2, 149, 160n.122.1, 192n.151.a, 195n.161.a, 222
  accompanies VH to Guernsey, 21–22, 158n.112.a
  attends VH's Académie acceptance speech, 88
  death of, 24, 203, 209n.177.1
  fiancée dies, 193n.154.1
  final illness of, 24, 203, 208n.175.a, 209n.176.a
  meets JD, 161n.126.a
  sends away his mistress, 156n.103.b
  translates Shakespeare, 228
  writes to JD, 181, 193n.155.1

Hugo, Georges (I), 196n.166.a
Hugo, Georges (II), 196n.166.a, 201, 204, 209n.178.a, 210n.180.a, 214, 221, 222
Hugo, Harper Richard, 138
Hugo, Jean, ix
Hugo, Jeanne, 205, 210n.180.a, 222
Hugo, Léopold, 222
Hugo, Léopoldine ("Didine"), xi, 17, 20, 88, 90, 109n.49.2, 222
  as angel, 168, 189n.135.a, 191n.141.1
  death of, 91, 110n.53.1
  gravesite, 196n.166.1
  marries, 109n.50.1
  as VH's copyist, 162n.130.2
  wedding of, 88–89
Hugo, Victor ("Toto"), 222–23
  Académie acceptance speech, 88, 109n.49.1
  affair with Blanche Lanvin, 24
  affair with Léonie Biard, 17–19, 20, 22, 41n.71, 41n.77, 110n.56.1, 110n.57.1, 110–11n.58.1, 111n.59.2, 126, 134, 153n.82.a, 154n.83.1, 154n.89.1, 154n.90.1, 156n.101.b, 217–18
  affection for Claire Pradier, 20, 78n.29.1, 112n.63.1
  aristocratic title, 42n.109
  and the Assemblée constituante, 104–6, 114n.70.1, 114n.77.1
  at Auteuil, 208n.175.a
  becomes JD's lover, ix, 10
  bust by Lebeuf, 179, 192n.152.2
  charity on Guernsey, 192n.149.1, 193n.153.1
  children write to JD, 131
  death of Léopoldine, 17
  drawings engraved by Chenay, 190n.139.1
  "dry guillotine" speech, 119, 152n.78.1
  elected to Senate, 215n.183.a
  expresses contempt for Napoleon III, 155n.97.a, 156n.101.a
  fondness for omnibus rides, 113n.67.b

Hugo, Victor ("Toto") *(continued)*
  goes into exile, 20, 130
  infidelities, xi–xii, 16, 24, 41n.68,
    41n.77, 113n.67.1, 133–34,
    202–3, 204, 208n.*175*.2,
    209n.*176*.a (*see also* Biard,
    Léonie)
  letters to adult sons, 42n.92
  letters to JD, 31
  letters to Léonie Biard, 31,
    153n.*82*.a, 154n.*83*.1
  letters to wife, x
  lithograph by Noël, 8
  meets JD, 9
  miniature portrait by Alaux, 52,
    73n.*9*.1
  need for written word, 15
  parsimony of, 14–15, 23, 40n.63
  protests extradition of Communards,
    206n.*170*.1
  pursues Alice Ozy, 225
  records own sexual activity, 41n.68
  removes to Guernsey, 158n.*112*.a
  removes to Jersey, 156n.*101*.a
  returns from exile, 23, 206n.*168*.1,
    206n.*169*.1
  returns to Jersey, 166
  and the revolution of 1848, 102–3,
    114n.*69*.1
  sells *Les Misérables*, 170
  and the Shakespeare banquet, 179,
    192n.*152*.1
  spurns Napoleon III amnesty offer,
    162n.*128*.1
  superstition of, 23
  survives anthrax, 160n.*121*.1
  suspects JD of infidelity, 15
  visits Belgium from Guernsey,
    189n.*136*.2, 189–90n.*136*.1
  visits Waterloo, 189n.*137*.1
Hureau, Mme (schoolmistress),
  110n.*54*.1

Ida, Mlle. *See* Ferrier, Ida

Jacques II (Vanderburch), 58, 75n.*18*.2
Jadin, Louis, 226
Jane Osborn (Biard), 218

Jeanne Vaubernier, 10
"*Je ne veux qu'être aimée*" (Drouet, ed.
  J. and S. Charpentreau), 32
Jocrisse (acquaintance of JD and VH),
  213
Joly, Anténor, 78n.*31*.1
Jourdain (upholsterer), 49, 72n.*4*.2
Journal des débats, Le, 217
Juliette Drouet ou "la dépaysée"
  (Pouchain and Sabourin), 33

Karr, Alponse, 8–9, 10
Kettly ou le Retour en Suisse (Duvert
  and Paulin), 5
Koch, Louis, 15, 18, 42n.87,
  206n.*169*.1, 223
Koch, Renée Gauvain, 15, 223. *See also*
  Koch family
Koch family, 73n.*11*.1, 151, 162n.*129*.a
Krafft, Laure, 3, 62, 65, 71n.*1*.1, 83,
  223

Labarne(?) (physician), 128. *See also*
  Cabarrus
Lacroix, Albert, 170, 178, 184,
  190n.*138*.1, 190n.*140*.1,
  192nn.*151*.1–2, 194n.*159*.1
Lanvin, Antoinette, 92, 110n.*54*.2, 223
Lanvin, Augustine, 223
Lanvin, Blanche, xii, 24, 107n.*44*.3,
  201, 208n.*174*.2, 208n.*175*.2, 223
Lanvin, Jacques-Firmin, 107n.*44*.3, 223
Lebeuf (sculptor), 192n.*152*.2
Légende des siècles, La (Hugo), 21, 152,
  160n.*120*.3, 161n.*127*.1, 162n.*129*.1,
  162n.*130*.1, 224
Lehaene, Alice. *See* Hugo, Alice
Lemaître, Frédérick, 6, 9, 13, 78n.*31*.1,
  79n.*34*.1, 120, 153n.*79*.c, 224
Lemoine (physician), 98
Lemonnier (Peace Congress organizer),
  204
Lenclos, Ninon de, 103, 114n.*71*.1
Lesclide, Richard, 214, 216n.*185*.2
Lettre à la Reine d'Angleterre,
  158n.*112*.a
Lettres à Juliette Drouet, 1833-1883
  (Hugo, ed. Gaudon), 32

Lettres à Victor Hugo, 1833-1882
(Drouet, ed. Blewer), 32
Lettres familiales (Drouet, ed. Pouchain), 33
Liévenne, Anaïs, 156n.*103*.b
Livre de l'anniversaire, Le (Hugo), 11
Louis-Philippe, King, 114n.*69*.1
Lucrèce Borgia (Hugo), ix, 9–10, 159n.*115*.3, 224
Lucullus, Lucius Licinius, 136, 156n.*103*.1
Lusignan, princesse de, 216n.*184*.b
Luthereau, Jean, 223
Lycée Janson-de-Sailly, 213, 215n.*184*.a

Madame Bovary (Flaubert), 3, 226
Manière (lawyer), 58, 67, 75n.*20*.1
Marchandet, Françoise. *See* Drouet, Françoise Marchandet
Mari à bonnes fortunes (Bonjour), 80n.*40*.1
Mariage à province, Un (Biard), 218
Marie Tudor (Hugo), 12–13, 52, 55, 73n.*8*.2, 74n.*15*.1, 219, 224
Marion de Lorme (Hugo), 9, 43n.*1*10, 219, 224
Marre, Mme (schoolmistress), 110n.*54*.1
Mémoires de Madame Ludovica (Boyé), 36n.*16*, 226
Mendès, Judith Gautier, 30, 207n.*173*.1, 220
Mère rivale, La (Bonjour), 80n.*40*.1
Meurice, Paul, 157n.*108*.1, 206n.*169*.1, 224, 227
Misérables, Les (Hugo), xiii–xiv, 11, 14, 20, 21, 102–3, 108n.*47*.1, 113n.*68*.1, 165, 171, 187–88n.*131*.1, 189–90n.*137*.1, 190n.*140*.1, 191n.*143*.1, 191n.*144*.1, 224–25
   banquet for, 174, 191n.*145*.1
   Fantine published, 173
   sold to publishers, 170, 190n.*138*.1
Moi, Le, 207n.*171*.1
Moine, Le (Fontan), 6–7, 10, 12
"*Mon grand petit homme...*" (Drouet, ed. Souchon), 32
Monk, The (Lewis), 6
Musset, Alfred de, 215n.*183*.d
Musset, Paul de, 213, 215n.*183*.d

Napoleon I, 156n.*101*.a
Napoleon III, 153n.*81*.a, 225
   amnesty offer by, 151, 162n.*128*.1
   coup d'état, 20, 127–29, 135, 154–55n.*94*.1, 155n.*100*.2, 156n.*102*.a, 174, 184, 191n.*146*.a, 195n.*161*.a
   denounced by Hugo in *Les Châtiments*, 218
   vetoes Shakespeare banquet, 179, 192n.*152*.1
Napoléon le petit (Hugo), 156n.*101*.a, 225
Napoléon ou Schönbrunn et Sainte-Hélène (Dupeuty, Régnier, and Detourbey), 6
Nicodème dans la lune (fairy play), 152n.*79*.2
Nicolle, J. P., 138
Nicolle, Mme, 166
Noël, Alphonse-Léon, x, 8, 9
Notre-Dame de Paris (Hugo), 6, 220, 225

Odéon, 6, 7
Oeuvres complètes (Hugo, ed. Massin), 32
Orientales, Les (Hugo), 209n.*175*.1, 225
Orléans, duchesse d', 114n.*69*.1
Ozy, Alice (Julie-Justine Pilloy), 18, 41n.*77*, 225

Peace Congress, Lemonnier's, 204, 210n.*180*.1
Peers of France, 76n.*26*.2
   VH admitted to, 110n.*57*.2
Pernot family (property owners), 96, 111n.*61*.1
Perrinet Leclerc (Lockroy and Anicet Bourgeois), 8, 10
Peruzzi, Simone Luigi, 4, 7
Petites Epopées, Les (Hugo), 146, 160n.*120*.3. *See also Légende des siècles, La*
Pierceau, Mathilde, 57, 62, 65, 69, 75n.*17*.2, 79n.*38*.a, 83, 84, 88, 107n.*43*.1, 225
Pilloy, Julie-Justine. *See* Ozy, Alice
Pinel, Scipion, 4, 7

Pinson, Lt. Alfred, 22, 192n.*148*.1, 221
Plessy, Jeanne-Sylvanie, 94, 111n.*58*.1
Popular Theatres of Nineteenth-Century France (McCormick), 33
Pradier, Charles-Simon, 2
Pradier, Charlotte, 20, 226
Pradier, Claire, xi, 4, 49, 53, 68, 84, 92, 95, 223, 225–26, 228
   affection for her father, 42n.82
   as angel, 148, 161n.*123*.a, 168, 189n.*135*.a, 191n.*141*.1
   at boarding school, 72n.*4*.1
   drawings of, by James Pradier, 34
   Drouet's efforts to procure support for, 41n.71
   gravesite, 42n.87
   Hugo promises to support, 16
   illness and death of, 41–42nn.79–80, 97–100, 107n.*43*.1, 111n.*62*.1, 112n.*63*.1, 112n.*64*.1, 112n.*65*.1
   James Pradier's relationship with, 19–20
   love for father, 42n.83
   parentage, 2
   relationship with Hugo, 69
   at the Saint-Mandé pension, 110nn.*54*.1–2, 111n.*59*.1, 219
   VH's affection for, 78n.*29*.1
Pradier, James (Jean-Jacques), 2–4, 34, 35–36nn.10–11, 36n.16, 36n.21, 41n.71, 42n.82, 64, 72n.*4*.1, 217, 223, 226, 227
   attempted assistance to JD, 37n.26
   called "a stupid cretin" by JD, 37n.25
   and Claire's illness and death, 19, 20, 98, 111–12n.*62*.a
   Claire's love for, 42n.83
   marriage, 37n.24, 37n.27
Pradier, John, 226
Pradier, Louise d'Arcet, 3, 4, 36n.16, 37n.23, 37n.24, 226
Pradier, Thérèse, 20, 226
Propos de table de Victor Hugo (Lesclide), 216n.*185*.1
Proudhon, Pierre-Joseph, 194n.*159*.1

Quatrevingt-treize (Hugo), xiii, 226

Racine, Jean, 62, 77n.*26*.a
Rage and Fire (Gray), 33
Rampe et les coulisses, La (magazine), 7
Rayons et les ombres, Les (Hugo), 210n.*180*.1, 226
Redouté, Pierre-Joseph, 3
Rhin, Le (Hugo), 226
Ribot (Ribou), Mme (moneylender), 4, 5, 7, 9, 72n.*6*.2, 85
Rivière (mourner), 99
Rochereuil, Emile, 223
Roi s'amuse, Le (Hugo), 226–27
Ruy Blas (Hugo), 13, 65, 67, 78n.*31*.1, 78n.*32*.1, 79n.*34*.1, 119, 152n.*79*.1, 152n.*79*.b, 159n.*116*.b, 214, 216n.*185*.1, 224, 227

Sainte-Beuve, Charles-Augustin, 11–12, 23, 221
Saint-Hérem (dinner guest), 213
Satyre et Bacchante (Pradier), 3, 36n.11
Sauva[...], Mme (dressmaker), 104
Savant, Jean, 36n.20, 41n.77
séances, 157n.*106*.1, 157n.*107*.b, 157n.*108*.1
Sévigné, Mme de (Marie de Rabutin-Chantal), xii–xiii
Shylock (Dulac and Alboise), 6, 7
"Si dans ce grand Paris, ô charmante infirmière..." (Hugo), 207n.*171*.1
Siler, Douglas, 33
Simple Histoire (Scribe and Courcy), 5
Société des gens de lettres, 213, 215n.*183*.e
Spontini, Gaspare-Luigi-Pacifico, 113n.*67*.1
Statues de chair (Pradier exhibition), 34
Strasbourg, (Pradier), 36–37n.23
"Sultane favorite, La" (Hugo), 209n.*175*.1

Teleki, Sandor-Alexandre, 136, 156n.*103*.1
Térésa, play, 10
Théâtre de la Porte-Saint-Martin, 5–6, 7, 218

Théâtre de la Renaissance, 78n.*31*.1
Théâtre des Funambules, 119, 153n.*79*.2
Théâtre du Parc, 5
Théâtre du Vaudeville, 5
Théâtre-Français, 64, 75n.*18*.1, 76n.*22*.2. See also Comédie-Française
Théâtre Petit-Lazary, 119, 152–53n.*79*.2
Thomas, Catherine, 222
Torquemada (Hugo), 25–26, 227
Toto. See Hugo, François-Victor; Hugo, Victor
Toute la lyre (Hugo), 207n.*171*.1, 227
Travailleurs de la mer, Les (Hugo), 21, 182, 184, 193n.*156*.1, 194n.*159*.a, 227
Trébuchet, Sophie, 222
Triger, Mme, 84, 107n.*43*.1
Triger (physician), 98, 112n.*63*.a
"Tristesse d'Olympio" (Hugo), 77n.*27*.1, 111n.*60*.1, 226

Ulbach, Louis, 178, 192n.*151*.2

Vacquerie, Auguste, 139, 195n.*162*.1, 213, 215n.*183*.d, 227
Vacquerie, Charles, 17, 109n.*50*.1, 110n.*53*.1, 222, 227
Vengeance, Une (Biard), 218
Vestale, La (Spontini), 113n.*67*.1
Victor Hugo (Robb), 33

Victor Hugo: L'Homme océan (Prévost), 34
Victor Hugo et Juliette Drouet (Guimbaud), 32
"Victor Hugo in front of Notre-Dame at Reims" (Alaux), 52, 73n.*9*.1
Victor Hugo in the Channel Islands (Cox), 33
Victor Hugo intime (Chenay), 219
Victor Hugo raconté par un témoin de sa vie (A. F. Hugo), 23, 185, 195n.*162*.1
Viennet, Jean Pons Guillaume, 62–63, 76n.*26*.2, 77n.*26*.a
Vilain, Victor, 36n.20, 100, 112n.*66*.1, 120, 153n.*80*.2, 219, 227–28
Voltaire (François-Marie Arouet), 210n.*182*.1

Watteville, Mlle (schoolmistress), 72n.*4*.1
Wheadon (barber), 142, 158n.*113*.2
William Shakespeare (Hugo), 21, 192n.*151*.1, 228
Wilmen, Mme (actress), 131

Yvan, Melchior, 133, 155n.*100*.1

Zélie-Paul, Mme (actress), 7
Ziegler, Jules, 3, 36n.20, 219